DISCARD

The Presidencies of
GROVER CLEVELAND

AMERICAN PRESIDENCY SERIES

Donald R. McCoy, Clifford S. Griffin, Homer E. Socolofsky
General Editors

George Washington, Forrest McDonald
John Adams, Ralph Adams Brown
Thomas Jefferson, Forrest McDonald
John Quincy Adams, Mary W. M. Hargreaves
Martin Van Buren, Major L. Wilson
James K. Polk, Paul H. Bergeron
James Buchanan, Elbert B. Smith
Andrew Johnson, Albert Castel
James A. Garfield & Chester A. Arthur, Justus D. Doenecke
Grover Cleveland, Richard E. Welch, Jr.
Benjamin Harrison, Homer E. Socolofsky & Allan B. Spetter
William McKinley, Lewis L. Gould
William Howard Taft, Paolo E. Coletta
Warren G. Harding, Eugene P. Trani & David L. Wilson
Herbert C. Hoover, Martin L. Fausold
Harry S. Truman, Donald R. McCoy
Dwight D. Eisenhower, Elmo Richardson
Lyndon B. Johnson, Vaughn Davis Bornet

The Presidencies of

GROVER
CLEVELAND

Richard E. Welch, Jr.

UNIVERSITY PRESS OF KANSAS

Published by the University Press of Kansas (Lawrence,
Kansas 66045), which was organized by the Kansas
Board of Regents and is operated and funded by Emporia
State University, Fort Hays State University,
Kansas State University, Pittsburg State University, the
University of Kansas, and Wichita State University

Library of Congress Cataloging-in-Publication Data

Welch, Richard E.
The presidencies of Grover Cleveland/Richard E. Welch, Jr.
p.   cm.—(American presidency series)
Bibliography: p.
Includes index.
ISBN 0-7006-0355-7 (alk. paper)
1. United States—Politics and government—1885–1889. 2. United
States—Politics and government—1893–1897. 3. Cleveland, Grover,
1837–1908. I. Title. II. Series.
E696.W45 1988   88-268
973.8'5—dc19   CIP

British Library Cataloguing in Publication data is available.

Printed in the United States of America
10 9 8 7 6 5 4 3 2 1

The paper used in this publication meets the minimum requirements
of the American National Standard for Permanence of Paper for
Printed Library Materials Z39.48-1984.

*To my students
at Lafayette College, 1958–88
—always a challenge
and not infrequently a great pleasure*

CONTENTS

FOREWORD

The aim of the American Presidency Series is to present historians and the general reading public with interesting, scholarly assessments of the various presidential administrations. These interpretive surveys are intended to cover the broad ground between biographies, specialized monographs, and journalistic accounts. As such, each will be a comprehensive, synthetic work which will draw upon the best in pertinent secondary literature, yet leave room for the author's own analysis and interpretation.

Volumes in the series will present the data essential to understanding the administration under consideration. Particularly, each book will treat the then current problems facing the United States and its people and how the president and his associates felt about, thought about, and worked to cope with these problems. Attention will be given to how the office developed and operated during the president's tenure. Equally important will be consideration of the vital relationships between the president, his staff, the executive officers, Congress, foreign representatives, the judiciary, state officials, the public, political parties, the press, and influential private citizens. The series will also be concerned with how this unique American institution — the presidency — was viewed by the presidents, and with what results.

All this will be set, insofar as possible, in the context not only of contemporary politics but also of economics, international relations, law, morals, public administration, religion, and thought. Such a broad approach is necessary to understanding, for a presidential administration is more than the elected and appointed officers composing it, since its work so often reflects the major problems, anxieties, and glories of the nation. In short, the authors in this series will strive to recount and evaluate the record of each administration and to identify its distinctiveness and relationships to the past, its own time, and the future.

The General Editors

ACKNOWLEDGMENTS

I am deeply indebted to the helpful librarians and staff of the Manuscript Division of the Library of Congress; the Harry Elkins Widener Library and Documents Division of Harvard University Libraries; the Boston Athenaeum; and the David Bishop Skillman Library at Lafayette College. I am equally indebted to Mrs. Carl L. Cooper, secretary and general manager of the History Department, Lafayette College. Hilda Cooper is a woman of awesome efficiency and a fine friend.

I also wish to express my appreciation to the President and Board of Trustees of Lafayette College and to its Committee on Advanced Study and Research, for grants of time and money, and to the American Philosophical Society of Philadelphia, for a generous research grant.

My greatest obligation is to my late wife, Christina Sedgwick Marquand Welch, a rare and talented person and a far-better writer than her husband.

Richard E. Welch, Jr.

Easton, Pennsylvania
September 1987

1

INTRODUCTION

The historical reputations of Grover Cleveland and Gilded Age politics have enjoyed a close if inverse relationship. Initially the Gilded Age was scornfully viewed as a period of shadowboxing politics between the Republican and Democratic parties as they carefully avoided political issues while waging a furious battle for political spoils. Grover Cleveland was usually portrayed as the only president with a claim to statesmanship, a doughty warrior of undeviating courage whose efforts to reform the civil service and revise the protective-tariff system furnished a salutary contrast to the corrupt and selfish politicians of the Gilded Age. Over the last generation, however, there has been a historiographical revolution of sorts. The reputation of Gilded Age politics has enjoyed a significant improvement, while the reputation of Cleveland has fallen to a low point. Now the Gilded Age is seen as a transitional period in which intelligent politicians—mostly Republican—made meaningful efforts to meet the political challenge posed by the post–Civil War economic revolution. Cleveland, on the other hand, is damned as a political anachronism, a porcine reactionary, a Bourbon!

The story of the improved reputation of the political history of the Gilded Age is quickly told; that of Cleveland's decline is more complicated.

Mark Twain and Matthew Josephson jointly fashioned the initial view of Gilded Age politics. In 1873, Mark Twain and his friend Charles Dudley Warner published a satirical novel which mocked the rascality, corruption, and greed of post–Civil War America by tracing the adventures of a bombastic professional promoter, Colonel Beriah Sellers. The shabby standards and materialistic aspirations of Sellers and his contemporaries were supposedly summarized in the book's title, *The Gilded Age*. It was one of Twain's lesser efforts, but the title has become a permanent feature in the lexicon of American historians and textbook writers. The dates of the Gilded Age have varied with the needs and convenience of the writer. Though usually it is confined to the 1870s and 1880s, it has occasionally been expanded to embrace the period from the end of the Civil War to the presidency of William McKinley (1865–96). Matthew Josephson chose the latter dates in his influential and iconoclastic study *The Politicos*, published in 1938.

Josephson echoed Twain's disgust with the business chicanery and cultural philistinism of the period but focused primarily on national politics. In Josephson's account, the post–Civil War presidents, senators, and congressmen were at best mediocrities and most usually the witting tools of the special interests and the robber barons. There was no difference between the major parties: both ignored the socioeconomic transformation of the United States as they concentrated on political spoils and partisan advantage. Political battles were but a shadow play, detached from the main stage where entrepreneurs fought to gain illicit fortunes and to fashion an America characterized by heedless economic growth and increasing social division.

Down to the 1960s, most United States history textbooks offered a tempered version of the Twain-Josephson characterization of the Gilded Age. Emphasis was placed on industrialization and urbanization. The politics of the period was judged to be almost irrelevant to economic and social developments, providing a dull interlude between the excitement of the Civil War and Reconstruction decade and the political reforms and contests of the Progressive Era. The Gilded Age was usually dismissed as a time of weak presidents, infrequent and ineffectual efforts at governmental regulation, and the increasing political authority of big business. Civil-service reform was seen as an exercise in rhetoric, and political battles over the tariff and the currency were judged peripheral to the central issue of social and economic inequality. For historians in the New Deal/Fair Deal period, the politicians of the Gilded Age were bearded conservatives fighting outmoded battles of little current relevance. Usually hostile to big business and champions of a strong national executive and effective federal regulation, these historians found the political struggles of the Gilded Age uninteresting and, consequently, were inclined to judge them insincere. Failing to see the obstacles to effective federal social and economic regulation in the post–Civil War generation and seemingly determined to impose the demands and aspirations of a later time on the American electorate of the 1870s and 1880s, these historians labeled the Gilded Age as a period of "negation," characterized by "the politics of dead center." The Gilded Age was portrayed as a time of lost opportunity and political inertia, when the issue of social injustice and the inequalities of an unmanaged economy were ignored.

Over the last generation a more complimentary view of Gilded Age politics has emerged. Recent historians have noted, for example, the extent of popular involvement in politics. In the 1880s, over 80 percent of eligible voters cast their ballots in presidential elections, a much-higher percentage than at any time during the twentieth century. More importantly, historians now question that these were years of governmental lethargy and political subservience to vested interests. Their narrative of Gilded Age politics is more complex and more interesting. The Gilded Age was "a time of intense conflict between old values and the pressures generated by massive change," a time of conflict between localism and nationalism, a time when efforts were first made to meet the problems created by the rise of the industrial city.[1] These historians do not proclaim the success of Gilded Age politicians in meeting these conflicts and problems; they do insist that politicians in the Gilded Age were not oblivious to the new challenges. They see the Gilded Age as a necessary transitional period in the nation's political history. In the opinion of H. Wayne Morgan, the Gilded Age witnessed the first " 'modern' American generation," and when one considers the demands it faced and the absence of tested solutions, "the generation's response to challenge was impressive."[2] Lewis L. Gould has argued that the politicians of the Gilded Age compare favorably with those of any other era of American history: "They resorted, on occasion, to . . . , bribery, and corruption; yet excessive emphasis on the less savory aspects of the politician's craft obscures the degree to which they debated real issues, grappled with genuine problems, and sought workable solutions."[3] These revisionist historians make no claim that the political leaders of the Gilded Age invented the regulatory state; they do deny that Gilded Age politicians uniformly or consistently avoided what were for their time "the real issues."

Such historians as Morgan and Gould, however, tend to see the Republican party as the instrument of change and the repository of foresight. It was politicians such as James G. Blaine who sensed the need to meet the challenges of a new era by means of a more active and energetic federal government. Consequently, as the reputation of the Gilded Age has experienced partial redemption, that of the sole Democratic president of the period has experienced a sharp decline. No longer is Grover Cleveland portrayed as the single presidential hero in an age of political mediocrity. Instead, he is now more often seen as the prime illustration of the outmoded politics and negative political philosophy of "Bourbon Democracy."

It was Allan Nevins who most persuasively fashioned the older view of Cleveland as the reformer statesman and the era's one claimant to presidential greatness. In his Pulitzer-prize-winning biography of Cleveland, published in 1933 and subtitled *A Study in Courage*, Nevins portrayed Cleveland as John Bunyan's "Valiant-for-Truth." If not a great constructive statesman, Cleveland was "immovable in his honesty" and "unflinching in his fortitude." His faith in democracy "was a part of his very being" and his political aims "embraced nothing less than the whole national welfare." In his efforts to improve the civil service, further the identification of the South with the nation, bring honesty to the departments of the federal government, educate the American people to the economic errors of high protectionism, and preserve the soundness of the nation's credit and currency, he deserved the title of reformer and "became a symbol of civic staunchness." Cleveland was a symbol as well of political morality and stubborn independence. He stood forth as an example of "courage that never yields an inch in the cause of truth, and that never surrenders an iota of principle to expediency."[4]

Henry Steele Commager wrote in a popular college textbook that Cleveland alone of the presidents of his generation "had some suspicion of the significance and direction of the economic changes that were transforming the country" and dared to challenge "the pressure groups that were using the government for selfish purposes."[5] Richard Hofstadter, writing in 1948, offered a more qualified version of Cleveland's contribution but still concluded that Cleveland was "the sole reasonable facsimile of a major president between

4

Lincoln and Theodore Roosevelt" and "the flower of American political culture in the Gilded Age."[6]

The general acceptance of this favorable view of Cleveland is illustrated by his ranking in the famous "Schlesinger poll." The distinguished Harvard professor Arthur M. Schlesinger, Sr., asked some seventy-five fellow-historians in 1948 to rank United States presidents by some unspecified criteria of "greatness." One can legitimately believe that this exercise was little more scientific than a poll determining the best high-school football team in the nation's history or the best-dressed men in public life. There was, however, a remarkable degree of agreement that Cleveland was a praiseworthy president. Cleveland was ranked eighth among all U.S. presidents and was awarded the classification "Near Great."[7]

Subsequent polls, however, have indicated a rather steady drop in Cleveland's ranking and historical reputation. The most recent poll, conducted in 1982 by Robert K. Murray and Tim H. Blessing, showed Cleveland finishing seventeenth, the last among those presidents classified as "Above Average."[8] There are historians who would place him still lower, and among those, none has been more influential than Horace Samuel Merrill.

In three books published between 1953 and 1957, Merrill portrayed Cleveland as the exemplar of those members of the Democratic party identified with the selfish wishes of a sector of the business and financial community. These were the Bourbon Democrats, supporters of the status quo, sworn antagonists of agrarian radicalism, social reform, and governmental regulation. Conservative spokesmen for the railroad, commercial, and exporter interests, the Bourbon Democrats sought "to prevent control of the government by farmers, wage earners and inefficient, irresponsible, corrupt officeholders"; and Grover Cleveland was their symbol and champion. Cleveland was a man who placed property rights over human rights and was convinced that "to serve business was to serve the nation as a whole."[9] Distrustful of governmental regulation and paternalism, he was equally distrustful of those who would threaten the dominance of the probusiness wing of the Democratic party. When Cleveland proclaimed that public officials were "trustees of the people," he had reference only to "the right people."[10]

Currently, the strictures of Merrill are more generally accepted by historians than is the praise of Nevins. Such respected students of the Gilded Age as Vincent P. De Santis, Morton Keller, and Walter T. K. Nugent emphasize Cleveland's conservatism and see his administrations as essentially negative in character and accomplishment.

De Santis describes Cleveland as a man incapable of understanding the changes generated by the rise of industrial capitalism and "unsympathetic to the needs and protests of the nation's farmers and workers." Cleveland's famous vetoes were the product of a sincere antipathy to governmental paternalism and monetary inflation, but they had the effect of endearing him "to the conservatives and businessmen." Believing that governmental interference with the natural laws of political economy was "futile and wicked," Cleveland, in the last analysis, was "an extreme conservative."[11]

Morton Keller finds Cleveland the embodiment of "the traditionalism and solidity of the Bourbon Democratic political style" and "the preeminent Bourbon Democrat," while Walter T. K. Nugent, after giving Cleveland the rather contradictory label of "an honest, decisive negativist," offers the judgment that Cleveland's first administration was primarily responsible for earning the Gilded Age its "where-were-the-real-issues" reputation.[12] Robert F. Wesser and John G. Sproat give equal emphasis to Cleveland's identification with Manchester School economics and limited government. And when Arthur M. Schlesinger, Jr., sought in 1979 to convince the readers of the *New Republic* that the Democratic party should dump Jimmy Carter in favor of Edward Kennedy, he found in Grover Cleveland the perfect whipping boy. In an article entitled "Who Needs Grover Cleveland?" Schlesinger declared that to find Carter's equal as "an ideologically conservative Democratic president, one must go back to Grover."[13]

Although many recent historians have followed Merrill's lead in characterizing Cleveland as the leader of "Bourbon Democracy," few have bothered to define the term with any precision. It usually has derogatory implications, but its definition has been flexible as to reactionary intent and sectional coverage. Perhaps the most specific definition is to be found in Merrill's study *Bourbon Democracy of the Middle West, 1865–1896*:

> These post–Civil War Democratic leaders [of the Middle West and Northeast] were Bourbons in the sense of being wealthy, self-esteemed, self-appointed guardians of an already fixed pattern for living and making a living. They were protectors of the existing, although accelerating, course of the industrial revolution. They jealously guarded this machinery of material progress against threats from restless farmers and wage earners.

The Bourbon Democrats, Merrill's argument runs, were further characterized by a firm conviction that the primary responsibility of government was to remove any man-made obstacles to the operation of natural economic laws and to keep taxation to a minimum. First and last they were spokesmen for the business interests—particularly those engaged in commerce, trade, and railroad management—and their "patron saint" was Grover Cleveland.[14]

Other historians have implied a link between the Bourbon Democrats of the Northeast and the Middle West and those of the South Robert Wesser claims that there was a close alliance between such Bourbon leaders as Daniel Manning and William C. Whitney of New York and "the Southern Redeemers who represented the new order in Dixie—corporation lawyers, factory owners, railroad men, and merchants."[15] John M. Dobson, Morton Keller, and R. Hal Williams see less of an alliance than a "loose aggregation" between southern and northern conservatives in the Democratic party; but in varying degrees, they also stress the negativism of Bourbon philosophy. Keller even implies a similarity with the nineteenth-century Bourbons of France when he writes of "a political attitude that forgot nothing and learned nothing."[16]

This study of the Cleveland presidencies will both ignore and dispute the identification of Cleveland with the amorphous term "Bourbon Democracy." If that term has any meaningful utility, it has reference to certain spokesmen of "the New South" who achieved a position of dominance in several states of the Southeast in the decade following Reconstruction. It is inaccurate and insufficient as a description of the ambivalent political philosophy of Grover Cleveland or the mixed record of his two nonconsecutive administrations. Cleveland was by certain criteria a political conservative; he was not a reactionary, nor did he favor the rule of the masses by the self-chosen few.

The Gilded Age deserves its historiographical redemption, but acknowledgment of the contribution of James G. Blaine and William McKinley in achieving a Republican electoral majority does not require the derogation of Grover Cleveland. If Cleveland does not deserve the undiluted praise accorded to him by Allan Nevins, neither does he provide a parallel to the Bourbons of France or South Carolina. Whatever Cleveland's fears of "agrarian radicals" and "free-silver demagogues," he was a believer in popular government. Nostalgic for the Jacksonian past, he was not unaware of the new problems posed by the development of industrial trusts and monopolies. There is a seductive simplicity in labeling all intraparty enemies of William

Jennings Bryan as Bourbon Democrats, but the label provides little understanding of the evolving goals of Grover Cleveland or the variegated record of his administrations.

The contradictions and ambiguities of the Cleveland presidencies were, in part, the result of a continuing tension between Cleveland's inherited political faith and his assertive, aggressive personality. One cannot understand the record of either administration or their surprising similarity of objectives without first attempting to analyze the inherent conflict between Cleveland's political philosophy and personal temperament.

2

THE CONTRADICTIONS
OF PHILOSOPHY
AND PERSONALITY

One is tempted to picture Grover Cleveland as a rather simple man, if not indeed a dull one. One can easily obtain quotations from his speeches that would imply that his political philosophy was restricted to a series of dogmatic statements in behalf of limited government and the protection of property and that his personality was that of an Eagle Scout mouthing truisms about duty. In point of fact, neither Cleveland's political philosophy nor his personality was without ambiguities and self-contradictions. As there was a measure of difference between Cleveland's rhetoric and his actions, so was there a greater difference between the blunt, stolid, forthright persona displayed to the electorate and the ambitious, irritable, sensitive person behind the public mask. More importantly, Cleveland's proclaimed political ideology was often at odds with his assertive political personality. Although he pledged public allegiance to a Whiggish version of the presidency—the chief executive restricted to administrative duties and abjuring a role in the legislative process— Cleveland's aggressive insistence on presidential independence led him to exercise increasing control of the executive branch and then to seek influence over Congress and national legislation. Similarly, although Cleveland gave lip service to states' rights, his determination to revise federal land and Indian policy in the West and to put an end to the Pullman strike encouraged expansion of the authority of the federal government. On several occasions, Cleveland's inherited political philosophy confronted his assertive political personality and was defeated in the encounter. During his second administration, journalists would note the personal coloration in the language of his state papers, and his political enemies criticized his monarchical arrogance. Cleveland's efforts to direct Congress were more frequent during his second term, but contradictions of ideology and personality were present throughout both administrations.

It is necessary to analyze in turn the ambiguities of his political philosophy and temperament, but it is the continuing tension between his proclaimed ideology and his personality that provides the essential key to understanding the aims and failures of the Cleveland presidencies.

Grover Cleveland never wrote an essay entitled "My Political Philosophy," and the student of his presidencies should be careful not to claim for Cleveland a systematic philosophical position. Cleveland was not a deep thinker; he was rather suspicious of public persons who had a speculative turn of mind. He had no taste for theoretical and abstract ideas, and he prided himself on being a practical man who met issues and problems as they arose. His social and economic philosophy was neither deliberately formulated nor cast in stone. Many of his political principles were unconsciously borrowed, and although he declared his identification with the imperishable truths exemplified by the words and actions of Thomas Jefferson and Andrew Jackson, he was prepared to acknowledge the need to adapt the verities of the past to changing conditions.

With caveats proclaimed, an attempt will be made to evaluate Cleveland's political beliefs respecting the powers and functions of the presidency, states' rights and the authority of the federal government, the correlation of economic progress and individual economic freedom, and the political role of morality and religion.

Cleveland usually took the public position that the primary role of the president was that of an executive officer and administrator, charged to carry out the policies formulated by the legislative branch. His career prior to the presidency, however—as mayor of Buffalo and as governor of New York—featured a readiness to employ the executive veto, and he showed an equal readiness as president. The exercise of the veto power, although a negative approach to legislative involvement, is not an example of executive restraint. Cleveland adopted a more activist conception of presidential power with his State of the Union message of December 1887, in which he demanded the revision of the protective-tariff system.[1] Throughout his presidential tenure, however, Cleveland was prepared not only to serve as a censor of congressional legislation but to insist upon the unrestricted authority of the president within the executive branch of the federal government. He was equally determined, however, to proclaim his allegiance to the constitutional principle of the separation of powers. Even when, in his second term, he vigorously used his patronage power to force Congress to repeal the Sherman Silver Purchase Act, he found it necessary to assure himself that he was only frustrating mischievous obstructionists who would prevent the intelligent majority in Congress from exercising its true will and intent.

Cleveland took great pride in his election to the presidency, an office that he considered to be without a superior anywhere in the world. At times he was prepared to imply that it had divine sanction. Responding to a toast at the centennial celebration of the settlement of Clinton, New York, Cleveland declared: "That the office of President of the United States does represent the sovereignty of sixty millions of free people is to my mind a statement full of solemnity; for this sovereignty I conceive to be the working out . . . of the divine right of man to govern himself and a manifestation of God's plan concerning the human race."[2]

Cleveland was convinced that the president was, by constitutional design, the people's tribune. Of all the officers of the government, only he had been elected by the nation at large. Consequently, the president had a particular obligation to stand guard over politicians who abused the public trust and over any Congress that passed unwise legislation under the inspiration of popular excitement or political cowardice. When fighting a senatorial effort to restrict the president's power to appoint and dismiss federal officeholders, Cleveland not only claimed executive independence under the doctrine of separation of powers but referred as well to the president's national constituency. The president was responsible not to the Senate but to the people.

It would be false to claim that the "modern presidency" began with the tenure of Grover Cleveland or that he saw himself as the prime-minister type of president, charged with the responsibility of initiating legislation. Cleveland's efforts to influence legislative policy were usually confined to his annual messages, the exercise of the executive veto, and, on occasion, the purposeful delay of patronage appointments in the hope of influencing the votes of individual senators and congressmen. Only in the tariff struggles of 1886–88 and

1893–94 did he attempt an active role in seeking to influence the specific provisions of legislative bills and then but clumsily. Unlike his successor, William McKinley, Cleveland never appreciated the relationship between the president's role as party leader and the measure of his effectiveness in influencing congressional legislation. There have been few presidents, however, who by their personal temperament and conviction of righteousness had a stronger desire to see Congress abide by their wishes. Cleveland's self-assertiveness and willingness to assume responsibility virtually guaranteed that for all his rhetoric about abstaining from "interference with the legislative branch and its constitutional responsibilities," he would frequently discover in such interference a presidential duty.[3]

Cleveland had more difficulty in adapting his inherited antipathy to the expansion of the power of the federal government than in revising his conception of presidential authority. Although never a true believer in states'-rights doctrine, he entered the presidency with a strong suspicion of the growing authority of the national government. In part this was the result of his identification of congressional economic legislation with favored treatment for special interests. Cleveland never renounced his belief that the regulative and directive powers of the federal government should be carefully limited, but he was prepared to modify that belief in behalf of presidential authority, the rights of Indians, the preservation of the shrinking national domain, and the chastisement of striking railroad workers.

Cleveland was not above using fear of the federal government to political advantage, as he did in his attacks on the stillborn Federal Elections bill in the campaign of 1892; but his frequent warnings against the expanding scope of federal legislation were more often the response of a strict constructionist of the Constitution than of a partisan campaigner currying sectional support. In his fourth annual message to Congress, after his electoral defeat in 1888, Cleveland warned against the "impatience of constitutional limitations of Federal power" and the "increasing tendency to extend the scope of Federal legislation into the domain of State and local jurisdiction." Congress must always take care to preserve "the partitions between proper subjects of Federal and local care and regulation." No consideration of "expedience or sentiment" should be allowed to destroy those partitions.[4]

Cleveland's fear of the undue centralization of political authority in the federal government was supported by what he judged to be the wise warnings of his political heroes, Jefferson and Jackson.

12

But it was supported as well by his convictions in regard to the importance of governmental economy. Federal legislative experiments in uncharted waters would be costly and could only add to the tax burden of a people already suffering from the hidden taxation of an unjust and illogical protective tariff.

By the current lexicon of American politics, such convictions may be judged conservative. They were, however, at one with the beliefs of many middle-class Americans in the 1880s and 1890s and cannot easily be labeled reactionary. These convictions, moreover, did not prevent Cleveland from signing the Interstate Commerce Act of 1887 or from calling for a permanent federal panel of arbiters to promote the settlement of labor-management disputes. Cleveland was suspicious of constitutional innovation and legislative experiment, and he identified most readily with an older America that was passing; but he was prepared to acknowledge certain problems associated with the evolution of urban, industrial America and to accept a modest expansion of national responsibility in meeting the challenges of the new order.

Cleveland's views on the proper limits of federal authority were closely related to his ideas respecting the free market and to his frequent imprecations against governmental paternalism. Cleveland had little interest in economic theory, and there is no record that he ever pronounced the words *laissez faire*; but in harmony with most Americans of his day, he assumed that there was a close correlation between individual economic freedom and national economic progress. For some Americans, of course, laissez faire had always been defined as an absence of governmental restrictions and governmental assistance to the special interest they identified with their own well-being. Grover Cleveland's interpretation of "economic freedom" was less biased: he believed that the government should not offer favored treatment to any group or locality. Cleveland was as suspicious of governmental favors as of governmental regulation.

There were occasional compromises on both counts; Grover Cleveland was not an ideological purist but a well-meaning politician. A consistent theme throughout both administrations, however, was his conviction that governmental paternalism could only encourage a dangerous dependence on the federal government, destroy the American tradition of local charity and self-help, and undermine the independence and therefore the virtue of the citizenry. Governmental paternalism could, indeed, erode the very foundations of popular government if ever the electorate should see the government not as an institution of their creation demanding their loyalty but as

13

a source of gifts and privileges. Paternalistic government could only change the relation of the citizen to the government; instead of being a sovereign, the citizen would become a dependent.

Cleveland's veto message of 1887 denouncing a congressional act that would have provided free seed for the drought-stricken farmers of Texas has often been cited as an illustration of his callousness and blind conservatism. It is better read as the plea of a troubled president anxious to sustain the traditions and values of an idealized past:

> . . . the lesson should be constantly enforced that though the people support the Government, Government should not support the people. . . . Federal aid, in such cases, encourages the expectations of paternal care on the part of the Government and weakens the sturdiness of our national character, while it prevents the indulgence among our people of that kindly sentiment and conduct which strengthen the bond of a common brotherhood.[5]

Nine years later, when vetoing a rivers-and-harbors appropriations bill, Cleveland wrote in almost identical terms as he warned against "a vicious paternalism" that would encourage the belief that popular attachment to the government should "rest upon the hope and expectation of direct and especial favors." The mission of the national government was not the distribution of favors but "the enforcement of exact justice and equality."[6]

Cleveland, together with a majority of his compatriots, pledged an automatic allegiance to the free marketplace. He would have dismissed the modern concept of national economic planning as socialistic nonsense. Wrong governmental monetary policies could cause financial panic, but economic depression could not be cured by legislative action or appropriations from the national treasury. In line with the tenets of nineteenth-century liberalism, Cleveland believed that the economic function of government was not to shape the direction of the nation's economy but to assure a fair field for all and to encourage free and unfettered competition. Government could not promise social or economic equality; but it could try to remove man-made obstacles to equal opportunity. How this could be done in an era when industrial combination and monopoly appeared to flourish as never before, he did not know. He did not ignore the problem. Indeed, in his annual message of December 1888, he addressed it at length; but his fear of the consequences of governmental interference inhibited his efforts to find a national legislative solution.

Geoffrey Blodgett has identified the central dilemma of the Gilded Age as "the polar isolation" of political reality and economic thought: "The most powerful developing economy in the world lurched toward maturity without a theory to guide the national politicians who promoted it."[7] Blodgett is correct, if by *theory* one refers to a logically consistent body of principles applicable to changing social and economic conditions. Surely Cleveland could not claim to possess a guiding economic theory. In conjunction with many of his compatriots, he believed in the sanctity of private property, had no quarrel with free-enterprise capitalism, found satisfaction in the nation's increasing industrial power, and declared that the regulatory powers of the national government should be limited to protecting individual economic liberty. But if he subscribed to a general laissez faire philosophy, he was more the utilitarian than the dogmatist. He was increasingly prepared to consider the possibility of some regulation of trusts and monopolies, if only he could be convinced that such regulation was constitutional and would not encourage bureaucratic paternalism. American citizens had no right to ask of their government either favors or charity. They could demand that their government provide economy, purity, and justice and, in the last connection, a president who worried over the political and economic power of industrial combinations even while he offered no solution of program or theory.

Grover Cleveland was a conservative insofar as he was an advocate of a strict construction of the Constitution and was instinctively opposed to legislative innovation that threatened to overturn the traditional values of the social and political order. He was not, however, an obdurate enemy of change. His beliefs respecting free enterprise and the proper limitations of the national government, as well as his convictions in regard to the differing responsibilities of the federal and local governments, did not prevent his acceptance of cautious reform. His primary allegiance was not to conservatism but to individualism. The perfect society was the society in which everyone was free to rise in accordance with his individual portion of ability, talent, and virtue.

Virtue was, with duty, a favorite word, and Cleveland was prepared to associate civic virtue with morality. In another illustration of the ambiguities of his political ideology and character, Cleveland was not only a politician and a utilitarian but also a practicing moralist. When he believed a policy was unwise, he was quick to denounce it as sordid and selfish. Issues were to be judged by moral as well as constitutional standards.

Grover Cleveland was not a religious or spiritual man, and those historians who have sought to interpret his policies in terms of his Presbyterian inheritance and the Calvinist creed have exaggerated the impact of his religious convictions.[8] Cleveland was the son of a Presbyterian clergyman and was careful to observe the Sabbath if there was no opportunity for hunting and fishing, but he had little interest in the metaphysics of religion. He was a man of conscience, but he possessed no religious world view, and there is little reason to believe that his devotion to hard money and fiscal responsibility was inspired by the teachings of John Calvin.[9] Cleveland never saw reason to doubt the creed of his boyhood, and he expressed irritation with those who sought rationalist explanations of scriptural passages.[10] As president, however, he spent the early morning hours not in prayer but in the dissection of fraudulent pension claims.

When Cleveland sought external support for his policy decisions, it was not to John Calvin that he turned but to Andrew Jackson. Cleveland and Jackson were in many ways highly disparate figures; surely Cleveland lacked the military aura and the frontier past of his hero, as well as Jackson's ability to generate enthusiasm among eastern laborers and western debtors. But when Cleveland spoke of "a better and purer day," it was often with reference to his undocumented picture of America in the Jackson era. Cleveland identified his fight against the unjust favoritism of the protective tariff with Jackson's fight against the Second Bank of the United States.[11] Jackson, too, had been in favor of hard money, governmental economy, and tariff reductions; had vetoed federal subsidies such as the Maysville Road bill; had been suspicious of involvement by the federal government with business enterprise. Moreover, Jackson had epitomized presidential independence and the authority of the righteous executive in contest with mischievous senators. While recognizing, if reluctantly, the problems created by the increased pace of industrialization, Grover Cleveland continued to praise "the purer and saner ideals" of an idealized Jacksonian past.

The tension between Cleveland's nostalgic preference for an earlier America and his confused recognition of the realities of the Gilded Age was illustrated by his message to Congress of December 1888. Its warnings were not those of a defeated politician venting spite on a stupid electorate; they reflected his romantic version of the American past, while they spoke to present dangers:

> [In former days] the pomp and glitter of Governments less free offered no temptation and presented no delusion to the plain

people who, side by side, in friendly competition, wrought for the ennoblement and dignity of man. . . .

[Today] our cities are the abiding-places of wealth and luxury; our manufactures yield fortunes never dreamed of by the fathers of the Republic; our business men are madly striving in the race for riches, and immense aggregations of capital outrun the imagination in the magnitude of their undertakings. . . .

We discover that the fortunes realized by our manufactures are no longer solely the reward of sturdy industry and enlightened foresight, but that they result from the discriminating favor of the Government, and are largely built upon undue exactions from the masses of our people. The gulf between employers and the employed is constantly widening, and classes are rapidly forming, one comprising the very rich and powerful, while in another are found the toiling poor. As we view the achievements of aggregated capital, we discover the existence of trusts, combinations, and monopolies, while the citizen is struggling far in the rear or is trampled to death beneath an iron heel. Corporations, which should be the carefully-restrained creatures of the law and the servants of the people, are fast becoming the people's masters.[12]

Grover Cleveland never saw fit to summarize his political philosophy or explain its ambiguities. The closest he ever came to a short summary was perhaps in a letter to a memorial meeting for Samuel J. Tilden, when he identified Tilden (whom he admired most temperately) with those beliefs that Cleveland wished to have associated with his own political position. Tilden, he declared, stood for limitation of federal power under the Constitution, public economy and honesty, protection of a sound currency, reform of the civil service, restriction of corporate privileges, executive independence, and undeviating allegiance to public morality and civic virtue.[13]

Cleveland's political philosophy was the result of many influences, among which were the demands of his personal psychology and temperament. The personality that Cleveland projected to the public was without ambivalence. He was the honest, forthright, blunt-speaking, fearless individual who stood leagues apart from compromising politicians or quibbling intellectuals. In fact, his personality was more complex and more interesting. In many ways he was a tangle of self-contradictions: humble and ambitious, courageous and cautious, practical and moralistic, irritable and kindly, aggressive and sensitive.

17

It was Cleveland's public posture that he never sought public office but that he accepted it from a sense of duty and at the sacrifice of personal desire and comfort. There was a large measure of self-deception in Cleveland's pose of the reluctant public servant. He was an ambitious man who relished political victory and enjoyed the prestige and dignity of gubernatorial and presidential office. Not a power-hungry man, he found satisfaction in exercising the power that came with those offices. The trappings of official position meant little to him; indeed, he often viewed them as sources of irritation. Formal receptions and presidential parades were a bore; ceremonial addresses, a tiresome chore. He cared little for pomp and circumstance and had no taste for dress clothes, rich food, or conspicuous consumption. He was ready to acknowledge his limited formal education and his lack of intellectual cultivation, but coexistent with a realistic acceptance of his deficiences was an unshakable conviction of the correctness of his policies and the superiority of his public virtue.

Cleveland saw himself in three consecutive elections as the best man for the Democratic nomination for the presidency and, consequently, as the correct choice of the American electorate. Ambition and self-assertion were diluted by spasms of humility but were never seriously threatened. If he did not possess quickness of wit or intellectual brilliance, he was certain that it was more important for a statesman to be of a practical mind, to subject issues to careful study before forming an opinion, and then to stick by his decision with adamantine obstinacy. Cleveland was a stubborn man, and he relished his reputation for obstinacy—obstinacy in behalf of the good and the right.

Cleveland also had the reputation of being close-mouthed, serious, and reserved; and this, too, he cultivated. With close friends and those he trusted, Cleveland could be gregarious and talkative; but he found a posture of stolid reserve useful when dealing with politicians and reporters; and he believed it well matched the dignity of presidential office. Lacking social graces, he found that it also served as a refuge during wearisome White House dinners and receptions.

During both of his administrations, Grover Cleveland was frequently charged with indifference to human suffering and poverty. Although quick to chastise laziness and scornful of those who would transform the federal government into a charitable agency, he had a warm and sympathetic side to his character. He was, as well, a man who was sensitive to popular opinion and regard. Cleveland took huge if concealed pleasure in his election victory of 1892, and when he became the object of increasing denunciation during the last years of his second term, he was deeply hurt. He pretended to care little for the insults of the ignorant and misled, but when he left the presidency, he was despondent for the future of his party and his place in history.

Cleveland was by nature stubborn, earnest, and conscientious. He did equivocate on occasion; he was at points prepared to shave his convictions in behalf of political expediency, as when he sought to gain partisan advantage from popular sentiment against the immigration of Chinese laborers; but Cleveland, more than most politicians of his day, sought to match his political actions with his sense of duty. While he undoubtedly saw political advantage in his posture as the independent statesman of inflexible will, standing apart from the machinations of lesser men, there was little of sham in the self-portrait. It was a stance required by his personality as well as by his determination to demonstrate that his meteoric rise within the Democratic party was the result of ability and virtue, not luck and the organizational machine of Samuel Tilden.

Another feature of Cleveland's personality was its contrary characteristics of patience and irritability, practicality and sentiment. Cleveland sought to give the impression of being a man who exemplified self-control and who never acted on impulse, whose every policy statement was the result of thorough study; and more often than not, this was the case. He was, however, known to express himself on occasion with the pettish irritation and explosive anger of a road-company tragedienne. Unimaginative and not easily moved by human misery in the abstract, Cleveland was seen to weep openly at the news of the death of a single child or an intimate friend. Scornful of maudlin do-gooders, he had a strong if covert streak of sentimentality and was ready to idealize the patriotic heroes of the American past. The Founding Fathers were judged to be without flaw, and he praised George Washington as a demigod. Cleveland deplored the efforts of certain historians to cast doubt on the validity of Parson Weems's story about Washington and the cherry tree. The students of the University of Michigan were told to ignore the siren voices that would deny the relevance of principles and morality in politics: the United States must never outgrow or discard the credo of truth, honesty, and goodness that had sustained George Washington.[14]

Whatever the complexities of Cleveland's temperament, the most interesting question for the student of his presidencies is the manner in which his constitutional temperament was frequently at war with his inherited political philosophy. For all his professed respect for the doctrine of separation of powers, Cleveland was a self-assertive executive who felt an obligation to influence the course of government lest stupid legislation endanger the traditions and welfare of the nation. For all his rhetorical allegiance to his party's tradition of limited government and executive restraint, Cleveland's advocacy of presidential independence and impatience of criticism made it likely that the institution of the presidency would be strengthened during his tenure in office and that the authority of the national government—at least in the area of its police power—would be augmented as well. Grover Cleveland claimed to despise personal politics, which he associated with the Stalwart Republican chieftains of the 1870s, but he dominated the executive branch as had no president since Abraham Lincoln. With his electoral victory in 1892, some reporters were already referring to the Cleveland Era.

Acutely conscious of his personal and presidential prerogatives, Cleveland was the individualist in politics who, while paying homage to the party of Jefferson and Jackson, felt free to try to refashion the party in his own image. That he failed has little bearing on the sincerity of the effort and its illustration of Cleveland's political personality. Cleveland's two terms were nonconsecutive, but they share many features in common. Of these perhaps the most interesting is that during both administrations, Cleveland's character and temperament determined his political position more often than did his Democratic political inheritance.

What marks the distinction between Cleveland's two presidential terms is not any major shift of political purpose but a difference in political climate. The years 1893 to 1897 would offer different challenges and a new cast of political antagonists in comparison with the years of his first administration, 1885–89. This study will analyze the major events of each presidential administration in turn. It is first necessary, however, to explain how a man who was known only to a handful of Americans outside the city of Buffalo in 1881 was chosen by the Democratic party to be its presidential candidate three years later.

3

★ ★ ★ ★ ★

"CLEVELAND LUCK": THE ROAD TO THE WHITE HOUSE

Grover Cleveland's rapid rise from obscurity to the presidency was attributed by certain contemporary observers to "Cleveland Luck"—the fortunate individual who succeeds beyond his deserts by being in the right place at the right time. No politician succeeds without a measure of luck, but good timing alone does not explain Cleveland's swift rise in the firmament of Democratic politics. Cleveland was a more skillful politician than has usually been acknowledged—a man able to capitalize upon opportunities not usually of his own making.[1] Diligence and ability, as well as the needs and heterogeneous composition of his party, explain "Cleveland Luck."

Grover Cleveland was born in Caldwell, New Jersey, on 18 March 1837, the fifth child of the Reverend Richard Cleveland and his wife, Anne Neal Cleveland. Christened Stephen Grover Cleveland in tribute to an earlier minister of the parish, he was born to a family of "good background" and very little money. The Clevelands were descended from colonial stock that had settled in the Connecticut Valley, and Cleveland's father was a Yale graduate of scholarly temperament whose ministerial career was marked by little fame and many moves. After serving a succession of small Presbyterian congregations in Connecticut, Virginia, and New Jersey, Richard Cleveland was called to a parish in Fayetteville, New York, in 1841. Grover spent his boyhood years in the central New York towns of Fayetteville and Clinton, and although the Clevelands never lacked for food or shelter, a ministerial salary of less than $600 a year provided no luxuries for a family of nine children. "Waste not, want not" was a necessity as well as a platitude, and if Grover in later years would shed much of the Presbyterian piety of his boyhood home, he never lost his early conviction that frugality was a virtue and extravagance a sin.

Cleveland's father died when Grover was sixteen, and the young man had to surrender his hopes of enrolling at Hamilton College. Instead, he went to New York City to assist one of his older brothers, who was a teacher in a school for the blind. Teaching had little attraction for Grover, however, and a year later he decided to head west to seek his fortune. The destination he had in mind was the city of Cleveland, Ohio, but his western adventure was cut short at Buffalo, New York. Stopping off to see an uncle, Lewis F. Allen, in that city, Cleveland was persuaded to stay and help prepare a pedigree herd book for Allen's prize stock of Shorthorn cattle. Buffalo would be Cleveland's home from 1855 to 1882, and in Buffalo he would find a congenial occupation in the practice of law.

Cleveland's uncle arranged for Grover to be accepted as a clerk and part-time law student in the Buffalo legal firm of Rogers, Bowen, and Rogers. Exhibiting previously hidden qualities of diligence and ambition, Cleveland spent his evening hours reading Blackstone's *Commentaries* and other standard works, and it was now that Cleveland discovered the mildly masochistic pleasure of working long hours under the self-imposed demand of duty. It was a talent he would never lose.

Cleveland was admitted to the bar in May 1858 at the age of twenty-two, and his subsequent progress in the legal profession of the growing port city of Buffalo was slow and certain. Never accused of brilliance by his fellow lawyers, he gradually obtained a reputation as a hard-working, always-reliable member of the bar, with a strong concern for professional ethics. He fastened on every case with a bulldog grip and was never satisfied until he had learned every feature. Suspicious of spontaneity and lacking eloquence, he usually memorized his court arguments, lest he forget a point and do injury to a client. Preparation, not inspiration, marked the good lawyer. Cleveland obviously defined the good lawyer in terms of his own strengths. If he had no talent for oratory and had received but sketchy training in the intricacies of the common law, he possessed an excellent memory, enjoyed digging for facts, and was prepared to work until two or three in the morning when organizing and memorizing his presentation to judge or jury.[2]

Such qualities promised success in the provincial bar of Erie County, and Cleveland realized that promise. By 1881, he was acknowledged as one of the more prominent and respected attorneys in the county, and in that year the New York Central Railroad Company offered him the position of general counsel for its business in western New York. He refused: he already had a savings account of almost $75,000, and the position would have required too much traveling to suit his comfort. Cleveland did not refuse because a connection with the New York Central could damage his political future; he refused because he was content with his professional success in Buffalo and was happy within the confines of his narrow circle of hunting and fishing male companions. In 1881, "Big Steve"—as he was known to a group of close friends—did not plan ever to get married or to be president.

In later years, partisan antagonists would grossly exaggerate the carousing life of Cleveland during his bachelor days in Buffalo. Cleveland was too conscientious in his professional endeavors to have had time for all the drinking, gambling, and fornicating that his enemies alleged. It is equally true, however, that Cleveland, during the 1860s and 1870s, did find relaxation in activities associated with "good old boys" male companionship. His sex life was fairly restricted, probably confined to a few brothel visits and a brief affair with a widow named Maria Halpin; but the restaurant-saloons of Buffalo, practical jokes and buffoon-style nicknames, fishing expeditions, and hunting camps stocked with whiskey and oft-told ribald anecdotes—all provided sources of pleasure and relaxation from the labors of the law.

Cleveland felt at ease only with male companions and with the customary and the familiar. He had little curiosity about other professions or other localities. A contented provincial, he had no desire to travel abroad, and it would be many years before he would see the Mississippi River or venture south of the Potomac. Nor did Cleveland find recreation in reading fiction or poetry or listening to music. He had little interest in what passed as cultural matters. He found sufficient occupation for his time in his profession; poker parties with such friends as Wilson S. ("Shan") Bissell, Oscar Folsom, and Charlie Goodyear; and sporadic labors in behalf of the Democratic party organization of Buffalo and Erie County.

Cleveland's political activity, prior to 1881, came in spurts. He had identified with the Democratic party by the election of 1856, finding little attraction in the abolitionist radicalism of the party of Frémont and Seward. During the Civil War years, Cleveland deserved the designation of a Union Democrat, but he did not volunteer for military service. Claiming, with fair justice, an obligation to provide financial support for his widowed mother, he had, when drafted, hired a substitute to serve in his stead. He advocated the Union cause, however, and probably deplored the impact that the Copperheads had on the reputation of the Democratic party. His first political labors were as a poll watcher and ward worker, and his first political office was as assistant district attorney in 1863. Defeated in his bid for the post of district attorney in 1865, Cleveland concentrated over the next five years on his law practice and then, in 1870, let himself be persuaded to run as the Democratic candidate for sheriff of Erie County. He held that post for two years, declining to run for reelection. For the next decade he took little part in local politics and was probably honestly surprised when, in the fall of 1881, the leaders of the Buffalo City Democratic Committee asked him to accept the party's nomination in the mayoralty race.

Buffalo was a city with a Republican majority, but the Republican organization had grown fat and lazy, while recent Republican city administrations had demonstrated a measure of greed and graft beyond the level of popular expectation. The business leaders of Buffalo were beginning to demand less extravagance and more efficiency, and the Democratic organization made the intelligent decision to select a new face and a man with a local reputation for probity and diligence.

In his letter of acceptance for the Democratic nomination, Cleveland wrote that he considered public officials to be "the trustees of the people." Democratic publicists would later tighten this far-from-original observation into the phrase "A public office is a public trust." Cleveland accepted the improvement, and the slogan would be prominent in all of his subsequent political efforts.

Cleveland won a decisive victory in the city election and was inaugurated as Buffalo's mayor on 1 January 1882. Although he served for only a year, he quickly gained the reputation of being a no-nonsense executive who was an enemy of graft and the friend of the taxpayer. He exposed a scheme to rob the city of $100,000 on a street-cleaning contract; he arranged for a new sewage system to be under the supervision of professional engineers, instead of friends of city officials; he vetoed various pork-barrel appropriations initiated by the City Council. Before his term was half over, Cleveland had gained the attention of certain prominent figures within the state

Democratic party, including Daniel Manning, friend and adviser of the party's gray eminence, Samuel J. Tilden.

Cleveland had obtained the mayoralty of Buffalo with little personal effort, but he was prepared to work—with calculated modesty—for the next rung on the ladder, the Democratic gubernatorial nomination. Fortunately, friends such as Daniel Lockwood and Edgar Apgar were prepared to promote his claim and willing to seize the opportunity provided by a party characterized by ideological confusion and factional division.

Gen. Henry W. Slocum and Roswell P. Flower were initially the leading candidates for the nomination, but neither provided a new face or a source of party unity. Cleveland's political friends would emphasize the superiority of the mayor of Buffalo on both counts, while carefully avoiding personal attacks on either Slocum or Flower. They also emphasized Cleveland's reputation as a reformer—a reformer of admirable caution and good sense; a man who would reform the state administration by improving its economical efficiency as well as its moral tone. Untainted by old quarrels or factional alignments, Cleveland would be a nominee around whom all sections of the state party could unite. For his part, Cleveland carefully avoided direct involvement in the canvassing labors of his friends and kept silent about his gubernatorial ambitions.

In 1882 the Republican party in New York suffered serious division as a result of a foolish act of interference by President Chester A. Arthur, who persuaded his secretary of the Treasury, Charles J. Folger, to seek the Republican gubernatorial nomination in opposition to the Republican incumbent, Alonzo B. Cornell. Heavy-handed tactics and promises of patronage gained Folger the nomination at the Republican State Convention, but the result was bitter resentment on the part of Cornell's supporters. The friends of Grover Cleveland could therefore argue that were the Democrats to choose a candidate such as the conscientious "Veto Mayor" of Buffalo, he would win the votes of many disgruntled Republicans in the general election and thereby assure a Democratic victory.

Cleveland's friends attempted a very difficult thing in the weeks before the Democratic State Convention met in September 1882. They trumpeted Cleveland's independence of organizational politics, while they sought to gain the support of the "County Democracy" faction, led by Abram Hewitt, conciliate the Tilden-Manning organization, and avoid inciting the antagonism of Tammany Hall or Boss Hugh McLaughlin's Brooklyn machine. In the process, suggestions of sympathetic cooperation were broadly distributed, but no hard-and-fast deals were made that could destroy Cleveland's public posture of independence. The posture was not hypocritical or insincere. Neither Cleveland's pride nor his sense of rectitude would allow him to serve as the catspaw of any group or machine. But Cleveland was not politically naïve, and he knew that he had to have organizational support if he was to have a chance at obtaining the gubernatorial nomination. By his own definition, he was a reformer; but reform had to pay respect to political reality. Cleveland was well aware that no politician secured office without the benefit of a well-organized band of political supporters, so he encouraged his friends to make overtures to Abram Hewitt and to Daniel Manning.

By the time the convention met in Syracuse on 21 September 1882, a growing number of the delegates were convinced that the selection of Cleveland offered the greatest likelihood of electoral success, and on the third ballot he gained the necessary majority. The convention adjourned amidst an unwonted display of party unity and enthusiasm. Only then did Cleveland pay a courtesy call on Samuel Tilden. According to the later reminiscences of a confidant, Tilden found Grover Cleveland to be "of somewhat coarse mental fibre and disposition" but "of great force and stubbornly honest in his conviction."[3]

With the support of a united party, Cleveland was victorious in the November election, benefiting from the division of the opposition and the votes of various self-proclaimed Republican Independents.

In his Inaugural Address at Albany on 1 January 1883, Cleveland promised an administration marked by honesty, economy, and the application of sound business principles to government. If it was not an exciting forecast, he was convinced it was what the times needed and what his particular abilities could best assure. He was prepared to work long hours, serve as quality inspector of the legislative product of the assembly, and prove to his old Buffalo companions that Big Steve had outgrown them and was now the respected leader of the Democratic party of New York. None of his Buffalo friends or supporters was offered a position in the new administration.

Grover Cleveland wished to project a dignified image, but he had no illusions that he could combine dignity with handsomeness of face and figure. Weighing over 280 pounds, he was a stout man who was called "Uncle Jumbo" by his nephews. Of average height, he had sandy brown hair, which was already beginning to thin at the top; pale blue eyes, under heavy lids; a strong Roman nose; a drooping brown mustache; a strong jaw, embellished by a double chin; and large hands with sausagelike fingers. His movements were slow and ponderous; his tenor voice was penetrating but flat in tone and cadence; his complexion was surprisingly pale for a man who enjoyed the outdoors.[4]

If Cleveland lacked beauty, he did not lack energy, and he entered upon his duties with self-assertive confidence. He had promised honesty and efficiency, and he had no self-doubts on either score. There could indeed be no question about his honesty, but the advocate of business efficiency in politics was not by all criteria a good administrator, chiefly because he was reluctant to delegate responsibility and because he approached the tasks of the state executive in the same way that he had worked as a Buffalo lawyer: he would prepare each case for himself. As governor, Cleveland listened to advice—particularly that of his aide, Col. Daniel S. Lamont—but he would not accept it unless he had investigated the matter for himself. As a result, his desk was always burdened by stacks of papers, despite his fourteen-hour workday, and his disposition suffered accordingly. Callers were often seen as instruments of unmerited harassment.

As governor, Cleveland supported certain modest institutional reforms designed to promote public supervision of the political process and used his veto power to curb legislative extravagance, unwarranted public-assistance programs, and improper interference with the rights of contract. In the latter connection, his most famous veto was that of the "five-cent fare bill." This bill mandated that the fare on the municipal elevated railroads in New York City be reduced to a uniform level of five cents. It was a popular bill, especially because the railroads were under the control of the monopolistic Manhattan Company, which was dominated in turn by the justly despised Jay Gould. Cleveland, however, was convinced that a mandatory reduction in fares was forbidden by the railroads' state charters.

Cleveland's veto of the five-cent fare on 1 March 1883, and certain other acts of executive censorship, generated brief outbursts of criticism, but more generally his veto messages encouraged a public perception that the new governor was a vigilant, incorruptible public servant and the watchdog of the state treasury. This was particularly true of veto messages that attacked laws granting privileges or immunities to particular corporations. With these vetoes, Cleveland proclaimed his enmity to governmental favoritism of any kind, whether to individual applicants for public charity or to banks and railroads searching for hidden subsidies.[5]

It was, however, Cleveland's battles with the chieftains and braves of Tammany Hall that secured most press attention beyond the confines of New York. Although he had accepted Tammany's aid in the election of 1882, he became convinced that the low political morals and patronage greed of John Kelley and his allies were harmful to the public interest, the state Democratic party, and the reputation of the Cleveland administration. He increasingly ignored Tammany's nominees when filling public offices, and he sought to prevent the reelection to the state senate of Thomas F. Grady, a Tammany stalwart. Some political calculation was involved here. Cleveland was aware of the poor reputation of Tammany among many Democrats throughout the country, who remembered the scandal of the Tweed Ring, and was aware that a clear separation between himself and Tammany Hall could enhance his reputation as the enemy of political chicanery. But Cleveland's determination to exert executive independence and to give New York an administration marked by integrity and economy made inevitable his opposition to the demands and political style of Tammany Hall.

It is impossible to determine just when Grover Cleveland began to entertain hopes for the presidential nomination of his party in the election of 1884. As early as December 1883 he had begun, in newspaper interviews, to speak on national issues and to advocate the revision of federal revenue laws, but it was only in the spring of 1884 that Cleveland indicated his aspirations by proclaiming his disinterest.[6] He informed the New York City lawyer Charles S. Fairchild that he regarded "any suggestion of my candidacy for a place higher than that I now occupy" as quite inadmissible on personal grounds.[7] Shortly before the Democratic National Convention was to assemble, he confided to Daniel Manning that although he was deeply gratified by reports that he was mentioned as "among those deemed worthy," he had "not a particle of ambition to be President of the United States."[8] It would seem that he protested too much and that Barkis was most willing.

Cleveland must, however, have thought his selection a long shot. He had served little more than a year of his gubernatorial term, and anxious for the prize were Democrats who could boast long years of service in state and federal government, such as Thomas F. Bayard of Delaware, Thomas A. Hendricks of Indiana, John G. Carlisle of Kentucky, Samuel J. Randall of Pennsylvania, and Allen G. Thurman of Ohio. There was even a diehard faction calling for Samuel J. Tilden to carry the Democratic banner once more and revenge the

"Steal of '76." Yet by the time the Democrats formally assembled in Chicago on July 8, Cleveland was clearly the front runner.

To say that Cleveland was seen as the candidate with the best chance of gaining victory in November is to offer a truth but not an explanation. The question persists: Why was this political novice considered to have a better chance than his more seasoned rivals? One part of the explanation can be found in the divided state of the Democratic party and the conviction that a "new man" might better inspire party unity in the fall campaign. The Democratic party still suffered North-South division and was beginning to experience division between its urban and rural elements, as well as between its recently naturalized recruits and its "native Americans." The Democratic party in 1884 was in many ways less a national institution than a cluster of state parties that gathered every four years in an effort to gain control of the presidency. In such a situation, a political figure who lacked a long political past and was not tainted by old factional quarrels had an understandable attraction.

There is an obvious parallel between Cleveland's appeal to the divided Democrats of New York State in 1882 and his appeal to the divided national party two years later. A new political personality, with a reputation for honesty and candor, Cleveland could provide a rallying point for a party beset by fragmentation. Moreover, in 1884, as earlier, he stood forth as a man innocent of ties to any machine while benefiting from organizational support.

With Tilden's less-than-heartfelt support, Daniel Manning maneuvered the Tilden-Manning machine behind the candidacy of Grover Cleveland in the spring of 1884, promoting Cleveland as Tilden's natural heir. Manning worked to neutralize the opposition of Tammany Hall and to obtain a strong majority of the New York delegation, while reminding Democratic leaders in other states of the importance of New York as a source of party funds and electoral votes. In three of the last four presidential elections the Democrats had selected a New York citizen as their standard bearer, and they must be persuaded to do so once again. As he surveyed the opposition, Manning became increasingly convinced that neither the old party warhorses, such as Thurman and Hendricks, nor the favorite sons, such as Randall, Bayard, and Carlisle, generated enthusiasm beyond their state or section. Moreover, none of them elicited praise from those Independent Republicans who would soon pridefully accept the disparaging designation of Mugwump.[9]

Much has been written about the influence of the Mugwumps in the selection of Cleveland by the Democratic National Convention and his subsequent victory over the Republican nominee, James G. Blaine. The Mugwumps magnified their influence beyond fact or evidence, but they did provide some aid to Manning and the other New York politicians who promoted Cleveland's nomination at the convention, and they provided a source of interest and entertainment in the election campaign of 1884.

The Mugwumps were a small band of dissident Republicans, largely confined to the states of Massachusetts and New York. In Massachusetts their more vocal members were James Freeman Clarke, Thomas Wentworth S. Higginson, Moorfield Storey, Edward Atkinson, Charles W. Eliot, Josiah Quincy, and Charles Francis Adams; in New York, Carl Schurz, Edwin L. Godkin, George William Curtis, and Henry Ward Beecher. Unhappy with many features of the political and social scene in the Gilded Age, these men were particularly unhappy with what they saw as the corruption of the political system by moneyed parvenus, patronage-hungry politicians, and boss-led machines. Of patrician sensibilities, they were convinced that the ills of the nation resulted chiefly from the moral corruption that characterized American politics, and they saw James G. Blaine as the very emblem of all they found distasteful. As Geoffrey Blodgett has observed, Mugwumpery was a state of mind, instead of an alternative to the two-party political system: "not an organization but a mood."[10] But the Mugwumps, although lacking talent for political organization, were quick to declare their "principles." They insisted that political morals were more important than legislative issues; that the most threatening national peril was political corruption; that in the next presidential election, voters should decide on the basis of the character and personal integrity of the candidate, instead of outmoded political battle cries.

The proclaimed moral superiority of the Mugwumps irritated many Americans, and critics questioned their virility as well as their practicality. They were sneered at as political hermaphrodites and mocked for their patrician airs and self-righteousness:

> Oh, we are the salt of the earth,
>   and the pick of the people too;
> We're all of us men of worth,
>   and vastly better than you![11]

Grover Cleveland was in many ways the polar opposite of Charles Eliot, president of Harvard University, and Edwin L. Godkin, editor of the *Nation*; but Eliot, Godkin, and other Mugwumps seized upon

Cleveland as the man who could initiate a new and cleaner era in American politics. If they made no thorough examination of Cleveland's political record, they convinced themselves that he deserved their unstinted praise. In June 1884, the *New York Times* published three columns of letters from various Mugwump luminaries, urging that Cleveland be selected by the Democratic party. Cleveland's very deficiencies encouraged confidence. It was to his credit that he was not brilliant, eloquent, flexible, magnetic: these were qualities needed by the demagogue, not the public servant who would purge the government of rascals and boodlers.

The Mugwumps were very sure of their enemies, the corrupt spoilsmen, and of the individual target of their animosity, James G. Blaine; but opposition was insufficient comfort; they must also be for someone. They selected Cleveland and, with unwonted familiarity, would refer to him occasionally as "Grover the Good." Their definition of reform was, of course, not unlike that entertained by Cleveland: both emphasized administrative reform rather than structural change. Efficiency and honesty, not regulation and innovation, were the ingredients of desired reform.

Whatever their subsequent claims, the Mugwumps did not obtain the Democratic nomination for Grover Cleveland. Cleveland's political managers made use of Mugwump intimations that were the Democrats to nominate a man of high political morals, the Mugwumps would bolt the Republican party; but in all likelihood, Cleveland would have gained the nomination had the little band of Mugwump leaders never put pen to paper. The editorial comment made by George William Curtis three days before the Democratic National Convention began on July 8 that Cleveland was a strong man "not because of his party but despite of it" was not the kind of statement that would persuade a Democratic delegate to change his vote in Grover's behalf.[12]

Mugwump praise was far less important than the quiet and effective labors of Daniel Manning and his lieutenants, Edgar Apgar, William Hudson, Smith Weed, and William C. Whitney. As a result of their labors, Cleveland led the first ballot with 392 votes. After a gentleman's agreement between Manning and Samuel Randall, whereby Randall secured a promise of virtual control over patronage distribution in Pennsylvania in a future Cleveland administration, and after a series of last-minute switches by bandwagon volunteers from other states, Cleveland had 684 votes when the second ballot was declared official. The Democratic party had selected its presidential nominee and found a new leader.

"Cleveland Luck" was involved but also the ability of Cleveland to rally to his side skilled political professionals while maintaining a surprisingly large measure of independence. He would maintain this posture—the product of personal character and political acumen—throughout the campaign of 1884. In that campaign, Cleveland gave few speeches and demonstrated intelligence and poise when confronted by the most trying experience of his political life.

The campaign of 1884 is usually characterized in textbooks as "the dirtiest campaign" in United States history. By some criteria the campaigns of 1928 and 1972 were dirtier, but certainly there has never been a campaign in which the public morality of one candidate and the sexual morality of his opponent received such unrelenting attention. This emphasis on the moral failings of the two candidates is often attributed to the lack of distinction between the platforms of the Republican and the Democratic parties and the failure of Cleveland and the Republican presidential nominee, James G. Blaine, to take decisive stands on the issues. But this is an unsatisfactory explanation.

There were differences between the party platforms and between the positions of the major party candidates. Although the Democratic platform gave much space to denunciations of Republican deviltry, it went on to advocate the reform of federal land-sales policy, the reduction of federal taxation and expenditures, the restriction of monopolistic combinations, and "a scrupulous regard for the rights of property as defined by law." The Republican platform emphasized the value of tariff protection for the expansion of the home market and the wages of American labor, continued effort in behalf of civil-service reform, and the importance of establishing "an international standard which shall fix [for all countries] . . . the relative value of gold and silver coinage." There is little doubt that both parties observed the tradition of avoiding specific proposals and took comfort in platitudes and generalities; but there were distinctions. Although there was no clear difference between the currency planks of the two platforms, the Republican document implied support for a more active federal government, whereas the Democratic platform evinced more deference to "the preservation of personal rights" and "the reserved rights of the states."[13]

As there were differences in emphasis between the two platforms, so were there distinctions in the campaign goals and strategies of the two candidates. Not only was Blaine the more active campaigner and the more practiced and polished speaker, but he sought to promote the issue of tariff protection as the centerpiece of

32

his campaign. Cleveland, on the other hand, emphasized the "honest administration of public affairs" and the elimination of governmental extravagance. Cleveland was at this time uncertain of his position on the tariff. Though inclined to favor a lower level of import duties, he sensed the political danger of the issue, was content with the clumsy straddle of the Democratic platform, and referred to the tariff only by indirection as he warned against the economic and moral dangers of the surplus in the federal treasury.

In the early weeks of the campaign—before scandals and mud-slinging began to dominate—Blaine sought to counter Cleveland's call for "corrective action" with demands for "constructive action" by the federal government. The latter would be expressed by a vigorous foreign policy, improvement of the nation's waterways, the encouragement of foreign commerce, and a national protective-tariff system that would band together all sections and occupational groups. Blaine hoped that those portions of the South that were becoming industrialized would be attracted to protection and the Republican party, and he thought that tariff protection, with its implied distrust of the British free-trade system, would appeal to Irish-Americans; but his chief object was to gain the electoral votes of New York, New Jersey, Indiana, and Connecticut, the traditional swing states in post–Civil War elections. Cleveland, however, would not cooperate in engaging in a debate on the tariff, and the electorate—having experienced a brief financial panic in May—was not generally in a mood to identify tariff protection and economic expansion.

The Democratic strategy was not to debate Blaine but to paint him as an example of the cupidity and the shabby political morals of a party too long in power. And there was material at hand for the palette of the partisan.

James G. Blaine was an able and intelligent individual who loved the game of politics and who was not above using his political position for personal financial gain. He was not the epitome of corruption as drawn by Democratic cartoonists, but he was a man who, in the phrase of a later day, was guilty of a "conflict of interest." The most publicized of his lapses involved the favorable ruling he had given, as Speaker of the House in 1869, in behalf of the Little Rock and Fort Smith Railroad. He had subsequently—by secret agreement—been allowed to sell the railroad's bonds on a highly generous commission. In the process, Blaine had written letters to a railroad executive named Warren Fisher, which had come into the possession of Fisher's one-time bookkeeper, James Mulligan.

Mulligan—inspired by civic outrage or mercenary greed—made a clumsy and unsuccessful attempt to blackmail Blaine, and the letters, by a confusing series of fortuitous events, fell first into the hands of Blaine and then into those of his journalistic enemies.

The more sensational dailies were not the only ones that had a field day with the revival of the Mulligan Letters scandal in the campaign of 1884, nor were those letters the only evidence that Blaine's professional ethics were, at the least, malleable. Charismatic as a speaker, Blaine was a babbler as a correspondent; and the campaign saw the revelation of the "Sanborn letter" and further disclosures from the archives of James Mulligan. Among the latter, particularly damaging was Blaine's endorsement to one communication requesting Mr. Fisher to "Burn this letter." Such a demand must imply a guilty conscience. In the editorial opinion of the *New York Times*, which displayed the new set of Mulligan letters on its front page, Blaine had exposed himself as "a prostitutor of public trusts, a scheming jobber, and a reckless falsifier."[14]

The *Times* was but one of six New York newspapers that, having supported the Republican James A. Garfield in 1880, now turned against the Republican nominee and gave their support to Grover Cleveland. Week after week, the *Nation* reprinted a series of Blaine's contradictory utterances in parallel columns, but the periodicals that most incited the ire of Blaine's managers were *Puck* and *Harper's Weekly*, for they contained the cartoons of Bernhard Gillam and Thomas Nast. Politicians, like photographers, have always tended to believe that a picture is worth a thousand words or, at the least, leaves a more lasting impression in the minds of the modestly literate. Nast's cartoons, which showed Blaine in fawning collusion with railroad entrepreneurs, were fairly acidic; but they were outdone by Gillam, who represented Blaine as the Tattooed Man, clothed in a breechcloth and seeking to hide from the audience a flabby body stenciled with notations of his alleged misdemeanors and phrases from his more suspicious correspondence.

Democratic politicians were not behindhand in their efforts to capitalize on that correspondence. They organized a great parade of "Democratic business men" who marched up Wall Street chanting "Burn this letter!" and who, on cue, would stop, draw out a presumed facsimile of a communication from Blaine to Fisher, light a match, and create a small pyrotechnic display to the applause of the bystanders. Presumably, some of these partisan firebugs were among the crowd of thirty thousand Cleveland supporters who, late in the campaign, formed a "Citizens' March" and traversed the length of

Broadway, ending at number 618, where a canvas picture twenty yards in width was stretched across the front of the building. This work of art pictured Fisher, with Blaine's letter in hand, hesitating before a lighted candle.[15]

It is difficult to discover whether these juvenile exercises were directed by the Democratic National Committee. Senator Arthur Pue Gorman of Maryland was the predominant figure on the National Committee during the campaign, and his chief lieutenants were Daniel Manning, William C. Whitney, and Cleveland's friend and aide, Daniel S. Lamont. Gorman and Manning were old pros who saw the course of safety in soft-pedaling the tariff and other controversial issues and concentrating on inefficiency in Washington and the superior political virtue of the Democratic candidate. They were prepared to encourage a comparison of the political morality of Cleveland and Blaine, and there is no evidence that they instructed their supporters at the precinct level to resist the temptation to descend from personal comparisons to character assassination.

For his part, Cleveland intervened on only one occasion. When an effort was made to cast doubt on the premarital innocence of Mrs. Blaine by allegations that the birth of her first child had followed the date of her marriage by less than nine months, Cleveland informed his political managers that he wanted them to put an end to such slanders.[16] Believing, and wanting to believe, that Blaine was a man of shabby political morals, Cleveland never requested an end to abusive cartoons or parades.

Cleveland's own role in his campaign appears at first glance to have been very small. After delivering a short acceptance speech to the notification committee from the Democratic National Convention, he gave only two campaign speeches, one at Bridgeport, Connecticut, and the other at Newark, New Jersey. Political caution had some influence in his decision to limit his campaign appearances, as did the advice of party managers, but more important was the fact that Cleveland was spending long days in Albany as governor and chief clerk and had a strong distaste for the preparation and delivery of campaign speeches. As is the case with most persons, he disliked doing what he did poorly, and he realized that he was a poor stump speaker. A public speech of any kind was a heavy labor, and he had no talent for extemporaneous address. It was neither cowardice nor modesty that limited his public appearances; it was the human desire to avoid appearing at a disadvantage.

Cleveland labored and sweated over the customary letter of acceptance, and its heavy-laden prose reflected its many drafts. Its only element of novelty was a call for a constitutional amendment limiting the president to a single term. Such a limitation would presumably eliminate the temptation that the president would serve not as a public servant but as an ambitious politician currying the support of an army of officeholders. In the balance of the address, Cleveland endorsed the Democratic platform, proclaimed allegiance to the principle of civil-service reform, urged governmental economy, and declared his opposition to such exercises of the police power as prohibition legislation. He advocated laws to promote the welfare of workingpeople but offered no advice respecting their objectives, other than a brief reference criticizing alien immigrants who had no intention "to become Americans."[17]

Similar themes characterized his speeches at Bridgeport and Newark, where he characterized the Republican forces as "a vast army of office-holders," long in power, corrupt to the core, and rich in resources of money and influence. That army stood as a barrier between the people and their government and as an obstacle to the reduction of governmental taxation and governmental extravagance.[18]

George William Curtis and other members of the Civil Service Reform League urged Cleveland to give specific promises that he would retain meritorious officeholders, irrespective of their party affiliation. They had to be content with a letter from Cleveland to Curtis, in which Cleveland promised to consider retaining such officeholders if they were not in positions central to the execution of administration policy and had not previously engaged in "obnoxious" partisan activity. Officeholders who had attended strictly to their public duty would not be dismissed arbitrarily "for party or political reasons."[19]

Cleveland's efforts to secure his election were chiefly confined to his financial contributions to the Democratic war chest and letters of advice to his political friends. While he wrote that he was relying on Daniel Manning "to keep me in the right shape," Cleveland's temperament would not allow him to refrain from giving instruction to the party managers, even as he acknowledged their greater experience.[20] The major test for Cleveland and his managers came with the Maria Halpin affair, and here it was Cleveland who determined party strategy.

When Cleveland was charged with fathering an illegitimate child and sending the victim of his lust to the insane asylum, he was attacked at what was presumably his greatest strength, his moral probity. Cleveland wisely decided to put forth a bold face and give his Democratic supporters and Mugwump allies no excuse for retreat.

They rallied under his guidance, and in a display of political leger-demain, Cleveland emerged from "the Buffalo scandal" with his reputation for courage and candor enhanced.

This had not been the intention of the *Buffalo Evening Telegraph*, when, on July 21, it had publicized Cleveland's sexual transgressions under the title "A Terrible Tale," or of the Reverend George H. Ball, D.D., a Republican loyalist who served as chief source and investigative reporter for revelations of the liaison of "Grover the Good" and Maria Halpin.

Maria Halpin was a widow of easy morals with whom Cleveland had had frequent sexual encounters during the year 1874. In the salaciously genteel language of the time, Maria had "bestowed her favors" on other Buffalo gentlemen as well. When Maria had become pregnant, however, and had given birth to an infant boy, it was Grover whom she selected as the child's father. Cleveland had admitted the possibility of his paternity and had agreed that the child be named Oscar Folsom Cleveland. Oscar Folsom was at the time his law partner and possibly another candidate for parental attribution.[21] Maria had subsequently fallen victim to an excessive appetite for liquor and had suffered a mental breakdown. Cleveland had then arranged for the institutional care of the mother and the adoption of the boy by a childless couple living in the western part of the state. Considering his obligations fulfilled, he never saw Maria or the boy again.

By the criteria of a later day, Cleveland's chief sin was less the act of fornication than his subsequent rather churlish treatment of Maria and the infant. It was, however, the sin of unchastity that most fascinated his contemporaries and threatened to defeat his presidential candidacy. The manner in which many editors and clergymen dwelt with salacious enjoyment on the details—real and imagined—of a liaison ten years in the past would suggest that the Maria Halpin episode provided some Gilded Age Americans with a welcome vent for sexual fantasies.

The Reverend George Ball of the Hudson Street Baptist Church in Buffalo relished his fame as a source of information on Cleveland's delinquency, and in an effort to sustain notoriety and promote Republican success, he expanded "A Terrible Tale" into an epic of moral depravity. Cleveland had made his bachelor rooms in downtown Buffalo "a harem" and, his lust unslaked, had foraged for victims "in the city and surrounding villages." The division between Cleveland and Blaine was that "between the brothel and the family, between indecency and decency, between lust and law . . . between the depradation of woman and due honor, protection, and love of our mothers, sisters and daughters."[22]

Lucy Stone commiserated with the readers of the *Woman's Journal* on the lamentable impact that Cleveland's example would have on impressionable male youth, and the president of Amherst College declared that Cleveland's stance as a paragon of virtue had been revealed as a sham and that he would now receive the support only of "voters of debauched moral sentiment." The editors of the Republican press expectedly offered a similar judgment after teasing their readers with allusions to "perverse enjoyments" and "bestial conduct."

The Republicans, having suffered partisan attacks on the character of their candidate, were understandably anxious to pay back in kind. As "Democratic business men" had engaged in childish imitation of Blaine's pleas to Mr. Fisher, so now their counterparts held parades in which vested businessmen of the Blaine persuasion pushed baby carriages, complete with dolls, and chanted in falsetto tones, "Ma! Ma! Where's My Pa!"

After the initial shock had subsided, Cleveland's supporters rallied to his defense with varying degrees of bravado. With Cleveland's approval, the State Democratic Committee requested a sympathetic minister to conduct a "thorough investigation," and the Reverend Kinsley Twining reported that "after the preliminary offence," Cleveland's conduct had been "singularly honorable, showing no attempt to evade responsibility, and doing all that he could to meet the duties involved, of which marriage was certainly not one."[23] Other political friends zealously spread a report that Cleveland was not the culprit but instead was a self-selected victim. It had been one of Mrs. Halpin's married admirers who was the probable father, but bachelor Grover had accepted the responsibility in an act of Arthurian chivalry.

Col. Thomas Wentworth Higginson informed his fellow Bostonians that unbroken integrity was more important than unbroken chastity, and Edwin L. Godkin solemnly told the readers of the *Nation* that although chastity was indeed a fine thing, "every man knows in his heart that it is not the greatest of virtues, that offences against it have often been consistent with. . . the qualities which ennoble human nature and dignify human life and make human progress possible."[24] Occasionally Cleveland's supporters went too far in their efforts to diminish the importance of sexual continence, as when the Reverend Henry Ward Beecher—whose own record was a bit spotty—informed a reporter that if every New Yorker who had broken the Seventh Commandment were to vote for Cleveland, he would carry the state by a large majority.

More interesting than the accuracy of Beecher's prediction is the role that Cleveland played in his own defense. When the *Buffalo Evening Telegraph* first broke the story of Maria's illegitimate child, Cleveland had sent his Buffalo supporters a three-word telegram: "Tell The Truth." At Cleveland's direction the telegram was made public, and it had the desired impact of repairing the confidence of his supporters. After sending the telegram, Cleveland appeared to ignore the scandalmongers and to leave his defense to such good friends as Charlie Goodyear, Shan Bissell, and Daniel Lockwood. In fact, Cleveland kept in close touch with these men, wisely advocating a policy of "no cringing." They were to acknowledge that Cleveland had fallen prey to temptation—but only once. They were to emphasize Cleveland's manly and generous assumption of responsibility for the infant boy, while avoiding allegations against any other parental claimant. They were vigorously to deny that Cleveland had ever entertained a woman "in any way bad" in the governor's mansion, and they were to be prepared for further mischief from Ball and his gang, particularly the production of letters from Cleveland to Mrs. Halpin. If such letters were produced, they would be forgeries and had to be exposed as such.[25]

In an age when propriety, at least in its public expressions, was much prized by the middle class, it is surprising that Cleveland's candidacy was not more seriously damaged by the Maria Halpin scandal. In explanation, one can cite the poor timing of the Buffalo Republicans, who might better have tossed their bombshell in October instead of July, Cleveland's politically shrewd posture of proclaimed candor and dignified reserve, and a cacaphony of events during the last month of the campaign, damaging to Blaine's electoral success. These last included the unexpected strength of the Prohibition party, the stubborn enmity of Roscoe Conkling, and the Reverend Samuel Burchard's weakness for alliterative denunciation.

There were a total of seven parties contesting the presidential election of 1884. They included the Equal Woman's Rights party, with Belva Lockwood as its presidential candidate; but the only "third parties" that threatened to influence the election results were the Greenback-Labor party and the Prohibition party. The former, led by the political chameleon Gen. Benjamin Franklin Butler, was seen as a threat primarily to the Democrats, and the latter, as a problem for the Republicans. Despite secret subsidies from the Republican National Committee, Butler's candidacy never caught fire, and the fear that he would steal the Democratic share of the labor vote in certain northeastern cities proved unfounded. The Prohibition party and its candidate, John P. St. John, exhibited greater strength than expected, particularly in upstate New York. This was hurtful to Blaine, because most members of the Prohibition party were former Republicans who had no use for Cleveland or the Democratic party.

Even more damaging to Blaine's chances of gaining a large majority of the popular vote of upstate New York, and therefore the state's electoral vote, was the refusal of Roscoe Conkling to bury the hatchet and forget past party rivalries. Conkling was no longer a Republican of national influence and aspirations—as he had been in the days of Grant's presidency—but he was still a power in Oneida County and was determined that the county organization would offer little help to Blaine's candidacy. In all probability, Conkling's ill temper was more damaging to Blaine than was the stupidity of Samuel Burchard, though it figures less prominently in accounts of America's "dirtiest election."

In the last days of the campaign, Blaine visited New York City, and among the various groups that were scheduled to demonstrate their partisan faith and optimism was a delegation of Protestant ministers. Their accidental spokesman was Samuel Burchard. At the conclusion of a rambling address, Burchard linked the Protestant and Republican creeds and assured Blaine that Burchard and his fellow clerics had no intention of deserting the Grand Old Party for one characterized by "Rum, Romanism, and Rebellion." A stenographer who was assigned to cover Blaine's visit reported Burchard's alliteration, and its insult to the Roman Catholic Church, to Senator Gorman at Democratic headquarters. Within hours, Gorman had arranged for handbills to be distributed to Manhattan precincts that had a large concentration of Irish-Americans.

Burchard's insult—which Blaine was slow to recognize and repudiate—undoubtedly lost the Republican leader some votes among the Irish of New York City, while it probably won some votes among "nativist Americans," who saw Catholicism as the enemy. The only thing that appears certain is that the influence of the "Burchard Affair" was exaggerated by Republican leaders at the time and has been exaggerated by many historians since.

Cleveland won the election by the narrowest of margins. His plurality in New York State was less than 1,100 votes. A shift of 550 votes would have given New York's electoral vote, and therefore the election, to Blaine. In the nation at large, Cleveland received 4,875,971 votes (48.5 percent); Blaine, 4,852,234 votes (48.3 percent). Because

Cleveland's margin of victory was so small, historians have engaged in lengthy debate as to "the key event," "the crucial factor." Some see the Mugwump rebellion as a prime consideration; others, the superior character of Grover Cleveland, the political malfeasance of Blaine, the Burchard Affair, or factional division within the Republican party.

The research of Lee Benson has conclusively shown that the secession of the Mugwumps was of limited influence. Blaine received solid support in areas of traditional Republican strength. The Republican percentage of the total vote was only 0.09 less in 1884 than in 1880, and the defeated Blaine received almost 400,000 more votes than had the victorious Garfield four years earlier.[26] The best explanation for the narrow margin of Cleveland's victory would seem to be the evenness of the strength of the two parties during the 1880s; and the best explanation for Blaine's defeat, the fact that the year 1884 witnessed a short-term economic slump—always a handicap for the party of the incumbent administration—and that Blaine and the Republican managers failed to conciliate Roscoe Conkling. Whereas Garfield had secured a plurality of 1,946 votes in Oneida County in 1880, Cleveland edged Blaine by a plurality of 69 votes in Conkling's county bailiwick in 1884.[27] One reaches the discouraging conclusion that Cleveland's victory in 1884 was perhaps less the result of his superior political morals than the result of the machinations of Roscoe Conkling, a man whose political ethics were far more suspect than those of James G. Blaine.

One can always view election results from two different perspectives: why the loser lost and why the winner won. Blaine lost through a series of misfortunes and the vindictiveness of an old enemy. Cleveland won because of his refusal to be shaken by the Halpin Affair, his quiet guidance of the hard-working Democratic-party managers, and his appreciation that in a program of cautious reform, governmental economy, and honesty in the public service, the Democrats had their best chance to persuade northern and western voters to forget the southern flavor of the Democratic party and trust that party with the administration of the national government.

One can better speak of "Democratic Luck" than "Cleveland Luck" when analyzing the election of 1884. In Cleveland the Democratic party had stumbled on the right man for the time. A more progressive or more conservative candidate perhaps would not have served them so well. The quietly ambitious and shrewd governor of New York—independent and yet cooperative—provided the answer for ending the Wilderness Years of the Democratic party.

Cleveland, despite his protestations against leaving his accustomed habitat and duties, was highly gratified by his victory. He saw it in part as a vindication against the slanders of the Reverend Mr. Ball and his cohorts. Cleveland would, indeed, never forget their attacks or the anger and hurt they had inspired.[28] Never again would he consider Buffalo his home, and his heightened distaste for prying journalists would influence his relations with the press for the rest of his political life.

As always, he sought solace in work. There were gubernatorial tasks to finish before he formally resigned in January, and there was the distasteful labor of writing an Inaugural Address.

4

THE CAUTIOUS REFORMER: CLEVELAND'S FIRST ADMINISTRATION

Democratic and Republican newspapers across the country devoted their lead editorials on 4 March 1885 to the inauguration of a Democratic president. Many made mention of the significance of the occasion for sectional reconciliation; several implied that the presence of a Democratic chief executive portended a political revolution. Few editors took time to discuss the state of the nation; none made reference to "America in transition."

This is not surprising, however. No generation sees itself as "transitional." That task is reserved for historians at a later date, and even they usually begin with an acknowledgment that every period of time is transitional by definition. Not, however, in equal degree. Historians are in general agreement that in the two decades after Appomattox, American economic society and its institutions experienced a significant transition. Between the assassination of Abraham Lincoln and the inauguration of Grover Cleveland, the face of America had changed in important ways, largely as the result of three social forces: industrialization, urbanization, and immigration. The last fifteen years of the nineteenth century would see these forces effect even more pronounced changes, but their impact on American society and institutions was already apparent by the advent of Cleveland's first presidency.

The impact of industrialization is perhaps the most obvious. The two decades following the Civil War witnessed the increasing domination of the factory system, the geographic expansion of America's industrial base, and a doubling of the nation's total manufactured product. By the end of the decade of the 1880s, the value of manufactured products exceeded that of farms and ranches. The expansion of the nation's railroad system was essential to the rapid growth of the manufacturing sector. By 1885, there were almost 140,000 miles of railroad track, and improved transportation facilities made possible the increased pace of industrialism as the railroad linked growing industrial towns with sources of raw materials as well as a national market. For some industries the railroad provided an even-more-immediate incentive to growth. The demand for steel rails spurred the increased application of the Bessemer process for converting pig iron into steel and encouraged the rapid development of the iron and steel industry as well as the expansion of anthracite coal mining.

The 1880s also saw a dramatic increase in the number of patents registered at the U.S. Patent Office and the establishment of a separate tool-and-die industry. New machine tools and inventions spurred the expansion of such comparatively new industries as steel and oil and helped to transform such older industries as flour milling, shoe and clothing manufacture, mining, and lumber. The increased application of the Corliss steam engine was but one symbol of the beginnings of a technological revolution and an industrialization process unmatched in pace by that of any other nation in previous human history.

The growth of cities was the inevitable accompaniment of the spread of industry and the factory system. In 1885 a majority of Americans still lived in a rural, agrarian environment, but almost a third of America's population of fifty-five million lived in cities, and twenty-five of those cities boasted populations of over one hundred thousand.

American cities could not claim to have solved the complex network of problems associated with urban transportation and communication, water supply, sewage disposal, and police and fire prevention, but in a few eastern cities, progress had been made in each of those areas. The 1880s saw the beginnings of the effort by a small corps of pioneer reformers to apply America's boasted technological prowess to the problems of the industrial city in an effort to make it more habitable as well as more efficient.

Every new arrival to such swollen, sprawling cities as New York and Chicago had problems of adjustment, but this was particularly true of the European immigrant. The impact of immigration on American society began with the settlers at Jamestown, but it is difficult to exaggerate the importance of immigration as a social force during the post–Civil War decades. Cheaper transportation facilities and the lure of jobs and economic improvement inspired a dramatic increase in the emigration of Europeans to America. During the 1870s some 2.2 million people emigrated; during the 1880s, better than 5 million, as European immigrants furnished almost one-third of the nation's population growth in these decades. Some traveled west to the Missouri Valley and some to the northern plains of the Dakotas, but a majority settled in the cities, where they often formed ethnic ghettos in an effort to sustain the traditions of the past, even while they sought to adapt to strange ways and fight an increasing sense of alienation. Sustained by the hope that the "Promise of America" would be fulfilled for their children, they made an essential contribution to American economic expansion and played an equally important role in the rise of the city.

The forces of industrialization, urbanization, and immigration had an obvious effect on the economic institutions of American society and had a more subtle and indirect impact on its social and political institutions as well. The relationship of industrialization to business cycles and recessions, the size of the industrial labor force, and the evolution of labor unions is easily traced, and so, too, is the connection between the development of a national market for American manufactures and the industrial-combination movement. The Knights of Labor and railroad pooling agreements were both a part of the American scene by Cleveland's first inauguration, and it would be but a few years before the American Federation of Labor and the Standard Oil Trust would make their appearance. The post–Civil War economic revolution—the trumpeted example of the beneficial effects of the open market, unfettered competition, and individual economic freedom—compelled people to depend increasingly on organizational instruments as they sought to gain an increased share of its promised benefits.

Industrialization, urbanization, and the increased rate of immigration had effects as well on national political institutions, but these effects were still largely concealed when Cleveland took the oath as the nation's twenty-second president. Farmer protests against the expanding power of the railroads had apparently done little to lessen the domination of the two major parties, nor had those parties adopted distinct or contrary philosophies respecting the impact and problems of industrialization. Election campaigns were still conducted to the accompaniment of torchlight parades, wide popular participation, and flamboyant oratory. Local issues and religious and ethnic identifications were more frequently the determinants of shifts in voting behavior than were such national economic issues as the protective tariff or the composition of the nation's currency, and neither Democrats nor Republicans could boast of a strong national party organization. The "nationalizing of America" was more apparent in its economic than in its political institutions. There were, however, signs of change and transition; the political system could not remain immune from the major social forces of the post–Civil War generation. The growth of cities meant increasing authority and sophistication for urban political machines; improved facilities of communication and transportation influenced campaign tactics and the distribution of campaign literature. Spokesmen for big business sought a more prominent role in the determination of party policy, and some of the organizational techniques of business were adopted by the political parties, especially the Republican party in the decade of the 1890s.

American politics was marked by the influence of local issues and local organizations throughout the nineteenth century. Cultural and ethnic pluralism, sustained by a continuing flood of immigrants, worked to limit the effectiveness of national political organizations, but if the impact of economic growth on American politics was often ambiguous, it was nonetheless real. Federal, state, and local governments played only a limited role in the development of the United States economy in the post–Civil War decades; but economic developments had significant long-term effects on the American polity.

Major party politicians were not seriously concerned with those effects in the mid eighties. There was, however, an uneasy appreciation on the part of a number—Cleveland among them—that the benefits of economic expansion were not without cost. Few had read Henry George's *Progress and Poverty*, published in 1879, but they were necessarily aware that their constituents did not unanimously share the sense of pride and confidence illustrated by the juvenile novels of Horatio Alger and other writers of the "Success Cult." Staple farmers began with the late 1870s to suffer "the long price depression," with periodic fluctuations that encouraged overproduction. Inadequate financing and discriminatory railroad practices inspired, in the next decade, the growth of Farmers' Alliances in the South and the Northwest. The early 1880s had seen the open-range Old Cattle Kingdom claim a territory equal in size to Spain or France, but with the "great blizzard of 1887," cattlemen who were

not able to adjust to the new ranch cattle industry would join southern cotton farmers and western wheat farmers as self-extolled victims of a changing economy.

The year 1885 was a prosperous one for American industry in
general, but over 5 percent of the industrial labor force was unemployed, and for a large part of that labor force, the average workday was thirteen hours, and wages barely provided a subsistence
standard of living. Unskilled labor in the North and agricultural
labor in the West and the South received but a small fraction of the
wealth created by the "second American industrial revolution," and
black Americans—with few exceptions—formed a socially segregated
economic underclass. The next decennial census listed 12.2 percent
of the population as nonwhite or colored. It did not list their share
of the total national wealth, but in all probability it was something
less than 3 percent.

Confidence, not discontent, characterized American society on
Inauguration Day 1885, and this confidence found justification in
the opening of a vast new West, an expanding railroad net, the
increasing production of coal, iron ore, and petroleum, and the ability of American factories to rival the production and surpass the
labor productivity of their British rivals. The agricultural domain
had doubled; American cities were exceeding the populations of the
ancient towns of Europe; each year more Americans were enjoying
central heating and indoor plumbing. But rapid and unregulated
economic development was exacting a price in increased economic
inequality and, with another decade, increased political dissent.
In March 1885, however, dissent was faint and muffled, and Cleveland's Inaugural Address spoke more to old values than to present
problems.

Grover Cleveland was a rather impressive figure as he took the
oath of office, using the little Bible that had been presented to him
by his mother forty years earlier. His beefy torso was encased in a
long-skirted, double-breasted Prince Albert coat, and he surprised
his audience in the Senate Chamber by delivering his address without notes or manuscript. If it was not the most eloquent of Inaugural Addresses, it remains the only one delivered from memory. True
to his courtroom style in Buffalo, Cleveland placed his hands behind
him and spoke for twenty-five minutes without hesitation or slip.

Cleveland promised his listeners, not innovation, but an administration that would achieve needed reform by means of economy,

efficiency, and a new spirit of public service. He indicated his concern for a sound currency and for a revision of the revenue system in a manner that would relieve the people of unnecessary taxation while paying proper regard to the interests of industrial capital and labor. Only in two areas, however, did he indicate a shift of governmental policy. When speaking of "the needs of future settlers," he declared his determination that the public domain be protected "from purloining schemes and unlawful occupation"; when speaking of the Indians, he indicated his hope for legislation that would promote "their education and civilization . . . with a view to their ultimate citizenship."

The composition of the nation's currency, the protective tariff, and labor-management disputes were issues of major importance in both of Cleveland's nonconsecutive terms. In all three areas his objectives and prejudices remained remarkably consistent. These issues must be discussed separately for each of his two terms, however, because external circumstances and public expectations were very different in the years of his second administration (1893–97). Cleveland's policies in regard to free silver, tariff revision, and labor during his first term (1885–89) will be analyzed in the following chapter. Other issues—such as administrative and civil-service reform, western land policy, the relationship between the federal government and the Union veteran, and the treatment of black Americans, Indians, and Chinese immigrants—figured most prominently in Cleveland's first administration and experienced little change in the years of his second term. This chapter will analyze Cleveland's failures and achievements in these areas for both presidencies.

Grover Cleveland placed great emphasis on the importance of improving the administration of the departments and agencies of the federal government, but he did little to improve the efficiency of the Executive Mansion. To modern eyes, Cleveland's presidential work schedule was both backbreaking and primitive. The White House staff during Cleveland's first term never exceeded a total of fifteen employees, and of these, only his private secretary, Col. Daniel Lamont, was of direct assistance in the performance of Cleveland's executive tasks. Known in Washington as Silent Dan, in tribute to his close-mouthed discretion, Lamont was the first man to give the position of presidential private secretary a measure of importance. Possessed of tact and endurance, Lamont was a helpful aide-de-camp. He was not, however, as some Washington observers thought, "the assistant president." Cleveland admired Lamont, and they dined together frequently, sharing a taste for whiskey and water as an accompaniment to the meal; but Cleveland's conception of presidential responsibility did not allow him to delegate his presidential duties. This conception found support in the stinginess of Congress, which had traditionally economized on appropriations for the staffing of the White House, whatever its readiness to spread largesse elsewhere. There was only one telephone in the White House, and when the steward was busy with other tasks, Cleveland frequently answered the summons of the phone or the doorbell himself. Each month he personally tallied the accounts of household expenses and made out the checks to pay the White House bills. In his first year as president, Cleveland had no stenographer and only limited clerical assistance. Even after a stenographer was hired, Cleveland, never comfortable giving dictation, continued to write his letters and the first draft of his public messages in longhand.

The Kentucky journalist Henry Watterson observed that Cleveland had "the poor man's love of work and trust in work," and there was truth in that statement.[1] What is more, Cleveland often fell prey to the "tyranny of the trivial." He was fascinated by detail, and this encouraged him to assume the self-imposed duty of exhaustively investigating pension claims, courts-martial in which the convicted persons sought a presidential pardon, and congressional appropriations for the construction of municipal post offices.

The pleas of office seekers took an inordinate share of Cleveland's time, despite his public announcement in the Washington press that petitioners should leave their requests with the respective departments and not seek a personal appointment with the president. His determination to appoint only the more capable and deserving Democrats encouraged him to spend many hours in examining the credentials of candidates for minor offices, and only an iron constitution allowed him to sustain a routine in which he slept only four to five hours a night, week after week.

Though he worked late, Cleveland was an early riser, and by eight o'clock was completing a substantial breakfast. He was at his desk in the large Oval Room on the second floor of the White House before nine, ready to work with Lamont on his official correspondence. From eleven to one he received congressmen and other visitors. After lunch there usually was either a cabinet meeting, on Tuesday and Thursday afternoons, or a public reception in the East Room, on Wednesday and Friday afternoons. Cleveland enjoyed cabinet meetings, where there was an agreeable mixture of formality and storytelling; but he loathed public receptions. The throng wishing to greet the president was pushed along at a rapid rate, and Cleveland developed a technique of grabbing the visitor's hand, giving it a slight squeeze, and then dropping it like a hot potato. Evenings were spent working in the library with Lamont. Cleveland successfully avoided most evening parties and invitations. Particularly was this true while he remained a bachelor.

It was with his cabinet that Cleveland demonstrated a measure of administrative talent. His first cabinet was one of the more able of the post–Civil War generation. Thomas F. Bayard of Delaware was secretary of state; Daniel Manning of New York, secretary of the Treasury; William C. Endicott of Massachusetts, secretary of war; William C. Whitney of New York, secretary of the navy; Lucius Quintus Cincinnatus Lamar of Mississippi, secretary of the interior; Augustus H. Garland of Arkansas, attorney general; William F. Vilas of Wisconsin, postmaster general.[2] Cleveland gained the respect of all of these men and developed warm friendships with Vilas and Bayard.[3]

Cleveland viewed the cabinet as his personal council. While he allowed all of its officers a large measure of independence in the day-to-day operations of their departments, it was understood that they were Cleveland's loyal lieutenants and were to avoid intramural quarrels or dissent. Cabinet officers were expected to observe the policies established by Cleveland for each executive department and then rely on the president to support them against the criticism of opposition congressmen, aggrieved office seekers, and complaining subordinates. In cabinet meetings, everyone was encouraged to speak, but no votes were taken. Cleveland would listen carefully to the opinion of each cabinet officer in turn, but he alone would make the final decision on administration policy. In similar vein, he refused to allow the formation of a kitchen cabinet, or inner circle of advisers, seeing such as a retreat to the days of President Grant and the Stalwart Republicans.

With the exception of the Treasury Department, the executive departments were still small. Although there were over 110,000 federal officeholders, only a small portion of that number had posts in Washington, and most of the departments remained understaffed throughout Cleveland's first administration. The State, Navy, and War departments shared the Executive Office Building, a block from the White House; phone service for all three departments was rudimentary; only a portion of their secretarial staffs was equipped with typewriters.

For the first two years of Cleveland's presidency, his unmarried sister Rose, a woman of stern and intellectual bent, served as hostess at White House receptions. This changed on the evening of 2 June 1886, when Cleveland was united in marriage with his twenty-two-year-old ward, Frances Folsom, in a brief ceremony in the Blue Room. The forty-nine-year-old Cleveland was the first incumbent president to be married in the White House, and the event was perhaps the most publicized episode of his first term.

Cleveland had kept his plans very quiet, hating the gossip that would ensue and seeking to protect his young fiancée from the "newspaper nuisances." Having been caught napping about Cleveland's marital intentions, the reporters now sought to gain a measure of revenge by following Cleveland and his bride to their honeymoon retreat at Deer Park in western Maryland. They took up their station a few hundred yards from the Clevelands' cottage and proceeded to engage in one of the more unattractive exhibitions of Paul Pry journalism. Cleveland's distaste for the press had been heightened at the time of the Maria Halpin scandal; it now achieved the level of undisguised animosity.

There is no reason to believe that Clevelands' marriage was inspired by a wish to extinguish rumors about his philandering bachelor days in Buffalo. Indeed, his admiration for his wife exceeded the usual level of devotion in September-May marriages. But had Cleveland ever thought that marriage would end the interest of the American press in his sex life, he was sadly mistaken. Press reports on Cleveland's honeymoon were marked by sniggering curiosity and veiled allusions to the dangers facing Mrs. Cleveland from her husband's girth and weight.

Cleveland's marriage had little influence on his White House work schedule. His pride in his wife's social tact and beauty made official receptions less onerous, and he now often made time for carriage rides with his bride in the late afternoon, but Colonel Lamont remained his most constant companion, and Cleveland's workday often continued to stretch into the early hours of the morning. Nor did his consideration for the American taxpayer diminish. He ordered the presidential yacht, the *Dispatch*, put into dry dock, paid his own expenses when he went on vacations and fishing trips, and insisted on personally paying for the hay that went to the White House carriage barn that was reserved for the president's private use.[4] Cleveland was, however, less parsimonious with his own money following his marriage. He encouraged his wife's shopping trips to New York, and he purchased a house and twenty-seven acres of land two miles north of Georgetown to serve as a retreat from the muggy heat of the Potomac basin. Cleveland was a happier man after his marriage, but he was not a more efficient manager of his time and energy. He would have insisted, however, that administrative efficiency in the Executive Mansion was less relevant to the nation's welfare than was administrative reform in the departments and bureaus of the executive branch.

Grover Cleveland frequently proclaimed his determination to improve the operations of the federal government by the tests of honesty and efficiency. The first half dozen cabinet meetings of the new administration were spent primarily in efforts to solicit from the department heads their plans for administrative reform. All promised to labor in the cause, and at least three—Manning, Whitney, and Lamar—would match promise with accomplishment. Before the end of the first year, procedural reforms had been effected in the various bureaus of the Treasury Department, an improved system instituted for the letting of contracts by the Navy Department, and a new concern exhibited for the rights of Indians and legitimate homesteaders by officials in the Interior Department. Cleveland's efforts at administrative reform were hampered by the fact that there was no overall executive budget. Each department submitted its own budgetary estimates directly to Congress. Moreover, the president's objectives were directed primarily to improvements in personnel and procedures. He was concerned less with departmental organization than with instilling what he liked to call "good business principles." There were, however, a few efforts at institutional reform, particularly in the Navy Department.

The rich and dapper William C. Whitney was perhaps Cleveland's most controversial cabinet appointment. His Wall Street connection and financial coups were viewed with suspicion by many western and southern Democrats, but Whitney proved to be an energetic and successful secretary of the navy. Building on the labors of his predecessor, William E. Chandler, Whitney reorganized the Navy Department while also urging Congress to appropriate funds for constructing several modern fighting vessels and assuring a domestic source of supply for armor plate and heavy naval armament. In these labors he had Cleveland's full support. Cleveland saw expenditures for a modern navy as essential to the national defense. A strong navy was not an instrument of provocation or territorial expansion, but a necessary protection against external enemies.[5]

Interior Secretary Lamar also may be credited with modest institutional reforms in the operations of the Land Office and the Indian Bureau, and at Cleveland's urging, Attorney General Garland sought to improve the system for selecting and paying federal marshals and United States attorneys and establish the first federal penitentiary.

By the perspective of a later day the most important reform achieved by Cleveland within the executive branch of the government was his successful assertion of presidential independence during his stormy battle with the Senate in 1886. To appreciate the significance of that battle, it is necessary to note the weakened position of the presidency in the two decades after Appomattox. The balance between executive and legislative power in the federal government had been destroyed by the Radical Republicans during the unhappy administration of Andrew Johnson, and its destruction had been sustained by the Stalwarts during the years of Grant. Hayes, Garfield, and Arthur had attempted to regain a measure of authority and independence, but with limited success. When Cleveland took office in March 1885, the executive was still the weakest of the three branches of the national government, the president having little control over appropriations and expenditures and restricted influence over the direction of public policy.

Cleveland's initial objective was not to increase presidential power but simply to prevent congressional efforts to usurp the authority of the chief executive. He stressed the constitutional doctrine of separation of powers and informed the press on 4 January 1886 that it was his intention to respect the "entire independence of the executive and legislative branches."[6] If he expected that the Republican-controlled Senate would reciprocate with promises not to limit the independence of the president, he was soon disappointed. Senate Republicans were in a contentious mood and were determined to demonstrate the hypocrisy of Cleveland's stance as a civil-service reformer. They would force him to admit that partisan animus alone dictated his appointments policy, and in the revised Tenure of Office Act they believed they had the necessary tool.

The original Tenure of Office Act of 1867 had given the Senate a veto power over presidential efforts to remove civil officers who had been appointed with senatorial consent. In 1869 the act had been revised. No longer did a president have to charge officeholders with criminal misconduct before he could suspend them, and no longer would a president have to provide the Senate with "the evidence and reasons" for his action. The revised act allowed the president, during a Senate recess, to suspend an officer within the executive branch and appoint a temporary replacement, subject to later Senate confirmation. The president would, however, have to submit the names of all replacements within thirty days after the Senate had reconvened. The revised Tenure of Office Act of 1869 lessened the obstructionist authority of the Senate, but presidential control over the dismissal of civil officers in the executive branch was still restricted. It was the intention of the Republican senators to expand that restriction.

The Senate Republicans caucused and decided to refuse to confirm Cleveland's appointments unless he produced all documents bearing on the suspension of the former officeholder, as well as the nomination of his successor. Senate committees began to demand that the respective departments and cabinet officers forward this information, insisting that as all executive offices had been created by congressional action, the Senate had the right to investigate suspensions as well as to evaluate nominations. Cleveland saw the demand as an invasion of presidential authority. If the president could not control the staffing of the executive branch, administrative reform would be endangered if not rendered impossible. His cabinet officers were instructed not to submit any papers concerning suspensions but to continue to provide "official papers" in support of nominations submitted for senatorial confirmation. Cleveland and the cabinet officer in question would determine which papers were "official." The Senate should not be allowed to engage in a hunting expedition and, in the process, to publicize confidential or irrelevant communications.

The Senate Republicans now sought a test case, and George F. Edmunds, the crusty chairman of the Senate Judiciary Committee, believed he had found such in the suspension of Republican George M. Duskin as United States attorney for the southern district of Alabama and his replacement by Democrat John D. Burnett. When Cleveland had submitted Burnett's name to the Senate, it had been sent to the Judiciary Committee, which now instructed Attorney General Garland to forward all papers relating to the management and conduct of the United States attorney's office in Alabama. Cleveland instructed Garland to refuse to submit any papers relating to Duskin's suspension, and Senator Edmunds then persuaded the Senate, on 25 January 1886, to adopt a resolution formally directing Garland to transmit copies of all requested documents. The battle was joined, and it was understood by both sides that it was a battle over more than the installation of Duskin's successor. At stake was the president's ability to assure the cooperation of officials who would have responsibility for executing administration policy, the proper breadth of the investigatory powers of the Senate, and the issue of presidential control over papers deposited in executive departments. Cleveland recognized the dimensions of the struggle, and they became clear to others when a caucus of Republican senators fashioned four resolutions, which in effect sought to assure control over the federal bureaucracy by the Senate majority.

The resolutions fashioned by the caucus would subsequently be the subject of a formal recommendation to the Senate from the Judiciary Committee. The committee called for the formal censure of Attorney General Garland and urged the Senate to withhold confirmation of any presidential nominations until the president had agreed to provide a full explanation for the suspension of the nominee's predecessor.

Cleveland met the challenge with his message of 1 March 1886. It was addressed to the Senate, but it was directed as well to the American public. It was one of Cleveland's more concise and well-written state papers. After a brief historical summary of the presidential appointment power and the Tenure of Office Act, Cleveland proceeded to justify his refusal to bend to the Senate's will on the grounds of statutory and constitutional interpretation. The demand of the Senate was possibly supported by the original Tenure of Office Act but found no support in the amended version. He would not concede the constitutionality of either version but would emphasize the illogic of the Senate's claim that if Congress had created an office, one branch of Congress had the right to dictate its operation. It was for the president to determine what papers should be classified as official, and the Senate had no authority to require an explanation for the suspension of an officer who was judged unsuitable for the execution of administration policy. The Constitution required the president to "take care that the laws be faithfully executed." In exercising his executive function, the president was responsible only to the people and must not suffer the obstruction of the Senate. If the Senate found the president unfaithful to his duties, there was the recourse of "the judicial process of trial on impeachment."[7]

Cleveland's message inspired considerable support from the public and the press. Those passages claiming the right to withhold information of a confidential nature and to exercise presidential discretion in the classification of "official papers" might strike a different response among Americans of a later generation who had suffered the imperial presidency of Richard M. Nixon; but in the 1880s, many Americans appreciated the need to correct the imbalance between the executive and legislative branches and supported the president. There were, of course, dissenters. Not only partisan Republicans but certain Mugwumps criticized Cleveland for his resistance to the Senate's demands. Carl Schurz supported the Senate's position on the ground that total disclosure of documents relating to removals and appointments would expose the tactics of the spoilsmen and increase the public demand for further civil-service reform.[8]

For his part, Senator Edmunds took Cleveland's message as a personal affront and proceeded to work diligently to obtain Senate approval for the resolutions authored earlier by a Republican caucus. The resolutions passed, though only by a narrow margin and in spite of several Republican defections. To Edmunds's disgust, however, many Senate Republicans, sensing the unpopularity if not the constitutional weakness of their position, began to stage a strategic retreat. The issue of Attorney Duskin's suspension became moot when it was discovered that his term of office had expired several months earlier. Attorney Burnett was then quickly confirmed, and within a few months the Senate ceased to demand papers from cabinet officers respecting suspended officials and began to confirm their successors. By mid December 1886, Senator George Frisbie Hoar, a devout Republican whose allegiance to the Constitution exceeded his love for the Grand Old Party, proposed the complete repeal of the original Tenure of Office Act. Cleveland had the pleasure of signing the repeal bill on 3 March 1887. With its passage, Congress formally abrogated its claim "to control presidential discretion in suspending or removing officials in the executive branch."[9]

The battle with the Senate over Cleveland's authority to remove unwanted officials had a significant impact on his conception of the duties of the presidential office. It would not be long before he would be defining executive authority not only in relation to the separation of powers doctrine but also in relation to the president's responsibility to exercise influence over legislative policy. More usually that influence would find negative expression; during his first term, Cleveland would send 304 veto messages to Congress, more than the combined total of all of his predecessors. There were, however, positive expressions as well. One example would be Cleveland's message of December 1887 urging revision of the tariff. Had not Cleveland fought and won the contest over the Tenure of Office Act, it is doubtful if he would have broken precedent by devoting his third annual message exclusively to the issue of the tariff. It was only gradually that Cleveland came to relate "the independence of the Executive" with efforts to advise and direct members of Congress; but if the evolution was gradual in pace, it was consistent in direction. The modern presidency does not begin with Grover Cleveland, but Cleveland made a necessary contribution to its development when he contested the claims of the Republican Senate and thereby helped to right the balance between the legislative and the executive branches of the federal government.

The covert purpose of the Senate Republicans in that fight had been to reveal Cleveland as a false friend to civil-service reform, and several recent historians have made a similar judgment.[10] Grover Cleveland was not a false friend to civil-service reform, but neither was he a "civil-service reformer," as that term was defined by Schurz and other members of the Civil Service Reform League. Grover Cleveland was a loyal member of the Democratic party who supported the idea of ridding the civil service of corrupt and inefficient spoilsmen. He did not ever claim a more exalted position.

Months before he took office he explained his middle-of-the-road intentions in a letter to George William Curtis. He wrote that the incoming administration would be a Democratic administration but that there would be no "arbitrary dismissals" for party or political reasons. Current Republican officeholders in non-policy-forming positions who had not made themselves obnoxious by using their offices to serve party ends would be allowed to finish their four-year terms. The implication was clear that "offensive partisans" would be removed before the four years were up and that other Republicans, upon the conclusion of their term of office, most likely would be replaced by meritorious members of the Democratic party.[11] Cleveland proclaimed his advocacy of the principles of civil-service reform, but he made no promise to create a nonpartisan corps of federal civil servants. The goal was to improve the honesty and the efficiency of the civil service while righting the current imbalance of party membership among federal officeholders. The improvement of administrative efficiency was the primary objective, and reform of the patronage system could only be gradual.

As with most efforts of limited reform, Cleveland's attempt to strike a middle course was certain to find its critics. It was Mugwump criticism that Cleveland found most irritating. For their part, the Mugwumps, having earlier exaggerated Cleveland's identification with the movement for civil-service reform, believed that they had reason to chastise Cleveland for his failure to stand true to the cause. The ultimate goal of the Mugwumps was a nonpartisan civil service, and they saw the eradication of the spoilsman as a panacea for the nation's social ills and an avenue for establishing their own political importance. Though they did not expect total political neutrality in Cleveland's appointment policy, they were prepared to judge his sincerity by two criteria: his retention of honest, Independent-leaning Republicans and his rejection of the recommendations of the professional politicians of the Democratic party. They saw no reason why good men who had been appointed by Garfield and Arthur should be dismissed when their four-year terms had expired; they worried that the terms "offensive partisanship" and "pernicious partisan behavior" would prove too elastic and too dependent on individual definition.

As Mugwump recommendations were ignored and Republican officials lost their place, Mugwump criticisms grew sharper. In his report of 1887, George William Curtis, president of the Civil Service Reform League, asserted that "tried by the standards of absolute fidelity to the reform . . . , it is not to be denied that this Administration has left much to be desired." A year later, he observed that despite the association in the public mind between the Cleveland presidency and the cause of reform, the league could not regard his administration as "in any strict sense of the words a civil service reform administration."[12]

Cleveland found such criticisms to be captious and erroneous. Curtis was so concerned with civil-service reform that he was unable to appreciate that it was subsidiary to the greater need of administrative reform; Curtis was too naïve to understand that if a president were to institute a nonpartisan plan for the distribution of patronage, he would destroy both his influence with his party and the possibility of accomplishment on any front. Cleveland saw the more vociferous Mugwumps as impractical men, who "with supercilious self-righteousness discredit every effort not in exact accord with their attenuated ideas."[13]

It is difficult, after the passage of a century, to capture the emotional quality of the battle over civil-service reform. It has a dusty flavor, and one is tempted to see civil-service reform as the fetish of a self-satisfied minority determined to find a rationalization for ignoring social and economic problems. There is a crumb of truth in such a judgment, but for many voters in the Gilded Age the issue of civil-service reform divided politicians into two classes: the proponents of a partisan civil service as an instrument for party management and their critics. Cleveland belongs in the latter category, together with the Mugwumps and many Half-Breed Republicans. They differed over the pace and the ultimate goal of reform, but all saw it as essential to the more effective operation of the federal civil service. Even after the passage of the Pendleton Act of 1883, the president and his immediate subordinates were responsible for filling a hundred thousand posts in the federal bureaucracy. Expansion of the classified list appeared essential if an administration was not to devote its energies to the importunities of claimants for office and the distribution of patronage. With some justice, the reformers associated an expansion of the merit system with needed improvement in the efficiency of government. One of the most persuasive students of civil-service reform has written:

> The operation of the spoils system compounded political localism. . . . It perpetuated a primitive, personalized politics, enforcing patterns of mutually demeaning dependence between politicians and job-seekers which depressed the chances for longevity, experience, and technical competence in the clerical administrative staffs of government. . . . The spoils system may have been the most enervating illness in American life.[14]

Civil-service reform did not guarantee better government, but at least it would have the likely result of transferring the civil servant's loyalty from the patron who had secured him his position to the department or bureau where he worked. It is true that with the spread of the merit system, both parties would come to depend more on corporate contributions for financing election campaigns, and this would enhance the political influence of business. For the United States during the last decades of the nineteenth century, however, the cost-benefit ratio of civil-service reform was positive.

Did Cleveland's first administration see such reform in practice? Did Cleveland deserve the censure of the Mugwumps or the self-congratulation of his own appraisal? Cleveland's appointment record was at best erratic, and the membership of his Civil Service Commission was weak; but Cleveland did make a significant contribution by promoting needed rule changes and by revising and extending the classification system.

During his first year, Cleveland made a determined and time-consuming effort to evaluate the qualifications of applicants for vacancies on the nonclassified list. He rejected the recommendations of

Samuel Tilden and other important Democrats and machine bosses; he retained in office a few Republicans after the completion of their four-year terms, and he generally sought to improve the personnel standards of the federal government.[15] By the spring of 1886, however, worried by a rising rebellion within the ranks of Democratic leaders and party workers, Cleveland showed an increasing willingness to allow Adlai E. Stevenson, the first assistant to Postmaster General Vilas, to stretch the definition of "offensive partisanship" and replace Republican post-office workers by the thousands. There was a similar cleansing operation in the custom service and among internal-revenue collectors. Cleveland's appointment record was best where the civil-service reform movement was strongest, as in Massachusetts, and at its worst where reform effort was negligible, as in Maryland and Indiana.[16] This fact assumed added importance because the Pendleton Act required that federal appointments be apportioned among the states and territories according to population. The requirement served to enhance the influence of Democratic politicians in states where the public had shown relatively little interest in civil-service reform.

Cleveland's concessions to the patronage demands of party politicians were encouraged by his growing conviction that Republican officeholders were, for the most part, ill-wishers for the success of a Democratic administration. There was also the fact and the rationalization that when he took office, the federal civil service was staffed almost exclusively by Republicans. With the passage of time, the terms of Republican incumbents expired, and this afforded Cleveland a welcome opportunity to fill these "vacancies" with "good men of our party." When Cleveland left the presidency in March 1889, some 75 percent of the one hundred thousand nonclassified workers had been replaced, with fourth-class postmasters furnishing a large share of the total.

Cleveland did little to improve the personnel of the Civil Service Commission during his first term, but he contributed to the improvement of the federal civil service by promoting new rules of procedure and classification and by extending the classified list. On 14 July 1886, Cleveland issued a general letter to officeholders, warning them against using their position for electioneering efforts "to manipulate nominating conventions [or] . . . control political movements in their localities."[17] This order was erratically enforced, but it marked the beginning of a movement to divorce officeholders from partisan campaigning. Cleveland then called the commission's attention to the lack of uniformity in a classification system that permitted persons to enter at a particular grade in one department without examination, while in another department, persons at the same grade were required to pass an examination. At his urging, many of these inconsistencies were corrected. Cleveland also advocated examinations for promotions within the classified service and a general revision of classification categories.

Cleveland's most important effort to extend the merit system came during the last months of his first term, after his defeat in the presidential election of 1888. It represented, in part, a desire to limit the patronage authority of his successor and to give various Democratic officeholders a better chance of longevity in the public service. An order of 3 December 1888 directed that employees of the railway mail service—five thousand railway postal clerks—be added to the classified list. There were other extensions as well. When Cleveland left the White House in March 1889, the classified list had expanded from sixteen thousand to twenty-seven thousand officeholders.

It was during his second administration that Cleveland made his most permanent contribution to the merit system, and, again, this was by way of changes in rules and coverage.

In his second term, partisan considerations often dominated Cleveland's appointments policy, particularly in respect to the State and Treasury departments. The membership of the Civil Service Commission was strengthened, however, and Cleveland's retention of Theodore Roosevelt was the occasion for much praise by the Civil Service Reform League. Indeed, with the appointment of George Lyman as a commission member, that body was for more than two years composed of two Republicans and one Democrat. Cleveland, moreover, saw that the commission received additional staff and clerical assistance. The expansion of the classified list obviously enhanced the authority of the commission, and in 1895/96, Cleveland signed orders revising civil-service rules and adding forty-four thousand positions to the civil-service list.

Cleveland brought under the protection of the Pendleton Act a larger *percentage* of the federal bureaucracy than has any other American president. By the time Cleveland left Washington for a second time, more than 40 percent of a now-enlarged corps of federal employees were on the classified list. When he had first entered office, less than 12 percent had enjoyed that protection, and only a small part of the increase had occurred during the interim presidency of Benjamin Harrison. The extension of the merit system had a slow but incremental effect in making the federal civil service less political and more professional. For this extension, Grover Cleveland, however mixed his motives and inconsistent his patronage practice, deserved the thanks of later presidents, who would be less badgered by the importunities of office seekers and who could rely on a more capable corps of officials to execute their policies.

In the eyes of the Grand Army of the Republic, Cleveland was less a civil-service reformer than an enemy of the statutory requirement that Union veterans receive preference in the distribution of public offices. Leaders of the GAR bemoaned every removal of a Republican officeholder who could claim to have worn the Blue and every appointment of a former Confederate. They had no use for Cleveland's contention that veteran preference applied only when candidates were of equal fitness.

Cleveland came to office determined to promote the reconciliation of North and South, believing that sectional animosities were an anachronism and an obstacle to national economic progress. It was an intelligent objective, but it ignored the power of memory on both sides of the Mason-Dixon Line. He deeply resented GAR allegations that as a "slacker" who had avoided military service, he was unsympathetic to the soldiers who had saved the Union. One of Cleveland's first acts as president had been to restore the rank and pay of the ill and impoverished Ulysses S. Grant, and he was prepared to make frequent references to the sacrifices of the Union dead. He was determined, however, that patriotism not serve as excuse for an extravagant public-welfare program.

Cleveland saw the Pension Bureau as a prime target for administrative reform, and under the direction of the new pension commissioner, John C. Black, who was himself a disabled pensioner and a member of the GAR, the bureau was reorganized with perceptible improvement in investigation procedures and the speed with which claims were settled. During Black's first year in office, the Pension Bureau did a larger business than at any time in its history and at a reduction in operating costs for the government. The Pension Bureau was a part of the executive branch of the government, and Cleveland optimistically hoped that its improved efficiency would deter Congress from interfering in its operations by passing private pension bills to assist veterans whose claims had been rejected after careful examination.

It was, of course, Cleveland's vetoes of some 228 of these private pension bills that would raise the ire of the GAR. These bills were introduced by a senator or a congressman seeking to aid a constituent and to curry favor by a demonstration of hand-to-heart patriotism, and they were usually passed in large bunches by voice vote during late-hour sessions of the Senate and the House, with only a scattering of members in attendance. Cleveland viewed these private pension bills as a particularly insidious form of governmental favoritism. They represented an intrusion into the proper business of the executive branch; they added to the costs of the federal government; they encouraged flagrant dishonesty. In his veto messages, Cleveland revealed an unexpected taste for satire as he mocked the pension claims of a veteran who attributed his poor eyesight to a bout of diarrhea when in the service or one who traced his current attacks of epilepsy to the loud report of artillery guns heard twenty-two years earlier. Many of these messages contained constructive suggestions as well as mockery, but none found an appreciative audience in Congress. Cleveland often assumed the professorial mantle as he instructed Congress in the flaws of the bill in question and explained that it was a disservice to the honest disabled veteran to put fraudulent claimants on what should be an unblemished role of honor.

Cleveland might have pointed out that although he was the first president to dare the wrath of the veterans' lobby by vetoing private pension bills, he approved many more than he disallowed. Of some 2,099 private pension bills passed by Congress, 1,871 either received Cleveland's approval or became law without his signature. Where Cleveland may be faulted was not in his determination to veto the more fraudulent claims but in the excessive time and energy he expended in investigating each private pension bill. This was a task he would have done better to have delegated to subordinates. Here the stern call of duty became confused with the pleasurable irritation of the hair shirt.

The relations between the GAR and Grover Cleveland evolved from dislike to enmity with his veto of the Dependent Pension bill of January 1887. This bill would have given a pension of twelve dollars a month to every Union veteran who could claim that he was at present incapable of earning his living by physical labor. There was no requirement to show that his present "disability" had any connection with war service. The same pension would also be given to the parents or widow of a dead veteran if they claimed that they were unable to secure a livelihood by daily labor. The GAR had been lobbying for such a bill for many years, and it excoriated Cleveland's veto.

In his veto message, Cleveland decried the severance of pension rights and service-incurred disability. The bill would inspire an army of claims hunters and put a "premium on dishonesty and mendacity." It would transform the pension system into a public charity program, and its probable cost would be enormous.[18]

Fast upon the heels of Cleveland's veto of the Dependent Pension bill came the "infamous" flag order. The captured battle standards of various Confederate regiments had been gathering dust in Washington basements for twenty years, and Adj. Gen. Richard C. Drum and Cleveland's secretary of war, William Endicott, suggested that as a gesture of sectional reconciliation, they be returned to the states of their origin. When Cleveland issued the necessary executive order, Republican partisans and professional patriots had a field day. The commander of the GAR implored God to "palsy the hand" that had issued such a traitorous order. Finding that such a transfer of governmental property required congressional sanction, Cleveland backed off and rescinded his order. But in the eyes of many officers of the GAR, he had revealed himself as one who would traduce the Union soldiers who had shed their blood in capturing these symbols of secession and treason. Threats were uttered that if Cleveland dared to attend the Grand Encampment of the GAR in St. Louis, he would be verbally insulted if not physically assaulted.

Cleveland had earlier accepted the invitation of Mayor David R. Francis to go to St. Louis to review the GAR encampment and parade. Francis now shamefacedly had to suggest that Cleveland postpone his visit, and Cleveland wrote a public letter withdrawing his earlier acceptance and chastising those who defamed the nation's chief magistrate because they disapproved of acts performed in the course of duty. Those who would use the GAR for partisan purposes dishonored the Union dead; those who trafficked in sectional hatred were enemies of national progress; those who would insult an incumbent president endangered the dignity of "the people's highest office."[19]

In spite of his best efforts, Cleveland failed as an agent of sectional reconciliation. Such events as the furor over the "rebel flag order" increased the sectional sensitivities of the South. During Cleveland's first administration, the GAR became a blatantly political instrument, the veterans' lobby aligned itself more closely to the Republican party, and the citizens of the South found reason to feel rebuffed in their efforts to demonstrate their identification with the national government. Cleveland may be credited with the reform of the Pension Bureau, but in his broader aim—to serve as an apostle of sectional harmony—he failed.

A declared enemy of governmental paternalism for many claimants—veterans seeking unwarranted pensions, industrialists demanding higher tariff duties—Cleveland nonetheless displayed a paternalistic attitude toward black Americans, Native Americans, and, for a time, Chinese immigrants. One of the more difficult problems of analysis for students of Cleveland's presidencies is his racial attitudes and policies. The evidence is both limited and contradictory. Cleveland would have earnestly denied that he was a racist, and by the standards of his day, his racism was comparatively benevolent.

The provincial bar of Buffalo during the 1860s and 1870s had not encouraged an interest in cultural pluralism, nor had it afforded opportunity for personal contact with blacks, Indians, and Chinese. Cleveland never gave much conscious thought to questions of racial distinction, but he seems to have operated on the belief that although all residents of the United States deserved equal justice and fair play, only white Americans were capable of appreciating the greatness of the American past and providing leadership for its future. Emancipation had not freed black Americans from slavery-bred ignorance and thriftlessness; the Indians still exhibited the characteristics of their savage past and had to be carefully introduced to white civilization as wards of the state; Chinese immigrants demonstrated cultural and moral differences that made their assimilation into American society difficult if not impossible.

Cleveland respected certain blacks as individuals, but he was no admirer of black Americans in the mass. He liked and trusted his White House steward, William Sinclair, a black man, and together they would go over the monthly bills while companionably munching ham sandwiches. It was chiefly southern blacks whom he tended to view as deficient in education and character. In part this was the result of his acceptance of myths about Radical Reconstruction. As was true of a growing number of northerners by the 1880s, Cleveland associated the Reconstruction experiment with federal bayonets, Republican carpetbaggers, and "Black Rule." Exaggerating the role of southern blacks in the carpetbag governments, Cleveland identified black voters and politicians not only with the evil designs of the Republican party but also with extravagance and disrespect for property rights. "The tragic scar" of the Reconstruction decade was the product of ignorant blacks as well as Republican partisans and their Scalawag allies. Cleveland never publicly criticized the Fourteenth and Fifteenth amendments to the Constitution, but in all probability he believed it had been a mistake to give freedmen the rights of citizenship and the vote without a period of training and apprenticeship.

During the campaign of 1884, partisans of Blaine had predicted that were the Democrats to gain the presidency, the old Confederate generals would come to power in Washington and seek the repeal of the Civil War amendments. Only a few blacks believed the rumors that Cleveland's victory meant the reestablishment of slavery, but many entertained a natural anxiety about the new Democratic administration. In his Inaugural Address, Cleveland sought to allay their fears:

> In the administration of a government pledged to equal and exact justice to all men, there should be no pretext for anxiety touching the protection of the freedmen in their rights, or their security in the enjoyment of their privileges under the Constitution and its amendments. . . . All discussion as to their fitness for the place accorded them as American citizens is idle and unprofitable, except as it suggests the necessity for their improvement.[20]

It was a carefully worded statement, designed to give the lie to Republican charges while not unnecessarily offending the southern "Redeemers," and it obtained a measure of praise from northern black politicians. Frederick Douglass declared that it "was all any friend of liberty and justice could reasonably ask."[21]

Though politically inspired, Cleveland's promise to protect "the freedmen in their rights" was not necessarily insincere. Cleveland viewed the Constitution as secular Scripture, and the Civil War amendments were a part of the Constitution. He was, indeed, prepared to make a few efforts—though only a few—in behalf of the political opportunities of black Americans. Cleveland appointed no black postmasters in the South, but he did allow the Republican Douglass to retain his position in Washington as recorder of deeds, and when Douglass later resigned, Cleveland appointed another black man, James C. Matthews, to take Douglass's place. When the Senate balked at confirming Matthews, on the ground that he was a resident of New York City instead of the District of Columbia, Cleveland resubmitted the nomination with a message proclaiming his wish to tender "to our colored fellow-citizens just recognition."[22] Cleveland appointed a handful of blacks to consular and other positions, and he requested Congress to take steps to prevent loss for the depositors of the government-approved Freedman's Savings and Trust Company. This, however, was the extent of Cleveland's first-term efforts in behalf of black Americans.

Nor was the record more impressive during Cleveland's second term. Blacks were discriminated against in the hiring and firing practices of various government departments, such as the Bureau of Engraving and Printing; and Secretary of State Richard Olney informed Cleveland that it was unwise to appoint "colored men" as consuls in South America. Their appointment was resented by the proud Latins, and "the colored appointees who have been sent there have not proved efficient public servants." It was, however, proper to appoint a black as consul at Santos, Brazil: Santos was afflicted with yellow fever, "for which reason a colored person has usually been selected for the position."[23]

Cleveland did not wish ill to black Americans, but he believed that it was to their former white masters, not the federal government, that southern blacks should look for assistance and guidance. Intelligent, conservative southern Democrats, such as Lucius Lamar, could best protect them from the racism of upland whites or the manipulative designs of southern Republicans. When Cleveland visited the Piedmont Exposition in October 1887, he interrupted his paean of praise for the economic revival of Atlanta, "risen again from the ashes of destruction," to call for understanding and cooperation between whites and blacks as well as the North and the South. "Designing demagogues" should not be allowed to endanger harmony on either front. Blacks should see in education the true path for gaining the respect of their fellow southerners, especially practical education in agricultural and mechanical subjects.[24]

During his second term, Cleveland read with satisfaction Booker T. Washington's famous address at the Atlanta Cotton Exposition. He found the "Atlanta Compromise," with its advocacy of trade education for blacks and its denial of aspirations for social equality, to be both wise and irrefutable. Cleveland wrote to Washington: "Your words cannot fail to delight and encourage all who wish well for the race."[25] Cleveland had earlier made a financial contribution to a black trade school, and when writing to a black correspondent, he had offered the prophecy that it was only through education that the black American would achieve full citizenship: "If our colored boys are to exercise in their mature years the right of citizenship, they should be fitted to perform their duties intelligently and thoroughly."[26]

Even when expressing concern for the improvement of "colored boys," Cleveland's tone carried the implication of wishing well to persons of inferior status. In this, of course, he was at one with his times. It was a rare politician in the Gilded Age who remained immune to notions of white superiority, and the self-consciously righteous Mugwumps often matched the politicians in their readiness to ignore the promises of the Fifteenth Amendment and let the South take care of its "Negro problem."

For a Democratic president there was a special temptation to see the issue of black rights as a matter best left to the South. No Democratic presidential candidate had a chance of victory without the support of the Solid South, and rare was the southern Democrat who favored political equality for the black man. Cleveland was surely aware of this fact, and although he held no brief for vigilante methods and although he deplored lynchings, there is no evidence that during his second term he ever spoke out against the rising tide of Jim Crow ordinances in the southern states. Nor did he find fault with the Supreme Court decision that upheld the constitutionality of segregated public education. Indeed, on two occasions, Cleveland publicly denied that he had favored "mixed schools" in New York City when he had served as governor. Believing that "separate schools [are] . . . of much more benefit to the colored people than mixed schools," he had never advocated the forced integration of the races.[27]

Political considerations, however, were not the primary factor in determining Cleveland's essentially negative attitude toward black Americans. When he addressed the Southern Education Society in New York in April 1903—long after his retirement from politics and long after he had reason to be concerned with the electoral votes of the South—he gave ample demonstration that though he hoped for the improvement of black Americans, he saw them as essentially inferior:

> I believe that neither the decree that made the slaves free, nor the enactment that suddenly invested them with the rights of citizenship any more cured them of their racial and slavery-bred imperfections and deficiencies than it changed the color of their skin. . . .
> I believe that among the nearly nine millions of negroes . . . there is still a grievous amount of ignorance, a sad amount of viciousness and a tremendous amount of laziness and thriftlessness. . . .

I am thoroughly convinced that the efforts of Booker Washington . . . point the way to safe and beneficent solutions of the vexatious negro problem. . . . I have faith in the honor and sincerity of the respectable white people of the South in their relations with the negro and his improvement and well being.[28]

Cleveland never claimed to be a reformer in his attitudes and policies toward black Americans. But he did in respect to the American Indian, and with some measure of justice.

When Cleveland took office, the Indian population was 204,000, scattered among some 171 reservations which embraced almost 135 million acres of land. Those acres were the object of desire by farmer settlers as well as cattlemen, sheepherders, and railroad entrepreneurs, all of whom considered the size of the reservations to be grossly in excess of Indian needs. The volume of their complaints increased when the Apaches under Geronimo began the last of the Indian wars. Geronimo's raids and subsequent capture represented the final stand of the Warrior Indian. Subsequently, the "Indian problem" centered on Indian lands and Indian assimilation; and throughout his presidency, Grover Cleveland exhibited a consistent interest in discovering a solution that would be fair both to the Indians and to the farmer settlers.

Much of Cleveland's concern for the American Indian can be traced to his conviction that they were wards of the nation, and he, as the nation's chief executive, was in the position of a court-appointed trustee. He could not view the Indian as his equal; rather he viewed him as a wayward but promising child in need of a guardian. The end goal should be the Indian's assimilation into white society, and the means to that end embraced education in American ways, instruction in the English language, land ownership in severalty, and the paternal guidance of the federal government. The federal government must protect the Indians against cattle barons, land sharks, and the railroads. And the Indians must be persuaded to forego their outmoded tribal ways and become freehold farmers; in the process, they would become civilized and Americanized and worthy of the privileges of United States citizenship. In the eyes of the social anthropologist of a later day, Cleveland was an enemy of tribal mores; by the standards of the 1880s, he was a reformer who sought to improve the lot of the individual Indian.

Cleveland took his stand as an Indian reformer in his first Inaugural Address. After noting the diversity of characteristics among the Indian population and reminding Congress of the status of the

Indians as "wards of the government," Cleveland wrote: "This guardianship involves, on our part, efforts for the improvement of their condition and the enforcement of their rights. . . . The ultimate object of their treatment should be their civilization and citizenship. Fitted by these to keep pace in the march of progress . . . , they will readily assimilate with the mass of our population." He urged Congress to authorize the appointment of six commissioners, who should investigate conditions on the reservations and make recommendations concerning ways to promote the self-support and educational progress of the Indian population. The commissioners should also offer their opinion as to which reservations "may be reduced in area" and which lands "not needed by Indian occupation" might be purchased by the government.[29]

Cleveland undoubtedly hoped to pacify western complaints by suggesting that some of the Indian lands would be available in the future for sale to white settlers. This fact, however, offers no necessary contradiction to Cleveland's declared intention to protect Indian lands from encroachment by the railroads, the cattlemen, and white squatters. During his first year in office, Cleveland terminated certain grazing and grass leases that had been obtained by fraudulent practices and revoked an order by President Chester Arthur that opened the Winnebago and Crow Creek reservations in Dakota Territory to white settlement. All persons who had made claim to land within the reservations were warned to vacate within sixty days. A year later, Cleveland vetoed a bill granting certain railroads a right of way through the Indian reservation in northern Montana.

Cleveland saw individual land ownership in severalty as the key to the assimilation of the Indian, and he was consequently a supporter of the efforts of Senator Henry L. Dawes of Massachusetts to push through Congress a measure that would encourage the Indians to surrender the tradition of tribal land ownership and allow reservation lands to be divided into individual parcels.[30] Eastern "Indian reformers" had supported this idea for many years, and Cleveland made no claim of authorship for the Dawes Act. His encouragement, however, helped to assure its passage.

Formally entitled the Indian Emancipation Act, the Dawes Act of January 1887 empowered the president to allot land within the reservations to individual Indians, contingent on tribal agreement. Each Indian (man, woman, and child) would receive from forty to one hundred and sixty acres, with the proviso that the allotment was inalienable for twenty-five years. The federal government would purchase all reservation land after the division had been made. These acres would be added to the public domain, and the money would be deposited in a special account in the United States Treasury and reserved for purposes of Indian assistance and education. The rights of citizenship would gradually be extended to those Indians who held land in severalty and thereby demonstrated their readiness to adopt "the habits of civilized life."

Cleveland signed and praised the Dawes Act, while subsequently offering the advice that it would be best to proceed gradually with the division of tribal lands, lest the end result be the "pauperism," instead of the economic and moral improvement, of the Indians. Individual land ownership alone would not assure "that independence of spirit and life which the Indian peculiarly needs." Improved education in the Indian schools and fluency in the English language were also essential: "Complete facilities of education" would assist the Indian race and "redeem the sin of their oppression."[31]

Cleveland's Indian policy during his second administration showed little change in objectives or practice. Secretary of the Interior Hoke Smith, like his predecessor Lucius Lamar, was instructed to see that the federal commissioners exerted no undue pressure on the Indians when encouraging them to divide reservation lands under the terms of the Dawes Act: "The good and welfare of the Indian should be constantly kept in view, so that when the end is reached citizenship may be to them a real advantage, instead of an empty name."[32]

There is no reason to doubt Cleveland's sincerity in his stated goal to assist and assimilate the American Indian. It is unquestionably true that the Dawes Act had the effect of placing large portions of certain reservations in the public domain and thereby increasing the economic opportunities of white settlers and land speculators; it is equally true that the alienation of the Indian from tribal culture and communal agriculture had, in the long run, a harmful impact on the economic welfare and independence of many Indians. Neither of these judgments, however, need deny that Grover Cleveland believed that the Dawes Act would improve the lot of the Native American. That act and the president who signed it received the praise not only of Carl Schurz but of the author of *A Century of Dishonor*, Helen Hunt Jackson.

There was little reason for Cleveland to believe that efforts to assimilate the Indian would bring political profit to himself or his party, and his disinclination to use the authority of the federal government to protect the civil rights of the freedman was more the result of racial bias than the influence of the South on Democratic political fortunes. It was only with the Chinese immigrant that Cleveland allowed partisan considerations to determine administration policy, and this after making a sincere if limited effort to protect the Chinese resident against vigilante attacks.

In December 1885, Cleveland brought to the attention of Congress the "outrages" being committed against alien Chinese laborers in Washington Territory, noting that "race prejudice is the chief factor in originating these disturbances."[33] Cleveland soon came to the conclusion, however, that so deep was the prejudice against the Chinese on the West Coast and so different were the cultural backgrounds of the Oriental and the Caucasian, that there could be no absorption of the Chinese into American society. Our immigration laws were designed "to invite assimilation and not to provide an arena for endless antagonism." The federal government had the duty to protect those Chinese who were already here and to restrict further Chinese immigration by negotiating a new Sino-American treaty.[34] He would find difficulties on both fronts, from the bigotry of race baiters in the West, who would continue their attacks on Chinese railroad and mine workers, and from a Chinese government sensitive to the association of immigration restriction and cultural inferiority.

Secretary of State Thomas F. Bayard began negotiations in 1887 on a treaty to prohibit Chinese laborers from entering the United States. In his correspondence with Bayard, Cleveland for the first time admitted his concern for the domestic political impact of the Chinese question. "A proper movement upon the Chinese question" would furnish for the Democratic party "another string to our bow."[35] By the spring of 1888, the two governments appeared to have reached agreement on a treaty to prohibit for twenty years the entry of Chinese laborers into the United States. Any Chinese immigrant presently in the United States would be denied the right of reentry if he returned to China, and the Chinese government would receive the sum of $276,619 to compensate Chinese residents in the United States who had suffered injuries at the hands of private American citizens. The Republican-controlled Senate delayed action on the confirmation of the treaty, and then the Chinese government had second thoughts. In an effort to reclaim a measure of diplomatic equality, the Chinese suggested that the duration of the ban be reduced and that the proviso barring reentry be revised.

With the presidential election fast approaching, Cleveland exhibited no desire to extend the negotiations or to conciliate the Chinese government. Without consulting Secretary Bayard, Cleveland encouraged a Pennsylvania congressman, William L. Scott, to introduce in the House of Representatives a bill to prohibit the return of any Chinese laborers who left the United States. The measure sailed through Congress, with both parties determined to exhibit their patriotic antagonism to the depravity of the thrifty Chinese. Cleveland signed the bill on October 1 and took the opportunity to inform Congress that "the experiment of blending the social habits and mutual race idiosyncracies of the Chinese laboring classes with those of the great body of the people of the United States has been proved by the experience of twenty years . . . to be in every sense unwise, impolitic, and injurious to both nations."[36]

During Cleveland's second term the "Chinese question" faded in importance both as a political issue and as a diplomatic problem. Cleveland's unstated belief in the inferiority of Chinese culture was made explicit, however, by his reluctance to exert himself when a member of the Chinese royal family visited Washington during a worldwide tour. Cleveland suggested that "Esquire Li Hung Chang" might best be greeted by firing off a bunch of Chinese firecrackers.[37]

Cleveland's bias against Chinese immigration stemmed largely from his conviction that desirable immigrants were those who would accept American values and meld into American society. Good immigrants were assimilable immigrants. Cleveland never had any use for nativist movements that would shut the door to European immigrants from southern and eastern Europe. Italians, Greeks, Slavs, Russian Jews—all were welcome as long as they intended to become permanent residents and would accept American ways. When accepting for the nation Frédéric Bartholdi's statue of *Liberty Enlightening the World*, Cleveland had proclaimed that Liberty's lamp would illumine the way "to man's enfranchisement."[38] He associated that enfranchisement with assimilation and the acceptance of the rights and responsibilities of American citizenship.

One of Cleveland's last official acts during his second term was to veto a literacy bill authored by Congressman Henry Cabot Lodge of Massachusetts, which would have barred all illiterates from entering the United States. In his veto message, Cleveland declared: "The ability to read and write . . . in and of itself afford, in my opinion, a misleading test of contented industry and supplies unsatisfactory evidence of desirable citizenship or a proper appreciation of the benefits of our institutions." Cleveland was a proponent of Americanization, even conformity, but not of exclusion.[39]

Having largely shed the Presbyterian dogma of his boyhood, Cleveland exhibited little or no religious prejudice. This was possibly the result of indifference as well as liberal sentiment, but with the single exception of the Church of Jesus Christ of Latter-day Saints, Cleveland cannot be charged with religious intolerance, and he criticized the Mormon religion almost exclusively on the ground that it sanctioned the practice of polygamy.[40] He cannot be exempted as readily from the charge of racial prejudice. Cleveland tended to view blacks, Indians, and Chinese immigrants as persons of inferior ability, and although he sought to assist the blacks on occasion and the Indians quite consistently, there was a patronizing note in his words and policies. Even at his most benevolent, Grover Cleveland never rose above the position of the conscientious trustee, determined to see the wayward minor protected from the unscrupulous and instructed in the duties of citizenship.

By the criteria of a later generation, perhaps Cleveland's most praiseworthy "reform policy" concerned his efforts to reverse a century of exploitation of the public domain, revise the federal land laws, and promote the cause of ecological conservation by enlarging the forest reserves and protecting the "desert land" of the Southwest. Although he was an easterner who never traveled further west than Chicago, Cleveland from the beginning of his presidency demonstrated a determination to protect the public domain from further spoliation and to protect the interests of the homesteader settler.

In his annual messages to Congress in 1885 and 1886, Cleveland urged that the land laws be revised so that cattlemen and timber companies could not monopolize huge tracts of land by means of the pseudo-homesteading claims of cowboys, lumberjacks, and other paid agents. The disposal of the public lands "should have in view the original policy which encouraged many purchasers of these lands for homes and discouraged the massing of large areas." When Congress proved slow to act, Cleveland, Secretary of the Interior Lamar, and Land Commissioner W. A. J. Sparks proceeded to issue executive orders to institute patrols against timber thieves and to require the destruction of fences that the cattlemen had erected in an effort to monopolize water courses and use the public domain as private grazing lands. Cleveland was determined to stop the "rapid appropriation of our public lands" by individuals and corporations that flouted the requirement of residence and cultivation for a five-year period.[41] In 1886, Cleveland stopped all sales by the Land Office in order to allow Commissioner Sparks to pursue a major investigation of fraudulent claims.

The railroads, as well as the cattle barons and the timber corporations, were seen as enemies of the "preservation of the public domain for future generations of homesteaders." The railroads had received "princely grants of land," which had been "diverted to private gain and corrupt uses." Particularly blameworthy was the manner in which the railroads were using their "indemnity lands" to cheat the homesteader. When in earlier years it had not been possible to arrange that the entire railroad land grant ran along the proposed route, the railroad had been allowed "indemnity lands" elsewhere. A large acreage was set aside from which the railroad could pick and choose at a later time. The railroad would wait until homesteaders had moved into an area and prepared it for cultivation; then the railroad would claim those acres as part of its indemnity. In a famous case in 1887, the Northern Pacific Railroad Company sought to expel a settler named Guilford Miller, whose homestead was in an area that the railroad now elected to designate as indemnity land. Cleveland came to Miller's aid and publicly condemned the manner in which the railroads were keeping large regions from legal homesteading: "The convenience of a corporate beneficiary of the Government" must give way before the claims of the pioneer settler.[42] In several instances, Cleveland forced railroad companies that had failed to fulfill their contractual obligations to the government to forfeit a portion of their land grant. By the end of his first administration, he could boast: "That over eighty million acres have been arrested from illegal usurpation, improvident grants, and fraudulent entries and claims . . . must afford a profound gratification to right-feeling citizens."[43]

In Cleveland's first term, he concentrated primarily on efforts to disallow fraudulent claims and thereby enlarge the federal domain available to homesteaders. He also made a few moves, however, in the direction of withdrawing land from private entry. Cleveland was concerned with the possibility of mining companies' monopolizing large portions of the so-called desert lands, and he ordered the Land Office to make irrigation studies. Those studies culminated in the Carey Act of 1894, the first federal law to support irrigation projects in the Southwest. The chief thrust of Cleveland's land policy during the years of his second administration was to withdraw certain forest lands from the public domain. By means of executive orders,

Cleveland turned twenty-five million acres of the San Joaquin Forest in California into a national reserve, and by the end of his second term, Grover Cleveland had doubled the size of the National Forest Reserve. Geoffrey Blodgett does not exaggerate when he writes: "But for Theodore Roosevelt's vastly more skillful flair for self-advertisement—Cleveland might be remembered as our presidential pioneer in imposing sanity on federal land use policy."[44]

During neither of Cleveland's presidential terms did any American speak about environmental protection, and few spoke about the conservation of natural resources. Grover Cleveland was, however, if only half-intentionally, an environmentalist and a conservationist. By his efforts to fight the plunderers of the nation's natural resources and to save the national heritage of the public domain from further exploitation, Cleveland scored his most important success as a reformer.

5

★ ★ ★ ★ ★

LABOR, SILVER, AND TARIFF REFORM DURING CLEVELAND'S FIRST ADMINISTRATION

Problems of labor unrest, silver coinage, and tariff revision figured largely in both Cleveland administrations. During his first term, the tariff issue saw Cleveland make his boldest effort to influence the policy position of the Democratic party. In lesser measure, he sought the same objective when championing the cause of voluntary arbitration in labor disputes and urging the repeal of the Bland-Allison Silver Coinage Act. Linking his efforts in all three areas was an earnest but confused concern to discover the proper relation of the federal government to the operations of the American economy.

Although recent historians have stressed Cleveland's probusiness bias and disregard for the needs of the laboring classes, the evidence does not support the picture of an administration devoted to the interests of capital and mindless of the interests of industrial labor. Instead, it shows a president worried by labor unrest, worried by the unsavory business practices of the railroads, and worried by the dangers of an expanded economic role for the federal government.

Cleveland was the first United States president to send to Congress a message dealing exclusively with the problem of labor-management disputes. From a twentieth-century perspective, its proposals were timidly insufficient, but Cleveland's predecessor was Chester A. Arthur, not Franklin D. Roosevelt.

Cleveland had carefully watched the progress of the strikes against Jay Gould's southwestern railroads in 1885/86, and on 22 April 1886 he sent a message to Congress requesting legislation that would establish a permanent board for the voluntary arbitration of labor disputes. In his analysis of the need for such an agency, Cleveland took the position of the even-handed observer. He offered first the opinion that "the discontent of the employed is due in a large degree to the grasping and needless exactions of employers and the alleged [government] discrimination in favor of capital" and then the judgment that "the laboring men are not always careful to avoid causeless and unjustifiable disturbance." The federal government should encourage the practice of voluntary arbitration and should create a three-person commission of labor charged "with the consideration and settlement, when possible, of all controversies between labor and capital." It was better to have an arbitral body in permanent operation rather than to create ad hoc boards in the midst of disputes. Such a permanent agency would hopefully prevent damaging strikes, and its existence would "be a just and sensible recognition of the value of labor and of its right to be represented in the departments of the Government."[1]

Congress subsequently passed a voluntary arbitration bill that was inferior in many respects to Cleveland's proposal: it was restricted to railroad disputes; arbitral boards would be established on an ad hoc basis; the membership of each special board would be composed of railroad employees and managers, instead of "regular officers of the Government," as Cleveland had advocated. This was not, however, the only labor legislation during the years of Cleveland's first term. Bills were passed prohibiting the importation of contract labor, legalizing the incorporation of national trade unions, and authorizing the president to appoint a commission to investigate labor conflicts and to serve as a board of conciliation. Cleveland signed all three measures. If none addressed the basic grievances of labor in an age of industrial combination, neither did they reflect a president and a Congress oblivious to the relationship of industrial expansion and labor disputes.

To the demands of certain labor leaders that the federal government investigate and regulate the abuses of business, Cleveland offered little sympathy. He was not a dogmatic disciple of laissez-faire economics, but he was determined to respect what he saw as proper constitutional restrictions on the powers of the federal government. A government that began to interfere with the operations of private business enterprises was a government more likely to fall prey to the temptation to grant special favors to particular business interests. There did seem reason, however, to exercise a measure of federal regulation on interstate railway carriers.

Cleveland was critical of such railroad entrepreneurs as Jay Gould and was disgusted by the way in which certain of the transcontinentals had obtained large governmental subsidies and land grants, only subsequently to fail to fulfill their contractual obligations. When the Supreme Court, in the *Wabash* case of 1886, denied the power of the individual states to regulate interstate railway traffic, Cleveland belatedly joined the forces demanding federal action. In his annual message of December 1886, he declared that "the expediency of Federal action" in the field of railroad regulation was "worthy of consideration," and when Congress finally passed the Interstate Commerce Act of 1887, he signed it.[2]

The Interstate Commerce Act was, in retrospect, both a pioneer piece of legislation in federal governmental regulation and a disappointment. Designed to discourage the discriminatory practices and the excessive charges of the nation's railroads, it prohibited rebates to favored shippers, forbade railroads to charge more for short hauls (in noncompetitive regions) than for long hauls, outlawed pooling agreements, and established the five-member Interstate Commerce Commission (ICC) to conduct investigations of railroad practices. The ICC had no authority to fix rates, but it should seek to assure that rates were "reasonable and just." Powers of enforcement and punishment were left to the federal courts. The act proved difficult to administer. In the two years following its enactment, there was some rationalization of rate structures and a modest reduction in rate differentials; but by 1890, lawyers for the railroads, taking advantage of the vague language of some sections of the Interstate Commerce Act, had begun a successful campaign to weaken its prohibitions, assisted by the decisions of a conservative federal judiciary.

The Interstate Commerce Act had received Cleveland's signature but not his unmixed blessing; for he had doubts about the constitutional soundness of "government by commission." He did not publicize those doubts, however, and appointed to the new Interstate Commerce Commission respected individuals such as Thomas M. Cooley, former dean of the University of Michigan Law School, untainted by ties to the management and financing of the nation's railroads. Cleveland hoped that the ICC would encourage fair competition among the railroads, and he was convinced that only the federal courts could determine when a rate increase was unjustified and beyond the constitutional protection of the rights of property.

Here, as so often, Cleveland was the self-assessed reformer, inhibited by a distrust of governmental intrusion. The ideal would be a self-regulating economy in which no entrepreneur would seek excess profits or engage in dishonest practice and in which labor and management would see their mutual interest and cooperate in beneficial harmony.

Those who classify Cleveland as a conservative disciple of governmental inaction offer as prime evidence his veto of the Texas seed bill. The grain farmers of Texas were suffering from drought and were in need of seed grain, and Congress passed a law early in 1887 endorsing an appropriation of $10,000 to provide these farmers with free seed. In his veto message, Cleveland declared that the power and duty of the general government did not extend "to the relief of individual suffering which is in no manner properly related to the public service or benefit." It was the duty of the people to support the government, but "the Government should not support the people."[3]

The language of the message seemed to reflect a callous disregard for the plight of the nation's humbler citizens, but it is a mistake to extrapolate a single message into a systematic economic philosophy. Cleveland's rejection of aid to Texas farmers was no more characteristic of his administration than was his rejection of appropriations for a new post office in Allentown, Pennsylvania, or his rejection of the free use of the public domain by cattlemen and timber interests. All represented, in his eyes, instances of governmental favoritism and almsgiving at the expense of the taxpaying public. He can be criticized for not distinguishing between the plight of Texas farmers and the greed of timber barons; he can be criticized for failing to appreciate the need of western farmers for better credit facilities; but Cleveland was not a blind reactionary who was mindless of the economic woes of the poor. Instead, he was a latter-day Jacksonian Democrat who distrusted federal involvement in the economy and hoped that individual effort, private charity, and assistance programs at the local levels of government would mitigate the conditions of poverty and lessen the dangerous divisions in American economic society. The federal government could offer only indirect aid, and this within carefully observed constitutional limits. In his annual message of December 1888, Cleveland noted with satisfaction the work of the Bureau of Agriculture in checking the spread of "noxious insects," "destructive fungus growths," and "contagious diseases of farm animals." Agricultural research and the distribution of "practical information" were within the proper purview of the federal government in its efforts to promote the general welfare.[4]

For every day of his presidential tenure, Grover Cleveland was an enemy of monetary inflation and the antagonist of those who wished to inflate the currency by means of additional silver coinage. His opposition to free silver was unremitting; it was the result of his constant allegiance to Gresham's Law: "In the long run, cheap money drives dear money out of circulation."

Cleveland was convinced that the continued coinage of cheap silver dollars would drive gold from circulation as a monetary medium, and this could only result in destructive inflation at home and damage to our credit and trade abroad. Silver dollars were an instrument of dangerous monetary inflation because they were cheap dollars. Under the existing coinage ratio of 16-to-1, the silver in a silver dollar was worth only 80 cents—was worth only 80 percent of the value of the gold in a gold dollar. The answer was to stop the coinage of silver. Only in this way would the hoarding of gold be prevented and gold coins be available to banks, custom houses, and creditors.

Threats to the gold reserve in the United States Treasury would continually haunt the Cleveland presidency. The first of these threats surfaced in the month before Cleveland took office. Many eastern financiers offered dire warnings that the gold reserve was under attack as a result of the operations of the Bland-Allison Silver Coinage Act of 1878. That act required the government to purchase from $2 to $4 million worth of silver each month and to coin it into silver dollars. Cleveland was urged to assure the business community that he opposed the continued coinage of cheap silver dollars.

In the press of preparations for his inauguration, Cleveland accepted the help of Manton Marble, the former editor of the *New York World*, in drafting a public letter indicating his determination to seek the repeal of the Bland-Allison Act and to "continue in use the mass of our gold coin." This letter was published over Cleveland's signature—the only instance of ghostwriting during his political career.[5] But if the words were those of Marble, the convictions were Cleveland's own, as he made clear in his first annual message to Congress, on 8 December 1885.

This was Cleveland's major literary effort in behalf of the repeal of the Bland-Allison Act. Later messages would only repeat its warnings while meeting a similar lack of success. Cleveland insisted that the monthly purchases of silver had the consequence of accumulating an ever-larger supply of silver dollars in the Treasury, and the continued purchase of silver with gold held a real danger that the end result would be "the substitution of silver for all the gold the Government owns." The difference between the real value of gold and silver dollars would become increasingly apparent, "and the two coins will part company." The laboring man would see his wage dollar shrink in purchasing power, and the disappearance of gold as a circulating medium would mean both a sharp contraction in the volume of the nation's currency and general economic hardship. Congress had no duty more pressing than the repeal of the silver act.[6]

When Congress ignored his request, Cleveland and Secretary Daniel Manning sought to shore up the gold reserve by altering certain procedures in the Treasury Department. They discontinued President Arthur's policy of accelerating the redemption of government bonds, and wherever possible they used greenbacks for disbursements, in preference to specie certificates. Cleveland saw such departmental arrangements as necessary but not sufficient. He was angered by the failure of Congress to repeal the Bland-Allison Act, and he was increasingly irate at those Democrats in the House of Representatives who identified themselves with the silver forces and showed little concern for the state of the gold reserve. One of these Democrats was William R. Morrison of Illinois. Morrison introduced into the House a resolution that would have required the Treasury to employ all of its reserves over $100 million to the redemption of government bonds. Cleveland saw this as a menace to the gold reserve, and worked to secure the defeat of the resolution.[7]

The struggle between the silver men and Grover Cleveland during the years 1885 to 1888 ended in a deadlock unsatisfactory to both. Cleveland was not able to obtain the repeal of the Bland-Allison Act, the silver men were not able to push through Congress a bill authorizing the free and unlimited coinage of silver. Even had Cleveland acted more forcefully or with more political finesse, it is doubtful that he could have gained victory, so numerous were the silver men in both houses of Congress. Where Cleveland can be blamed is in his failure to offer an alternative to monetary inflation, an alternative means for lightening debt burdens and improving credit facilities for agrarian groups in the South and the Middle West. Cleveland defined his duty in terms of resistance rather than initiative. It was a position that in his second administration would generate mounting criticism.

The most dramatic example of presidential initiative during Cleveland's first administration was his State of the Union message of December 1887, which was devoted exclusively to the issue of the Treasury surplus and the need for a revision of the protective-tariff system. The message demonstrated Cleveland's evolving conception of the responsibilities of the presidential office and did much to determine the campaign emphases of the election of 1888. It was not, however, Cleveland's first labor as an advocate of tariff reduction. He had recommended tariff revision in two earlier annual messages— although with more brevity and circumlocution—and had sought to influence Democratic congressmen during the fight over the Morrison tariff bill of 1886.

In his first annual message to Congress, Cleveland had pointed to the growing surplus in the Treasury, described its effects on the money supply and business activity, and called for a revision of the protective-tariff system that would reduce governmental revenues and the cost of "necessaries" while taking into account the just claims of industrial labor and capital.[8] With Cleveland's encouragement, William R. Morrison fashioned a moderate tariff-reduction bill in the House Ways and Means Committee in the spring of 1886. Cleveland called key Democratic congressmen to the White House and urged its passage, but when Morrison in June moved that the House go into a committee of the whole to consider his bill, the Republican minority and the Democratic protectionists combined to defeat the motion, 157 to 140. The Morrison bill died, and a rebuffed president expressed his resentment. Cleveland put certain protectionist Democrats on his patronage blacklist and made preparations to force the fight for tariff reform in the next Congress.

He gave indirect notice to that effect in his second annual message of December 1886, when he observed that the American people would soon realize that the surplus revenue that was accumulating in the Treasury as a result of excessive import duties was "paid by them as absolutely . . . as if it was paid at fixed periods into the hands of the tax-gatherer." The revenue laws had to be revised to "cheapen the price of the necessaries of life and give freer entrance" to imported raw materials.[9]

The increasing surplus in the Treasury served as a catalyst for Cleveland's decision by the summer of 1887 to take the lead in the fight for tariff reform, but Cleveland's opposition to protectionism would outlast his worries about the Treasury surplus. Cleveland's argument in support of tariff reduction was based on two core beliefs: the Republican system of high protective tariff duties represented inequitable taxation; the Republican system of high protective tariff duties represented unjustifiable governmental favoritism. These beliefs remained constant. Other auxiliary arguments would be articulated in accordance with changing economic and political conditions, but at bedrock, Cleveland opposed high tariff duties because he believed they added to the cost of living and represented unwarranted favors for particular business interests.

Several recent historians have sought to associate Cleveland's tariff position with a strategy of economic expansion.[10] According to their thesis, the Cleveland administration saw that the home market was insufficient to absorb the increased production made possible by the post–Civil War economic revolution and decided that the only way to correct a price-depressing economic surplus and consequent unemployment and social unrest was to push exports and to expand U.S. foreign markets. Duty-free raw materials and lower tariff barriers could be means to that end. This is an interesting thesis, and it has a measure of validity with respect to the views of two of Cleveland's cabinet officers in his second administration; but it was Grover Cleveland who directed tariff policy in both administrations, and Cleveland was not a strategist of economic expansion. He was aware of the technology-overproduction-depression theory of free-trade propagandists David A. Wells and Edward Atkinson, but Cleveland had little respect for either man. When he made brief mention of "glutted domestic markets" and the desirability of encouraging exports, it was as a supplementary argument designed to increase political support for tariff reduction. From first to last, Cleveland argued that the system of protective tariffs needed revision because it raised prices, gave its beneficiaries excessive profits, and represented unwise governmental interference and favoritism. Grover Cleveland was more a throwback to the Democracy of Jackson and Polk than a prophet of twentieth-century United States economic diplomacy.[11]

Cleveland's analysis of the tariff problem took relatively little note of the international economic picture; its primary focus was on such domestic matters as governmental revenues, indirect taxation, price levels, and the "indefensible extortion" of certain monopolies and trusts. Cleveland's efforts to relate these matters can be criticized. It was, for example, by no means certain that a reduction in tariff duties would automatically shrink the Treasury surplus; by encouraging an increase in the quantity of imports, reduced duties might augment custom revenue even at a lower per-item assessment. Whatever its theoretical flaws, Cleveland's argument was essentially the old-fashioned one that high tariffs encouraged domestic manufacturers to raise their prices to the level of the duty-laden imported product, and this represented an unfair governmental grant of taxing power to the favored manufacturers and increased the cost of living for the laboring classes and a large majority of the American public. It would be false to claim that Cleveland was a pioneer advocate of "consumerism," but his tariff argument was more concerned with domestic prices than with foreign markets. Cleveland, unlike his predecessor Chester Arthur, showed little interest in reciprocity treaties; indeed, he often appeared to view reciprocal tariff agreements as a conspiratorial device to prevent the passage of a general tariff-reduction act.

The objectives of Cleveland's tariff policy have been the source of historical dispute and so, too, has been its motivation. He proclaimed that his sole motive was to do "what was right" and make the Democratic party "stand for something." Some historians have charged that Cleveland was less concerned with the cost of living of the laboring classes than with the electoral success of the Democratic party.[12]

By the time of his tariff message of December 1887, Cleveland had decided that he would seek reelection, and he naturally wished to divert the attention of the Democratic party from the divisive issue of free silver. It would be a mistake, however, to see Cleveland's message of December 1887 as a clever political trick. Cleveland was, indeed, well aware that many of the professional politicians in the Democratic party wished him to straddle or ignore the tariff issue. For every interest group that would favor tariff reduction—shippers, exporters, debtor farmers, manufacturers who imported their raw materials from abroad—there were others who would see it as a threat to their economic self-interest. Tariff reform could unite party factions in Massachusetts but divide them in Pennsylvania. Cleveland undoubtedly hoped that tariff reform would be a winning issue in the next presidential election, but he wrote his tariff message of December 1887 from motives of fear and conviction: fear that the Treasury surplus would incite governmental extravagance; conviction that the protective-tariff system was an agency of extortion and governmental favoritism.

Cleveland had once thought of calling a special session of Congress in 1887 to confront the issue of the Treasury surplus and tariff revision but decided, instead, to confine his annual message exclusively to the topic of revenue reform. Filling a dozen octavo pages of close print, Cleveland's message sought to provide an irrefutable argument for the immediate reduction of protective tariff rates. He began with an analysis of the manner in which the Treasury surplus was withdrawing money from trade, producing "financial disturbance," and "inviting schemes of public plunder." The accumulated surplus would soon represent almost a third of the country's circulating capital. It was the product chiefly of custom revenue, and it was here that Congress must direct its attention, and not to revenue from internal taxes on tobacco and whiskey. Those taxes served a social purpose and did not represent a burden on any portion of the people. The present tariff law, however, was a "vicious, inequitable, and illogical source of unnecessary taxation." It raised the price to consumers of imported articles "by precisely the sum" of the custom duty. It was not only the few who purchased the foreign article who paid the enhanced price; so, too, did the consumer of the domestic article, because the protected American manufacturer would raise his price to a level nearly equal to that of the duty-laden foreign import:

> . . . while comparatively few use the imported article, millions of our people, who never use and never saw the foreign products, purchase and use things of the same kind made in this country, and pay therefore nearly or quite the same enhanced price which the duty adds to the imported articles. Those who buy imports pay the duty charged thereon into the public treasury, but the great majority of our citizens . . . pay a sum at least approximately equal to this duty to the home manufacturer.

American industry was no longer in a state of infancy that might justify high tariff barriers against the competing goods of foreign nations. Nor were high tariffs necessary for the wage level of the American laborer. Tariff reduction could be accomplished without harm to the wages and employment of the factory worker; reduction in the excessive profits of certain manufacturers need furnish no excuse for reducing wages. The factory worker, like the farmer, was a consumer as well as a producer and must recognize that the present protective system raised the price of the goods that "he needs for the use of himself and his family."

Under the present system of high protection, competition among domestic producers had failed to prevent the tendency of domestic prices to rise to the level of the imported article, because competition was often "strangled by combinations quite prevalent at this time and frequently called trusts." These trusts had as their object "the regulation of the supply and price of the commodities made and sold by members of the combination." There was strong reason to believe that high tariffs fostered such monopolistic practices.

The solution was a revision of current tariff schedules that would significantly lower the duties on all necessities and abolish or lower the duties on raw materials used in American manufactures. This would reduce the cost of living in every American home and would give U.S. manufacturers a better chance in foreign markets. There would be advantage for all: consumer prices would decline, and American manufacturers would no longer see their growth only in terms of the exploitation of a protected domestic market.

Any suggestion that he was promoting the gospel of free trade was mischievous and erroneous. "It is a condition that confronts us—not a theory." The Treasury surplus must be reduced; the people must be relieved from unnecessary and unjust taxation: "The simple and plain duty which we owe the people is to reduce the taxation to the necessary expenses of an economical operation of the government, and to restore to the business of the country the money which we hold in the Treasury through the perversion of governmental powers."[13]

The reaction to Cleveland's message was predictably partisan. Although a few protectionist Democrats muttered their disagreement and some party politicians judged it an act of political folly, a majority of Democrats rallied to the call. A few dreamed dreams of perpetual party hegemony by means of an alliance between New England manufacturers in need of cheap raw materials, New York commercial interests, staple farmers in need of foreign markets, and the traditionally low-tariff southern states. Tariff reform could be related to the Jeffersonian-Jacksonian heritage of concern for the humbler citizen and the agrarian sections. It could help the party shed its negative image and identify itself with a positive approach to the nation's problems.

The Mugwumps now forgave Cleveland his compromises on civil-service patronage and cheered his efforts to identify his party with tariff reform. Some of the Mugwumps were free traders, and all identified lower tariffs with a salutary reduction in governmental interference with the operations of the marketplace.

Republican politicians were convinced that Cleveland had given them a winning issue. They would link his call for tariff revision with advocacy of free trade, subservience to Great Britain, and enmity to industrial prosperity and the standard of living of the American laborer. When Congressman Roger Mills of Texas introduced a tariff-reduction bill in the House of Representatives in the spring of 1888, the Republicans thought they had further reason to believe that Cleveland had played into their hands.

The Mills bill had Cleveland's blessing, but it was a measure both timid in scope and biased in favor of the economic interests of the South. The Mills bill called for tariff cuts averaging only 7 percent. Duties on sugar, rice, iron ore, and cheap cotton textiles were lowered very little; rates on finished iron products, glass, and high-quality cotton and woolen goods were slated for comparatively deep cuts.

The Mills tariff bill passed the House by a vote cast along strict party lines, but it was quickly pigeonholed in the Senate. The Republican majority in the Senate worked up its own tariff- and surplus-reduction bill, and then allowed both bills to die with the conclusion of the regular session of the Fiftieth Congress. Cleveland had the satisfaction of having identified his party with tariff reform, but that was the limit of his accomplishment. As he had achieved only a stalemate with the proponents of free silver, so now he could claim no more than a draw with Republican protectionists in his efforts for tariff reform.

There are, of course, historians who object to the term "tariff reform"; they insist that it carries the implication that lower tariffs were necessarily in the public interest and that "tariff reformers" were motivated by a concern for the general welfare.[14] There seems to be little profit in further debating this semantic question, but any student of the Cleveland presidencies is required to decide whether Grover Cleveland wished only to tinker with the protective-tariff system or to demand a significant measure of change. The answer would seem to be that he was both a cautious revisionist and a true believer. Cleveland was convinced that the existing system of tariff protection was a source of inequity and corruption, but unlike David Wells and other free-trade theorists, Cleveland did not wish to dismantle the protective system, only to rid it of its robber aspects. He wanted free raw materials and a major reduction in the duties on all articles that figured prominently in the food-and-clothing budget of the average American. He entertained no idealistic thoughts of a world free of all tariff barriers and economic rivalries. Too much the political realist not to fear the misrepresentations of his enemies, he emphasized that he wished no more than "a just and sensible revision of our tariff laws."[15] But this politically cautious gradualist was, in the context of his day, a tariff reformer. The system of high protectionism had become entrenched in United States politics ever since the Morrill Tariff of 1861, and a president who demanded revision in behalf of relief for consumers, a reduction of governmental subsidies to special interests, and the restraint of trusts and monopolies is not unduly praised when given the designation of reformer.

In his first-term efforts at tariff reform, Cleveland can be faulted on his timing and tactics. He might have done better to have delivered his tariff message a year earlier; he should have taken more immediate direction of the Mills bill when it was in committee and sought to correct its sectional bias. It is doubtful, however, that an earlier or better-balanced bill would have passed the Republican-controlled Senate. Where Cleveland primarily failed was in the area of public education. The tariff, with its many details and schedules, was a complicated business, and tariff revision was easily portrayed as a radical experiment that would subject the farmer and factory worker to the competition of the peasants and the low-wage laborers of Europe. Cleveland appeared to believe that he had done his duty once his message was published and he had successfully urged Democrats in the House to pass the Mills bill. He had little talent for mobilizing public opinion or generating publicity for his policies, and he would have considered a barnstorming tour to inspire grass-roots support to be beneath the dignity of the presidential office. He spoke about the need for "a campaign of public education" in behalf of tariff reform, but he left to others the labors of instruction.

When reviewing the record of Cleveland's first administration—its accomplishments and its failures—one hopes to find a consistent pattern that will allow conclusive judgments respecting Cleveland's claim to have fulfilled his promise to provide the nation with an example of a "reform administration." It is hardly enough to say that the record is "mixed"; but that must be the initial judgment. On one point, qualifications may be abandoned. During Cleveland's first administration, the presidency was reestablished as a branch of the federal government coordinate in authority with the Congress, and this was in large part attributable to the labors and personality of Grover Cleveland. The administrative reforms that he encouraged in the various departments, his extensive use of the veto power, his fight for executive independence during his battle with the Senate over the Tenure of Office Act, and his leadership efforts in such areas as Indian policy, western land policy, and tariff reform gave the executive branch a vigor and a morale that it had not known for twenty years. A naturally assertive disposition and a determination to associate himself with an improved level of integrity in American politics had encouraged Cleveland, by the summer of 1886, to take a more active role in the determination of legislative policy and the voting record of congressional Democrats. Cleveland did not possess the undeviating purity and courage that he sought to project, but he did enhance the dignity and the public reputation of the presidency and thereby gave it increased importance.

Cleveland may also be credited with having advanced the reputation of the Democratic party. He demonstrated little tact when dealing with party politicians, and his efforts at party leadership were erratic, but his first administration gave the lie to Republican charges that the administration of the federal government could not be trusted to a party controlled by Confederate brigadiers and states' rights ideologues. By the end of Cleveland's first term, the Democratic party had gained respectability in the eyes of all but the more extreme Republican partisans. Respectability is no guarantee of electoral success, as the election of 1888 would prove, but it is a long-term benefit for any political organization. The Democratic party of 1888 was a less heterogeneous and fragmented political institution than it had been in 1884. It could not boast effective party discipline or an efficient national organization, but it did appear to have a more coherent national purpose. At the least, Cleveland had begun to alter the public perception of the Democratic party as a party of drift, division, and nostalgic obstructionism.

Historical judgments that emphasize the lack of constructive legislation in the years of Cleveland's first term are understandable but exaggerated. There was no body of legislation that reversed the course of the nation's history, but there was the repeal of the Tenure of Office Act; the Presidential Succession Act; the Hatch Act, which established agricultural experiment stations; an act promoting voluntary arbitration in railroad labor disputes; an act raising the Bureau of Agriculture to departmental cabinet rank; the Indian Emancipation Act; and the Interstate Commerce Act. None of these was primarily the result of presidential initiative, but most received presidential support. In addition, there were executive orders to improve the efficiency and honesty of the Navy and Treasury departments; to restrict the political activity of federal workers; to enlarge the classified list; to reorganize the Pension Bureau; to prohibit the fencing of the public domain and protect its mineral and timber resources. For all his fears of governmental paternalism, Cleveland supported a number of measures that expanded federal authority.

There were no legislative results from Cleveland's efforts in the problem areas of the currency and the tariff. In part this was the result of his failure to place currency and tariff reform in the context of the rapid social and economic changes of the post–Civil War generation. But it was also the result of the fact that throughout his first administration the control of the two houses of Congress was divided between the major parties, and in neither house was there effective discipline and leadership. Congress was ill adapted to pass legislation that could significantly alter the economic status quo. Corporate interests were powerful in the Senate, and the House suffered from a set of rules that virtually assured continuous opportunities for obstructionism.

If one begins a review of Cleveland's first administration with a sense of disappointment that there is no collection of statutes to be identified as the "Cleveland Legislative Program," one ends with a sense of surprise that there was not less accomplishment. Cleveland offered no program to satisfy a twentieth-century progressive, but in his slow and often bumbling fashion, he had improved the public reputation of the federal government and had brought enhanced dignity and independence to the presidency.

6

★ ★ ★ ★ ★

DEFEAT, EXILE, AND VICTORY
(1888–92)

Although Grover Cleveland had once advocated a single term for an American president, he expected renomination in 1888. He believed, correctly, that the Democrats had no better man to defend and continue the policies of the Cleveland administration. Certain Tammany Hall enemies sought to block his renomination at the Democratic National Convention in St. Louis with prophecies that he would not carry New York State and by surreptitiously distributing a scurrilous pamphlet that charged Cleveland with bestial perversions during his Buffalo days and brutal treatment of his new wife.[1] Their efforts were ignored, and once the seconding speeches were over, Cleveland was renominated by acclamation.

The Democratic platform was less than inspiring, but Henry Watterson and other enthusiasts for tariff reform obtained a tariff plank that gave unqualified approval to Cleveland's message of December 1887 and the Mills bill. Identifying the protective tariff as tax legislation, the Democrats promised the American people "a fair and careful revision of our tax laws, with due allowance for the difference between the wages of American and foreign labor."[2]

The Republicans chose Benjamin Harrison, a former senator from Indiana, as their presidential candidate; and their platform, at least on the tariff issue, was forthright and specific: "We are uncompromisingly in favor of the American system of protection." If there were a need to reduce federal revenues, it should be done by the reduction or repeal of internal taxes.[3]

Students of the election of 1888 are unanimous in their judgment that the Republicans enjoyed a marked advantage in campaign organization and leadership. Led by Senator Matthew S. Quay of Pennsylvania, the Republican National Committee raised large sums from manufacturers worried by the alleged free-trade intentions of the Democratic party and oversaw the distribution of tons of campaign literature in cooperation with local Republican clubs and such special-interest agencies as the Iron and Steel Association. The Democrats were led by two men who demonstrated neither energy nor an interest in tariff reform: William H. Barnum, a manufacturer, and Calvin S. Brice, a railroad promoter. Cleveland had made no objection to their selection, perhaps because he had thought they would help to insulate the Democrats from the charge that they were seeking the total destruction of the protective-tariff system.[4] It was but one of many examples of Cleveland's failure of leadership in the campaign of 1888.

While Harrison was delivering eighty effective front-porch addresses from his home in Indianapolis, Cleveland confined his campaign labors to a short epistle to New York City Democrats, his acceptance letter, and a few letters to political friends.[5] Cleveland had claimed, in a letter to a supporter, that the campaign would be "one of information and organization." Every citizen "should be regarded as a thoughtful, responsible voter" and should be furnished with the means for "examining the issues involved in the pending canvass for himself."[6] He left to others, however, the task of furnishing these means. He hated the tiring, handshaking labor of campaigning and spent most of the campaign season in self-imposed seclusion. To the elderly Allen G. Thurman, the Democratic vice-presidential nominee, fell the chief burden of stumping in behalf of the national ticket. Tottering toward death, Thurman was unequal to the task.

Certain of Cleveland's supporters made an earnest effort to make good his hope that the campaign would be "one of information," and some were indeed more bold in their advocacy of tariff revision than was the candidate. Worried by the seeming success of Republican efforts to identify tariff reduction with free trade, Cleveland, in his few public letters, emphasized that the Democratic party intended to revise the tariff with conservative caution and a proper concern for the employment and wages of American labor. In the last weeks of the campaign, it was Harrison and the Republicans, not Cleveland, who insisted on directing public attention to the tariff issue.

The tariff argument of the Democrats was one that sought to balance a claim of moderation with a promise of lower prices and more economical government. The Republicans sought to identify the protective system with American nationalism, the interdependence of economic groups, and the patriotic assurance that American goods and American labor would have a monopoly of the home market. In Republican campaign posters, Harrison was shown against the background of the American flag; Cleveland, against the background of the British Union Jack. Harrison would protect the American farmer against imported wheat, beef, and wool and the American factory hand against the sweated labor of Europe. Protection meant prosperity for all economic classes. The manufacturer, the skilled worker, the professional, and the farmer would all prosper as American factories worked at full production and American farms found an increasing and stable market at home. George F. Hoar, the senior senator from Massachusetts, summarized the Republican argument in a campaign speech in October: the destruction of the protective system would necessitate heavy federal excise taxes and would be followed by lower wages for all and unemployment for many; the policy of protection by expanding production and stimulating competition cheapened the cost of all articles of consumption; protection generated profits for investments and lessened dependence on foreign capital; the primary purpose of the tariff system was to protect the living standards of all classes and sections.[7]

Cleveland had hoped to generate unity for the Democratic party around the tariff issue, but in the campaign of 1888, it was the Republicans who were the more successful in using the issue to rally the faithful and convince the committed to work harder for the cause.

The campaign of 1888 was not just a shadowboxing exercise in partisan rhetoric; there were distinctions of program and tradition between the major parties. The Republicans championed not only protectionism and federal aid to education and Union veterans but— at the state level—such issues of social control as temperance, secular schools, and Sunday observance laws. The Democrats proclaimed allegiance to tariff revision, governmental economy, and respect for state sovereignty and individual liberty. The campaign saw fewer torchlight processions and less personal animus than had the previous election, but partisans on both sides proclaimed the importance of victory, and there was a heavy voter turnout. Partisan identification remained strong throughout the eighties, and so did grass-roots participation in the political system.

The two episodes of the campaign that have received most attention in textbook accounts are the organization of the "floaters" by the Republicans in Indiana and the Murchison Letter. Each added a colorful footnote, but it is doubtful if either was of significance in determining the election result.

Indiana, traditionally a swing state in national elections, had a long history of vote buying by both parties. The Republican national treasurer, W. W. Dudley, sought to inject a bit of scientific organization into the process; he sent a circular note to the county leaders in Indiana, advising them to "divide the floaters into blocks of five and put a trusted man with necessary funds in charge of these five and make him responsible that none get away and that all vote our ticket." It was an incitement to bribery, but probably its chief effect was to raise the asking price of the floaters.[8]

The Murchison Letter was a ruse arranged by a Republican partisan in California named George A. Osgoodby, who had the bright idea of writing to the British minister in Washington and asking his advice about how a British-born U. S. citizen should vote. Was Cleveland a good friend of the old Mother Country? The British minister, Sir Lionel Sackville-West, a man of more credulity than intelligence, wrote back that any recent anti-British belligerence on Cleveland's part was the result of political pressures and that he was certain that Cleveland was an advocate of Anglo-American friendship. Sackville-West's letter came into the hands of Republican politicians in California and was soon given national publicity. The Republicans insisted that it proved that Cleveland was the puppet of Britain and therefore the enemy of Irish-Americans as well as tariff protection. An angry Cleveland, afraid that Sackville-West could serve the Republicans as the Reverend Samuel Burchard had served the Democrats four years earlier, demanded that the minister be recalled and, when the British failed to comply immediately, sent him packing. The affair showed Cleveland at his least courageous, but there is no reason to believe it determined the result of the election. Cleveland actually did better in certain Irish-American districts than he had done four years earlier.[9]

Largely as a result of increased Democratic margins in the South, Cleveland had a popular plurality over Harrison of better than 90,000 votes, but Harrison was victorious in the electoral vote count, 233 to 168. The key states were New York and Indiana: Cleveland had won them by narrow margins in 1884; now they fell to Harrison. The election of 1888 saw the return to power of the Republican party—the Republicans would control both houses of Congress as well as the presidency—but it saw no major shift of political allegiance among the electorate. Indeed, one of the more interesting features of the election results was the rough similarity of the voting pattern to that of the three previous presidential elections. Elections during the period 1876 to 1888 demonstrated the strength of partisan loyalty as well as the ability of chance events and local religious and cultural issues to tip the balance. In a period of political equilibrium, the party that was best able to rally the faithful usually gained the victory.

In the election of 1888, the tariff issue helped the Republican party to increase its vote in the Middle Atlantic and New England states, where it was traditionally strong; but the primary importance of the tariff issue for the Republicans was its utility as a scare tactic and as a patriotic rallying cry. Members of the Knights of Labor, as well as many manufacturers, were influenced by Republican predictions of a flood of sweated goods from Europe if the free-trader Democrats were to return to power. Republican propaganda was equally effective in associating protectionism with American patriotism and national pride.

The Republican party's large war chest, its ties to the GAR, the comparative vigor of its national organization, and its effective distribution of party literature among the expanding electorate in urban industrial areas were other factors that helped the Republicans achieve their narrow victory. Equally important, however, were the errors of the Democratic party and its presidential candidate. Cleveland's defeat can be attributed as much to his failure to orient and direct the Democratic campaign as to the inefficiency of Brice, Barnum, and the Democratic National Committee. Whether tariff reform could have proved a winning issue in 1888 will never be known, for Cleveland did not give it a fair trial. In his acceptance letter he chose to take a defensive position on the issue, and he subsequently retreated to a stance of above-the-battle monasticism.

An example of the latter was his posture of disdainful neutralism toward Democratic politics in New York. The thirty-six electoral votes of the Empire State would have gained him a majority of the electoral vote. The Democratic candidate for governor, David B. Hill, won the state by a plurality of over eighteen thousand votes, while Cleveland lost the state by some twelve thousand votes. The relations between Cleveland and Hill had been at best uneasy for several years, and Cleveland had refused to give formal endorsement to Hill's candidacy. There would be charges then and later that Hill had made an agreement with the Republican boss, Thomas C. Platt, whereby the Hill machine would agree to knife Cleveland and sell out the national ticket in exchange for Republican votes for Hill and for the Tammany candidate for mayor of New York City, Hugh J. Grant. Hill's political reputation had been constructed on the theme of undeviating party loyalty, and it is doubtful that he made any formal agreement with Platt. It is equally unlikely, however, that the supporters of Hill or Grant showed any enthusiasm for the national ticket. Less hauteur and more conciliation by Cleveland might have made a difference. As it was, election night saw the New York Republicans happily chanting

> Down in the cornfield
> Hear the mournful sound
> All the Democrats are weeping—
> Grover's in the cold, cold ground![10]

A defeated Cleveland was not a chastened Cleveland, as he made clear in what appeared to be his farewell address to national politics, his State of the Union message of 3 December 1888. This was in many ways a surprising effort both in tone and in content. At points it was a jeremiad against capitalist greed and big-business elites worthy of a Populist spokesman of the 1890s. It can, of course, be viewed simply as the embittered commentary of a politician anxious to take his whacks against the interest groups that he believed were responsible for his defeat. It is better read, however, as the reflections of a troubled conservative who feared for his country's future and sought to recall its happier Jacksonian past.

Cleveland now sought to place the cause of tariff reform in a larger context. The battle must continue, because the system of protectionism was but a symptom of a nation in danger of losing the virtues of republican simplicity in a mad scramble for material gain. Protectionism fostered trusts and monopolies and was part and parcel of a dangerous tendency towards increasing economic inequality and social unrest in American society. In the process, the proper relationship of the citizen and his government was being undermined, with dangerous consequences for the social fabric of the American nation:

> Upon more careful inspection we find the wealth and luxury of our cities mingled with poverty and wretchedness and unremunera-

tive toil. A crowded and constantly increasing urban population suggests the impoverishment of rural sections, and discontent with agricultural pursuits. . . .

As we view the achievements of aggregated capital, we discover the existence of trusts, combinations, and monopolies. . . .

. . . to the extent that the mass of our citizens are inordinately burdened beyond any useful public purpose and for the benefit of a favored few, the government, under pretext of an exercise of its taxing power, enters gratuitously into partnership with these favorites, to their advantage and to the injury of a vast majority of our people.

. . . .

Communism is a hateful thing, and a menace to peace and organized government. But the communism of combined wealth and capital, the outgrowth of overweening cupidity and selfishness, which insidiously undermines the justice and integrity of free institutions is not less dangerous than the communism of oppressed poverty and toil which, exasperated by injustice and discontent, attacks with wild disorder the citadel of rule.

He mocks the people who proposes that the government shall protect the rich and that they in turn will care for the laboring poor. Any intermediary between the people and their government, or the least delegation of the care and protection the government owes to the humblest citizen in the land, makes the boast of free institutions a glittering delusion. . . .

. . . .

[Andrew Jackson], in vindication of his course as the protector of popular rights, and the champion of true American citizenship, declared: ". . . it is not in a splendid government supported by powerful monopolies and aristocratical establishments that they [the people] will find happiness, or their liberties protection, but in a plain system, void of pomp—protecting all and granting favors to none."[11]

Cleveland offered only tariff reform and governmental economy as a prescription for the problems besetting America in a time of rapid economic transformation, but if the prescription was insufficient, the diagnosis was one of the more provocative offered by any political leader of the Gilded Age.

After witnessing Harrison's inauguration, Cleveland left Washington for New York, his public career apparently ended. Some Republican editorial writers indeed suggested that the presidency of Cleveland had been a political accident and would furnish but a small footnote in the history of the period. In New York, the Clevelands moved into a house at 816 Madison Avenue, and Cleveland soon accepted an autonomous association with the law firm of Bangs, Stetson, Tracy and MacVeagh. Pretending disinterest in the political scene, Cleveland occupied himself in the years 1889 and 1890 with his legal labors as a court-appointed referee and with the companionship of a small group of close friends that included Richard Watson Gilder, editor of the *Century*; Joseph Jefferson, the actor; Oscar S. Straus, a merchant-importer; Francis Lynde Stetson, a corporation lawyer; Dr. Joseph D. Bryant, a surgeon; Erastus C. Benedict, a financier; and L. Clarke Davis, editor of the *Philadelphia Public Ledger*.

In October 1891, Cleveland was proudly announcing to his old friend Shan Bissell of Buffalo the arrival of a baby girl, Ruth. Like many men who first become parents in their fifties, Cleveland was elated. He reported that he had "just entered the real world."[12] With parenthood—and Ruth would be followed by four other children over the next twelve years—came a greater concern for financial security. He had made a profit of almost $100,000 on the sale of his Washington home, Oak View, and his legal work brought him an income adequate to his current expenses; but he wished now to increase his capital for the sake of the future of his young family. He turned to his friend E. C. Benedict and, for the first time, became a stock-market investor, under Benedict's guidance.

Though some biographers have suggested that these years saw a turn to the right in Cleveland's political philosophy under the influence of a circle of corporate lawyers and financiers, there is little evidence to support their assumption. Cleveland did become more interested in making money, as was natural for a man with a much younger wife and a growing family, but he had always demonstrated a concern for property rights and the sanctity of contract. If he returned to public life in 1893 with a larger bank account and investment portfolio, he did not return with a determination to serve as the catspaw of big business. Frequent trips on Benedict's yacht did not alter Cleveland's political objectives or determine their ambiguity.

Although Cleveland refused to make any public comment on the first years of the Harrison administration and the legislation of the "Billion Dollar Congress" of 1889/90, he viewed both with mounting disapproval. He judged Harrison, incorrectly, as a weak man who was under the thumb of Secretary of State James G. Blaine and saw Blaine's "spirited," commerce-oriented foreign policy as confused in purpose and unduly belligerent in practice. The legislative program of the Billion Dollar Congress was even more blameworthy. The McKinley Tariff was a robber tariff;[13] the Dependent Pension Act was a piece of gross governmental favoritism that could only incite further raids on the Treasury by other interest groups; the Sherman Silver Purchase Act was a dangerous compromise with the free-silver forces; the new Reed Rules in the House of Representatives offered an example of tyranny by the majority; the effort to pass a Federal Elections bill was a shameful attempt to revive the sectional hostility of the Reconstruction Decade and erode the proper authority of state governments over the supervision of elections. The abortive Federal Elections bill was, in fact, a modest effort to make good the promise of the Fifteenth Amendment in behalf of black suffrage in the South. It would have made the federal circuit courts, instead of state governors and state certifying boards, the arbiters of congressional election procedures and returns. By its enemies it was labeled a "force bill," and Cleveland accepted that designation. Obviously, he saw the utility of the label for sustaining the Democratic allegiance of the South, but Cleveland was convinced that the measure represented a dangerous expansion of the power of the central government.[14]

It was only after the voters had expressed their distaste for the activism and expenditures of the Billion Dollar Congress in the congressional elections of 1890 that Grover Cleveland began to give serious thought to securing the prize of the Democratic presidential nomination for a third time. Cleveland limited his own participation in the congressional elections of 1890 to a few letters to tariff-reform clubs, urging their continued efforts in behalf of "fundamental principles."[15] He viewed the results, however, as an expression of support by a chastened electorate for the policies of Cleveland Democracy. It was an assessment of dubious accuracy.

Those elections represented a major defeat for the Republicans; the new House of Representatives would have but 88 Republicans and 235 Democrats—a Democratic gain of 78 seats. A number of factors had contributed to this apparent shift of political allegiance. At the national level, there was the Democratic success in attributing rising prices to the McKinley Tariff and the displeasure of many voters with the extravagant appropriations of the Billion Dollar Congress. In several states, however, it was probably local cultural and social issues that were the undoing of Republican candidates. This was a time when, to use the terminology of Samuel P. Hays, "community loyalties" still prevailed over emerging national "society interests"; and in states such as Iowa, Wisconsin, and Illinois, the Republican party was identified with temperance legislation, Sabbatarian laws, and other examples of interference with the personal standards and religious/cultural values of German Lutheran and Roman Catholic communities. Those communities found themselves in sympathy with Democratic opposition to pietistic laws and social activism under government direction. In a few states further west, agrarian unrest was of some benefit to the Democrats, now the party of the "outs."[16]

Cleveland, however, was a politician, not a political analyst. In the months following the congressional elections, he accepted several invitations to address party gatherings, and he took the opportunity to inform his fellow Democrats that the voters had expressed their approval of governmental economy and tariff reform. The falsehoods that had gained the Republicans undeserved victory in 1888—the baseless charges that the tariff reformers were British agents and wished harm to the American laborer—were no longer believed by the intelligent American voter.[17] Despite his claims to Daniel Lamont and others that he felt a "personal repugnance" about leaving the comforts of private life, Cleveland by the winter of 1890/91 was prepared to return to the political arena.[18] Before the year was over, he was ready to campaign for the Democratic nomination. Various influences were at work—apart from personal ambition and a desire for political vindication—and one of these was personified in the figure of Governor David B. Hill of New York.

Cleveland saw Hill, with some justice, as the epitome of the managerial politician who viewed politics as a game with but a single object—victory for self and party.[19] Cleveland early recognized that Hill was determined to gain the Democratic presidential nomination in 1892, and he believed that in pursuit of that aim, Hill would be willing to make deals with the free-silver forces, the protectionists, the spoilsmen, and other enemies of the true Democratic faith. Cleveland closely followed Hill's southern tours and was pleased to hear from Lucius Lamar and others about Hill's failure to gain firm pledges of support. Cleveland was increasingly convinced, however, that Hill could only be sidetracked if Cleveland's own friends were allowed, indeed encouraged, to offer the party a better choice.

The most important reason for Cleveland's unaccustomed energy in his own behalf was his fear that unless he entered the lists for the

Democratic nomination, the free-silver men might well control the Democratic National Convention in 1892. Cleveland was angered when Democratic leaders in Alabama, Georgia, and Virginia sought to counter the growing political strength of the Southern Farmers Alliance with predictions that the national Democratic party would adopt a free-silver platform, and he expressed his dismay when every state Democratic convention from Virginia to Texas gave rhetorical encouragement to the free-silver movement. By his famous "Silver Letter" of February 1891, Cleveland had sought to remind his party that a national currency of honest value was an essential part of traditional Democratic doctrine. Viewed by many at the time as a impulsive gesture by a man who was prepared to sacrifice his political future, the "Silver Letter" was, to the contrary, a declaration to his fellow Democrats that he had reentered public life with a firm determination to see that the Democrats fought the election of 1892 with a sound-money platform and a sound-money candidate.

Cleveland had been invited by a group of Democratic business-men in New York City to address a dinner meeting on the danger of free silver. Unable to accept, he took the opportunity of replying in a public letter in which he predicted disaster for the nation's credit if the United States were to embark upon such a "dangerous and reck-less experiment" as "free, unlimited and independent silver coinage."[20] In this letter, Cleveland left open the possibility of con-tinued coinage by means of an international agreement establishing a permanent coinage ratio for gold and silver;[21] but there was no qualification in his antagonism to monetary inflation.

There was, however, a measure of political calculation in Cleveland's "Silver Letter." Rather than having thrown away his chances for the Democratic nomination, he had assured himself the renewed support of eastern hard-money Democrats, as well as the members of Mugwump Reform Clubs. They were strengthened in their belief that Cleveland would oppose the reckless schemes of western radicals with uncompromising firmness. When Cleveland addressed a ratification meeting of the New York Democratic party at the Cooper Union in October 1891, some of the loudest applause came from such eastern capitalists as Henry Villard, William Whitney, and Charles Fairchild. These men were prepared to offer not only money but also time and managerial skill in behalf of Cleveland's nomination. Cleveland welcomed their aid.

He was not prepared, however, to write off other sections of the country in order to secure the support of eastern conservatives. He entered into active correspondence with many southern editors and politicians in 1892, urging them to remind southern Democrats of his labors in behalf of sectional reconciliation, his recognition of the difficulties of the southern farmer, and his criticism of the "force bill." Were the Democrats of the South to desert their party for the radical Populists, the result might well be the renewed political isolation of the South, Republican victory in the coming election, and another effort to obtain congressional passage of a "force bill."[22]

By the spring of 1892, Cleveland's readiness to accept the Democratic nomination was unconcealed.[23] In April, Cleveland delivered what, by his standards, was a rousing speech at the Providence Opera House. Excoriating the Republicans for their misrepresentations of Democratic proposals for tariff reduction and for their efforts to revive sectional prejudices, he attacked, for the first time, Republican promises to expand U.S. markets by means of bilateral reciprocity treaties: "If 'hypocrisy is the homage vice pays to virtue,' reciprocity may be called the homage protection pays to genuine tariff reform."[24]

Cleveland had the assistance and advice of George F. Parker as a self-appointed press secretary. Parker compiled a book of Cleveland's addresses and state papers for the years 1882 through 1891, and he encouraged Cleveland to cooperate with the press in order to gain wide distribution of his current speeches and public letters. In his role of publicity director, Parker sought to persuade Cleveland to view the press, not as an enemy, but as a public-relations instrument in his campaign for the Democratic nomination. Parker's task was made more difficult by the editors of the *Washington Post* and the *New York Sun* and their attempts at personal ridicule.

The editor of the *Washington Post* thought it newsworthy to indicate that Cleveland's attendance at the theater was limited by the fact that he was "too big and fat" to occupy an orchestra seat "with comfort."[25] It was the editor of the *New York Sun*, however, who was the more obsessed with Cleveland's weight. Charles A. Dana had gained a reputation as one of the nation's more vitriolic journalists, and one of the favorite targets for his venom was Grover Cleveland. After Cleveland's defeat in 1888, Dana had printed an entire column of quotations from medical works on the harmful effects of obesity, and in the spring of 1892 he sought to use the weapon of ridicule to block Cleveland's bid for the Democratic nomination. In the pages of the *Sun*, Cleveland was referred to as "the Perpetual Candidate," "the elephantine economist," or "the Stuffed Prophet."[26]

The waspish mockery of Dana gave Cleveland's supporters little concern. Under the leadership of William C. Whitney, and with the advice and encouragement of Cleveland,[27] they laid plans for a first-ballot nomination. Early in June, Whitney sent a confidential message to a dozen key Cleveland supporters, asking them to attend a conference at his house on West 57th Street.[28] Checking in with false names at different New York hotels, the twelve assembled at eleven o'clock on the morning of June ninth. Apart from Whitney, the major figures were William F. Vilas of Wisconsin, Donald M. Dickinson of Michigan, William L. Wilson of West Virginia, and Josiah Quincy of Massachusetts. They surveyed the delegations of each state and their probable first-ballot vote, made their choices for convention officials, and assumed responsibility for the continuous surveillance of probable Cleveland delegates. Their chief worry was that if Cleveland did not win on the first ballot, some dark horse, taking advantage of division within the New York delegation, might strike a deal with David Hill and his cohort, Senator Arthur Pue Gorman. Cleveland shared their worries, and he sent a flurry of messages to Whitney, requesting information, offering unneeded advice, and demanding that the planks of the Democratic platform be "plain and right."[29]

The Democrats convened on 21 June in the newly built "Wigwam" on the Chicago Lake Front. The giant hall, built in the shape of an Indian wigwam, could seat twenty thousand persons. Despite the now-traditional last-ditch effort of delegates from Tammany Hall, the result was foreordained, thanks to the labors of Whitney and his lieutenants. They had convinced a majority of the delegates that if the Democrats wished victory in November, they had best push the divisive issue of silver coinage into the background and give pride of place to tariff reform. Cleveland was the obvious leader for such a campaign.

After Senator John M. Palmer of Illinois had concluded his nominating speech for Cleveland, some of the delegates began to chant:

> Grover! Grover!
> Four more years of Grover!
> In he comes,
> Out they go,
> Then we'll be in clover!

The versification was feeble, but the optimism was understandable. Although Cleveland's first-ballot nomination owed much to Whitney's organizational talents and to Cleveland's own exertions, it was primarily the result of the realization of the convention delegates that Grover Cleveland was the candidate best respected by the rank and file of the party and by the Independent voters, and the man who offered the party the best assurance of victory.

At its last session, the convention chose Adlai E. Stevenson as Cleveland's running mate, primarily in the hope that he would help the party capture the state of Illinois.[30] Cleveland approved the selection, convinced that possible Democratic defections in the South and the probable machinations of David Hill in New York made Democratic gains in the Middle West essential.

Cleveland was highly pleased with his nomination. Having been dismissed by some political observers four years earlier as a political accident and having been attacked by the Hill-Gorman forces as the party's albatross, he saw his nomination as a personal vindication. He was also well aware that only one other Democrat had ever run in three consecutive presidential elections: his hero, Andrew Jackson. Having labored, somewhat surreptitiously, for the nomination, Cleveland was now prepared to work, quite openly, in the fall campaign. Victory in November would make complete the confounding of his enemies.

Some contemporary observers considered the campaign of 1892 dull; others called it dignified. Compared with the campaigns of 1884 and 1888, there were less partisan animus and less personal attack. For the first and only time in American history, the candidates of the two major parties had both seen presidential service, and this possibly encouraged good manners as did the temperamental reserve of the candidates. Henry Adams was more determinedly clever than accurate when he observed that Harrison "had no friends" and Cleveland "only enemies," but both men considered personal dignity a cardinal virtue and demagoguery a sin.[31] Another reason for the relative calm and civility of the campaign was the fact that the introduction of the Australian ballot had reduced the opportunities for election fraud. Nor could the Democrats complain of a "bought election" when they raised a campaign chest larger than that of the Republicans.

The relative absence of partisan rancor was not the result of a lack of issues or a mirror-image response by the major parties to those issues. Cleveland and Harrison offered contrary opinions on the tariff, the Homestead Strike, federal supervision of elections, and, to a lesser extent, the currency.

It was again the tariff issue that received the most attention in the campaign efforts of both the Democratic and the Republican parties. The Democrats attacked the McKinley Tariff Act of 1890 as a disgraceful example of class legislation, and the Republicans defended protectionism as an essential instrument of American prosperity and national patriotism. Cleveland, however, was in the position of a man fighting on two fronts, fighting both the Republican high protectionists and those Democratic tariff reformers who insisted that any level of protectionism was unconstitutional.

At the Democratic National Convention, the "tariff radicals" had persuaded a majority of the delegates to reject a rather mealy-mouthed plank favoring gradual and selective tariff revision and to accept a plank proclaiming any tariff in excess of immediate revenue needs to be unconstitutional: "We declare . . . that the Federal government has no constitutional power to collect tariff duties except for the purpose of revenue only, and we demand that the collection of such taxes shall be limited to the necessities of the Government when honestly and economically administered."[32]

Cleveland had been incensed by the success of the "tariff radicals" and had incorrectly attributed their substitute plank to a Machiavellian maneuver on the part of his Tammany Hall enemies. He threatened to repudiate the Democratic tariff plank in his letter of acceptance, but he finally decided on a more temperate approach: to dismiss the question of constitutionality as "a false issue." His irritation was in part the response of a politician afraid that the enemy would use the tariff plank to scare industrial labor and gain votes, but there was a more fundamental explanation. Cleveland never subscribed to the tariff-for-revenue-only position, and he did not believe that protection was unconstitutional. Cleveland was a tariff reformer in the mold of Andrew Jackson, not John C. Calhoun. Cleveland wanted significant reductions in the level of duties and the free importation of raw materials, but he considered it an error of fact as well as strategy to declare that protectionism was unconstitutional and therefore illegal. The Democrats should oppose the present tariff system because "in present conditions, its operation is unjust."[33]

The Republicans exhibited a like measure of caution as they promoted protectionism as part of a policy of "safe progression and development" based on "new factories, new markets, and new ships." Instead of defending the particular schedules of the McKinley Tariff, they were content to declare that "on all imports coming into competition with the products of American labor there should be levied duties equal to the differences between wages abroad and at home."[34]

Cleveland on several occasions mentioned the Homestead Strike when attacking the tariff argument of Harrison and the Republicans. The Amalgamated Association of Iron and Steel Workers, seeking to maintain wage levels at the Homestead plant of the Carnegie Steel Company in Pittsburgh, had met the resistance of Homestead's manager, Henry C. Frick. Frick ordered a lockout and employed strikebreakers and heavily armed Pinkerton guards. The result was a bloody labor war with casualties on both sides. The iron-and-steel industry was one of the prime beneficiaries of the protective-tariff system, and while the Republicans sought to persuade Frick to compromise with the strikers, the Democrats used the Homestead Strike as evidence that protectionism was no guarantee of a living wage for the American industrial worker. In his acceptance speech of July 20, Cleveland lashed out at those "made selfish and sordid by unjust government favoritism." The workingmen could expect little mercy from the interests that "received open subsidies," as demonstrated by "recent scenes enacted in the very abiding place of high protection."[35]

The issue that displayed Cleveland in the poorest light was that involving the federal supervision of local elections, particularly as those elections affected black suffrage in the South. Cleveland would have vigorously denied that he sought to pander to white racism in the South, but his repeated warnings against the "partisan intention" of the Republicans to obtain passage of the "force bill" indicated that he was more concerned with the Democratic allegiance of the South than with the intimidation of black voters.[36] Many Republican politicians were prepared to ignore their platform promise on this issue; but not Harrison, who gave unequivocal support to federal action in behalf of black voting rights.

On the currency issue, both parties had kind words for international bimetallism, but there were differences. The Democrats denounced the Sherman Silver Purchase Act as a "cowardly makeshift" and called for the repeal of the 10 percent tax on state-bank notes; the Republicans defended the Sherman act and opposed tax repeal. In his campaign letters, Cleveland gave relatively little attention to the currency issue, but offered no indication of compromise in his opposition to "free, unlimited and independent silver coinage." Support for repeal of the federal tax on state-bank notes was the only concession he would make in behalf of currency expansion.[37]

Cleveland's eagerness to win the election was apparent to his advisers if not always to himself. He took a more active role in the presidential election of 1892 than he had in any earlier campaign since he had been elected sheriff of Erie County. That role, however, was confined by political principle and personal inadequacy. Only with the greatest reluctance would he meet with the machine men of Tammany Hall, and he refused outright to embark on a speaking tour. There was an element of pathos in Cleveland's confession to the Democratic campaign manager, William C. Whitney: "I do dreadfully hate to exhibit myself. . . . Stumping on my part would be a mistake . . . I do not think I could be induced to undertake it in any circumstances."[38]

Cleveland was a man less jealous of his dignity than of his privacy, and he sought what for an active politician was nearly an impossibility—the complete separation of his public and his private life. Refusing to take political advantage of his handsome young wife, he instructed his supporters to discourage the formation of Frances Cleveland Clubs among women of Democratic persuasion. "The name now sacred in the home circle as wife and mother may well be spared in the organization and operation of clubs created to exert political influence."[39]

Cleveland was prepared, however, to interrupt and then cut short his summer sojourn at Buzzard's Bay, Massachusetts. In July he traveled to New York, where he delivered his speech of acceptance in Madison Square Garden before an audience of twenty thousand persons. He had been convinced that the formal notification meeting should depart from precedent. Instead of a semiprivate affair at the candidate's home, it should be transformed into a public occasion with illuminations and banners, followed by a public reception. Cleveland delivered a carefully organized address, emphasizing tariff reform and the danger of federal interference in local elections, and then greeted the party faithful with patient geniality.[40]

Cleveland made his chief campaign contribution, however, by writing letters. To party leaders he offered encouragement, to newspaper editors he offered praise, to William C. Whitney he offered advice.[41] Cleveland urged the Democratic National Committee to establish a "Western branch" in Chicago as a means of increasing the party's chances in Illinois and Wisconsin, and he offered to contribute $1,000 toward its establishment. He had earlier sent Whitney a check for $10,000, with the instruction that it should be listed as the contribution of "A Friend of the Cause."

To the end of the campaign, Cleveland remained fearful that Tammany Hall and the Hill machine would deny him the electoral vote of New York, but for several weeks he resisted all efforts by Whitney to arrange a meeting with members of the regular Democratic organizations of city and state.[42] Whitney finally had to warn Cleveland that unless he made some propitiatory gesture to assure a measure of harmony in New York, "You cannot carry this State."[43] Cleveland capitulated to the extent of agreeing to meet Edward Murphy, Richard ("Boss") Croker, and William Sheehan at the Hotel Victoria in New York City on September 8. The meeting was not a social success—Cleveland at one point threatened to resign the Democratic nomination and place the blame publicly on the New Yorkers—but it had the result of weakening the opposition of the Hill-Tammany machines and giving an appearance of party unity. Cleveland's New York supporters were consequently encouraged to make increased efforts in his behalf.

In none of his few campaign addresses did Cleveland mention the Populist party, but it was seldom out of his thoughts. The Populist party was an outgrowth of the Northwestern and the Southern Farmers' Alliances and had been formally organized as a national third party in 1891. A year later it held its first presidential convention in Omaha, Nebraska, selected General James B. Weaver as its presidential candidate, and fashioned a class-conscious platform directed toward federal assistance for the debt-burdened farmer and his potential ally, the industrial laborer. Among its many planks was a call for the free and unlimited coinage of silver at the ratio of 16 to 1. Cleveland considered its platform an example of demagogic radicalism, a view shared by his Republican opponent.

Some Democratic politicians in five traditionally Republican western states engaged in fusion negotiations with the Populists, in some cases encouraging Democratic voters to support the Populist congressional candidates and presidential electors, but their maneuvers received no support from Cleveland and Whitney. The Democratic National Committee sought to ignore the Populists where possible and to pretend that they represented only an extremist fringe with little support among the electorate.

General Weaver and the Populists won more than a million votes in the election of 1892 and thereby prevented Cleveland from obtaining a majority of the popular vote. This, however, was the extent of their impact on the results of the presidential election.[44] The popular vote stood: Cleveland 5,556,000; Harrison, 5,175,000. Cleveland's margin of victory in the electoral vote was still greater—

277 votes to 145 for Harrison and 22 for Weaver. Cleveland not only gained the votes of all the southern and Border States and those of the four swing states (New York, Indiana, Connecticut, and New Jersey), but he also upset political predictions by bringing Illinois, Wisconsin, and California into the Democratic column. If it was not a landslide, it was one of the more decisive victories of American politics during the Gilded Age.

One can argue that the election results represented a second repudiation of the Billion Dollar Congress and the Harrison administration, rather than an endorsement of the Democratic platform; one can argue that in a period of delicate party balance, it took but a few minor changes of voter allegiance to tip the balance of party control. Neither of these propositions, however, disproves Cleveland's own assessment that he had gained a historic victory. He had now received a popular plurality in three consecutive elections. Only Jackson had matched this feat; only Franklin D. Roosevelt would exceed it.

Cleveland had scored a political triumph. So, apparently, had the jubilant and seemingly united Democratic party. Professor Woodrow Wilson would shortly place his scholarly credentials behind a prediction that the Democrats were now the nation's majority party: "Signs are not wanting that the Republican party is going . . . to pieces, and signs are fairly abundant that the Democratic party is rapidly being made over by . . . the extraordinary man who is now President."[45]

When Cleveland took the oath of office for a second time on 4 March 1893, no observer, whatever his politics, would have predicted that within two years the Democratic party would be irreparably divided or that by the end of Cleveland's second term, he would be distrusted by a majority of his fellow Democrats and judged a presidential failure by Americans of all parties.

7

PANIC, DEPRESSION, AND THE CRUSADE AGAINST SILVER MONOMETALLISM

America had not stood still during the eight-year interval between Cleveland's first and second inaugurals. The social forces of industrialism, urbanization, and immigration continued to reshape economic and social institutions and indirectly encouraged significant developments in the intellectual and cultural life of the nation.

Grover Cleveland had little interest in such matters as the Darwinian revolution and its impact on American religious and scientific thought, but his personal intellectual limitations had not lessened that impact. By the 1890s the Darwinian revolution dominated scholarship in the natural sciences and, in its application to certain of the social sciences, had created a small civil war between those who would follow the lead of Herbert Spencer and William Graham Sumner and those others, such as Lester Frank Ward and Richard T. Ely, who would direct the disciplines of sociology and economics toward variants of Reform Darwinism. The impact of functionalism in economics and of pragmatism in law and jurisprudence was still uncertain during the early 1890s, but there were signs of increased activity and independence on the part of American scholars in many fields.

American painters, such as Thomas Eakins and Winslow Homer, were exhibiting an equal independence from European influence, as were, to a lesser extent, such writers as Mark Twain and William Dean Howells. Higher education was exhibiting growth and examples of curricular innovation. Johns Hopkins University and the new University of Chicago, with some of the older New England universities, were seeking to distinguish more clearly the objectives and requirements of graduate study, and state universities, teachers' colleges, and agricultural and mechanical colleges were expanding in number.

At least a dozen American cities had established art galleries and orchestras, even as they were wrestling with the problems of clean water, sewage disposal, and tenement housing. Rare was the city of any size that did not offer its residents at least three rival newspapers that supplied wire-service news and boilerplate features, and the 1890s provided the more intellectually ambitious with a wide range of literary magazines and journals of opinion.

By the time of Cleveland's second inaugural, institutional change had spread from the economic and political arenas to those influencing education, intellectual beliefs, and social values. The second Cleveland presidency, however, would confine its attention to problems inspired by the accelerated transition of the American economy. With the 1890s, an increasing number of discontented farmers and workers began to demand that the federal government address the problem of the inequitable distribution of the wealth produced by the post-Civil War economic revolution.

At his second inauguration on 4 March 1893, Grover Cleveland again used the Bible that he had received as a young boy from his mother. He had placed a bookmark at the Ninety-first Psalm, verse 12: "They shall bear thee up in their hands, lest thou dash thy foot against a stone." It was a soothing thought, but one that was soon confounded by political realities. A better augury of his second administration was the unseasonable Washington weather. Cleveland delivered his Inaugural Address in a cold drizzle, with snow upon the ground. His address was relatively brief and without surprises. He pledged that his administration would respect the need for economy and civil-service reform, would revise the tariff and maintain a "sound and stable currency," and would attempt to curb monopolies and trusts while observing the limitations that the Constitution placed on the powers of the central government.[1]

Among the shivering spectators were the members of Cleveland's second cabinet. They were not, on balance, as distinguished a group as those who had formed his official family eight years earlier, but

114

this was partially the result of Cleveland's difficulties in obtaining the men he wanted. For secretary of state he first thought of Chief Justice Melville W. Fuller and Thomas Francis Bayard, both of whom declined, before he settled on Judge Walter Q. Gresham, a maverick Republican who had supported Cleveland in the recent campaign. After Charles S. Fairchild had declined the post of secretary of the Treasury, Cleveland selected John G. Carlisle of Kentucky, one of his better choices and one of the few cabinet officers who possessed a strong political base within the Democratic party. After several earlier choices had declined the position of secretary of the navy, Cleveland offered the post to Hilary A. Herbert of Alabama. Cleveland flirted with the idea of appointing a Confederate veteran, Fitzhugh Lee of Virginia, as secretary of war, before selecting his long-time aide, Daniel Lamont. Another old friend, Wilson S. Bissell of Buffalo, was appointed postmaster general; and Richard Olney, a political novice and successful railroad lawyer, was chosen as attorney general after another Massachusetts Democrat, Josiah Quincy, refused a cabinet appointment. Uncertainty and declinations also characterized Cleveland's appointments to the cabinet posts of secretary of the interior and secretary of agriculture. The final choices were, respectively, Hoke Smith of Georgia and J. Sterling Morton of Nebraska. Both were hard-money men who had fought "the Populist craze."[2]

Although it was not a strong cabinet, it would prove to be a loyal and united cabinet. In his official family, Cleveland would find the solace of agreement and friendship, but he would receive no criticism or correction when those offerings might have served him better than unanimity. Few of its members had played an important role in party politics, and they would have little influence with party members in Congress. In the coming battles over the currency and the tariff, they would not be able to furnish the political finesse that their chief both lacked and disdained.

Cleveland's second term was overshadowed by financial crisis and economic depression. It is possible that a president with more foresight and flexibility and a party with greater unity and stronger congressional leadership might have ridden the economic storm with less political damage, but no president or party could have avoided a large measure of difficulty or the likelihood of a loss of popular favor. Throughout American history, hard times have damaged the party in power, and the depression that followed the Panic of 1893 was lengthy and severe. Only the Great Depression of the 1930s would have a greater social and political impact.

Although Cleveland would place chief blame for the Panic of 1893 on the diminishing gold reserve in the Treasury and the consequent fears of the business community that the government would be unable to fulfill its promise to back all treasury notes, silver certificates, and greenbacks with gold, there were more fundamental causes. The "Baring Panic" in London and the Panama Scandal in Paris had disturbed international financial markets, the nation's banking system was inadequate to the needs of a modern industrial economy, certain industries had expanded beyond current demand, and a major portion of the nation's agricultural sector had been in a depressed state since the mid 1870s. The precipitating factors, however, were an increased flow of gold to Europe—$87 million during the fiscal year ending June 1893—and the declining gold reserve in the Treasury.

The Sherman Silver Purchase Act, which required the government to purchase 4 million ounces of silver a month at the market price, caused a drain on the gold reserve, and the generous appropriations and pension largesse of the Harrison congresses also had taken their toll. As expenditures had increased, custom revenue had declined. Several of the rate schedules of the McKinley Tariff were so high that they had resulted in a reduction in imports and custom revenue. Moreover, a declining percentage of custom duties were paid in gold, while other governmental receipts were increasingly being paid in greenbacks and the new silver certificates.

The Panic of 1893 is usually given the birthday of May 4, when the National Cordage Company went bankrupt, or May 5, "Industrial Black Friday," when a wide range of stock prices fell precipitately. Banks began to call in their loans, credit dried up, and business failures increased week by week. Depositors withdrew their money from state and national banks, six hundred of which closed their doors, a majority of them in the West and the South. Railroads proved particularly susceptible to the financial panic. Before the year was over, the Philadelphia and Reading, the Erie, the Northern Pacific, the Union Pacific, and the Atchison, Topeka, and Santa Fe railroads had been forced into receivership. They were joined in bankruptcy by fifteen thousand other businesses.

By mid August, *Bradstreet's Report* estimated unemployment at one million persons; other estimates suggested two million, or nearly 15 percent of the industrial labor force.[3] Unemployment totals rose to 20 percent during the winter of 1893/94, "perhaps the worst in the country's history as an industrialized society."[4] The depth of the depression was reached in the middle of 1894, but depression conditions continued for another two years.

The depression of 1893–96 eventually hurt all classes and sections, but it was particularly the agrarian regions that suffered, because for the farmer it was the culmination of a long price decline for agricultural staples. By 1894, corn was selling at ten cents a bushel; cotton, at six cents a pound; and mortgage foreclosures had reached record proportions. Eastern newspaper editors attributed the farmer's problems to glutted world markets, overproduction, and inefficiency; but western and southern farmers attributed falling crop prices to the tightness of money and blamed a conspiracy of eastern creditors and international bankers. It was now that the demand for free silver began to achieve the status of a crusade in the depressed agrarian regions of the West and the South. For the debtor farmers, the gold standard became a symbol of their position of economic subservience to eastern capitalists, while monetary inflation was seen as a guarantee of higher farm prices and an opportunity to pay their debts in the form of cheap dollars. Silver became a panacea for the oppressed agrarian debtor in his contest with the grasping urban creditor. With the market ratio of gold and silver approaching 30 to 1, silver dollars coined at a ratio of 16 to 1 would be an instrument of inflation and consequent prosperity. Advocates of free silver believed in the quantity theory of money: the greater the nation's monetary stock, the higher the level of economic activity and the better the price of farm staples.

Grover Cleveland was convinced that the silver craze was destroying confidence in the economy and that it was a major cause of the depression. Businessmen feared, with reason, that free silver would mean silver monometallism, the isolation of the United States in the world of international trade and finance, and economic disaster. Silver monometallism would mean a debased currency and reduced purchasing power for the American consumer. For the sake of the consumer public, as well as for the safety of the Treasury's gold reserve and the preservation of the nation's credit abroad, the silver craze must be defeated; and the first essential step was the repeal of the Sherman Silver Purchase Act.

Cleveland's analysis of the harmful effects of the Silver Purchase Act and of the danger posed by free and unlimited silver coinage was oversimplified though not necessarily erroneous. During the

1890s, international trade and the world's financial markets did rest upon gold as the basic means of international exchange. With India's decision to abandon silver coinage, the United States was the only major governmental repository for silver. Unlimited silver purchase and coinage could have meant the increased importation of silver, a still-more-precipitous decline in the market ratio of silver to gold, the continued hoarding of gold, and the abandonment of gold as the nation's monetary standard. During the depression decade of the 1930s, all industrial countries would leave the gold standard; in the 1890s, a policy of unilateral bimetallism by the United States could have meant a severe disruption of its foreign trade and a sharp reduction in the purchasing power of greenbacks and silver dollars.[5]

In Cleveland's eyes the protection of gold as the nation's monetary standard was not solely a money question; it was also a moral question. It involved considerations of honesty: honest value for the wages of the factory worker, as well as the honest repayment of debts. Cleveland was fully aware that the creditor class would benefit from his fight against "the cheapening of the dollar," and he saw no wrong in that fact. It was only just to require the fulfillment of a contract in the specified currency. He was equally convinced that the consumer public would be cheated by a debased and degenerated currency.[6] Cleveland's convictions that sound money was an essential mechanism for a free-market economy and that the preservation of the national credit was identical with the preservation of the gold standard were not the result of careful economic analysis: they were acts of faith. But that faith was shared by a majority of politicians and businessmen in all industrial nations during the 1890s.

As a latter-day Jacksonian, Cleveland believed that under ideal circumstances, the federal government should divorce itself entirely from the banking industry and should leave questions of currency supply to the operations of the marketplace. Over the past generation, however, Congress had involved the government with such questions, and it was now the duty of his administration to prevent the depreciation of the currency by demanding that Congress undo past mischief by repealing the Sherman Silver Purchase Act. Since the passage of that act, the government had bought more than $147 million of silver. The treasury notes used in purchasing this silver were redeemable in gold, and the result had been a dangerous decline in the gold reserve. In April it had dipped below the level of $100 million, which had long been thought to be the minimum necessary for assuring creditors that their demands on the government were redeemable in gold. With the gold reserve shrinking and with wor-

118

ried creditors converting other forms of legal tender to gold, the Silver Purchase Act had become a threat to the national welfare, and repeal would be an act of moral virtue as well as sound financial policy.

Even before his inauguration, Cleveland had been advised by New York merchants and bankers that he should call a special session of Congress to repeal the Sherman Act. He procrastinated for some months, however, hoping that the growing financial crisis would develop a bipartisan consensus. Optimistically, he believed that the dangerous condition of the gold reserve would rally a large majority of both parties to the cause of repeal. Repeal would then pass Congress as a bipartisan measure, without harming the Democratic party or the cause of tariff reform.

On June 30 he issued a call for a special session of Congress to convene on August 7. The unlikelihood that repeal could be arranged without dividing the Democratic party and damaging the cause of tariff reform was indicated by the statement of a leading silver senator, William M. Stewart of Nevada: "He calls Congress together now that he has a panic on hand, which he helped to make, to see if they will be more obedient to his imperial will."[7]

Before the special session convened, Grover Cleveland underwent an operation for carcinoma of the jaw and demonstrated a degree of physical courage and stoicism unsurpassed by any of his presidential predecessors.

In the early morning of May 5, Cleveland had noticed a hard rough spot, the size of a quarter, on the roof of his mouth. Thinking it was no more than an irritating canker sore, he had delayed mentioning it to the White House physician, Dr. Robert M. O'Reilly. On June 18, however, he asked O'Reilly to examine it. Dr. O'Reilly suspected a malignant growth and sent part of the tissue to Johns Hopkins University for confirmation. His suspicions confirmed, O'Reilly called in Dr. Joseph D. Bryant, Cleveland's friend and a well-known New York surgeon. Bryant advised an immediate operation, before the cancer could spread. Cleveland consented, on condition that the operation be kept a complete secret. He appreciated that if it were known that his life was in danger, there would be renewed panic on Wall Street. Vice-president Adlai Stevenson had a reputation as a compromiser and a sometime ally of the silver men.

On June 30, after signing the executive order calling for a special session of Congress, Cleveland left Washington for New York, ostensibly to take a pleasure cruise on the yacht of his friend and financial adviser E. C. Benedict. In cloak-and-dagger fashion, the operating team slipped aboard the *Oneida* as it lay at anchor in the East River. The team consisted of Bryant, who performed the operation; Dr. John Erdmann and Dr. William W. Keen, who assisted him; Dr. O'Reilly, who administered the anesthetic; Dr. Edward G. Janeway, a general practitioner; and Dr. Ferdinand Hasbrouck, a New York dentist. Late the next morning, as the *Oneida* slowly steamed up the East River, Cleveland was strapped into a chair against the mast and was given nitrous oxide while Dr. Hasbrouck extracted two upper bicuspids on the left side of his jaw. Cleveland then received a small dose of ether, and Bryant began the forty-one-minute operation. His assistant, Dr. Keen, many years later, described the extent of the surgery:

> The entire left upper jaw was removed from the first bicuspid tooth to just beyond the last molar, and nearly up to the middle line. The floor of the orbit—the cavity in the skull containing the eyeball—was not removed, as it had not yet been attacked. A small portion of the soft palate was removed. This extensive operation was decided upon because we found that the atrum—the large hollow cavity in the upper jaw—was partially filled by a gelatinous mass, evidently a sarcoma.[8]

Because of the use of a cheek retractor, Bryant was able to remove Cleveland's left upper jaw without any external incision. The absence of any outward scar made possible the long-kept secret of Cleveland's cancer operation.

Shortly before two o'clock, the operation was finished and Cleveland was helped to his stateroom. Two days later he insisted on getting up and walking the deck, and on July 5, after the *Oneida* had anchored in Buzzard's Bay, Cleveland rode its launch to the dock and trudged unassisted to his summer home, Gray Gables. But Cleveland's cancer surgery was not over. Ten days later, after an examination of the wound, Dr. Bryant decided to remove additional tissue. After the original surgical team had reassembled, a second operation was performed in the salon of the *Oneida* on July 17, the surface cauterized, and the wound repacked.[9]

Without the packing, Cleveland's speech was virtually unintelligible; with the packing, his diction was that of a person who had a cleft palate. It was now the task of Dr. Kasson C. Gibson, a New York dentist, to make a prosthesis of vulcanized rubber, which would serve as a substitute for Cleveland's left upper jaw. Gibson was established in a makeshift dental laboratory in a backroom at Gray Gables and proceeded to make a series of modifications on the original model. Cleveland initially found the artificial jaw a source of pain and discomfort, but with stoic determination he learned to ignore the discomfort and was able, by early August, to speak with clarity and strength. He wore it for the rest of his life.

Cleveland's cancer operation remained a secret until nine years after his death, when the then-eighty-year-old Dr. Keen wrote a piece for the *Saturday Evening Post* of 22 September 1917. There had been a single leak in the year 1893, but it had been quickly plugged. A journalist, E. J. Edwards, was told by a never-identified source that Cleveland had undergone major surgery, and he printed a story to that effect in the *Philadelphia Press*. Secretary of War Lamont, the only cabinet officer who was privy to the operation, made a public statement calling the story a total fabrication. The president was momentarily indisposed because of a tooth extraction. When Cleveland traveled to Washington on August 5 to send his repeal message to Congress, his appearance and voice were normal enough to give credence to Lamont's lie.

Cleveland never referred to his operation or to the discomfort of wearing an artificial jaw to anyone outside his immediate family. Nor did he ever speak about his fear of a recurrence of the cancer. There must have been many occasions, however, when depression over political developments was compounded by personal anxiety about an early death or a life of invalidism and its consequences for his wife and children. Cleveland had displayed a capacity for irritability from his earliest years, but friends noticed an increasing shortness of temper and a greater readiness to take personal offense at his political enemies during his second administration. This was possibly the result of the physical and psychological effects of his cancer operation as well as to the "machinations" of silverites and protectionists. Cleveland, who was proud of his stoic disregard of pain and was convinced that only the weak sought pity, would have denied any connection between his political behavior and his personal health. Intimations of mortality only made it more imperative that he do his duty and save the currency. He wrote to Thomas F. Bayard, now the U.S. ambassador to Great Britain: "I see in a new light the necessity of doing my allotted work in the full apprehension of the coming night."[10]

Early on the afternoon of August 8—a day when the muggy temperature in Washington exceeded 90 degrees—Congress, assembled in special session, received Cleveland's message demanding the repeal of the Sherman Silver Purchase Act. In the House of Representatives the repeal bill was under the direction of William L. Wilson, chairman of the Ways and Means Committee. Assisted by Cleveland's decision to withhold certain patronage appointments until Democratic congressmen had declared themselves, Wilson was able to muster a slim majority of Democrats in support of repeal. The White House had provided Wilson with a list of sixty-nine doubtfuls; and Wilson, with his lieutenants William Bourke Cockran and Amos J. Cummings, labored hard to maintain that majority.[11]

There was stiff opposition to the repeal bill on the part of many southern and western Democrats, such as the old silver crusader Richard Bland of Missouri and a new champion, William Jennings Bryan of Nebraska. Bryan delivered a three-hour oration against the "goldbugs," who would shrink the currency supply and lower prices, the better to increase the debt burden of the oppressed farmer. When Bland and Bryan offered an amendment to the repeal bill which would have authorized the unlimited coinage of silver, the Democratic congressmen divided 104 ayes, 114 nays. The repeal bill, unamended, passed by the comfortable margin of 239 to 108, but much of that margin was provided by the Republican minority. Republicans in the Senate were less cooperative, however. Most of them planned to vote for the repeal bill at the last moment, but until then they were anxious to encourage dissension among the Democratic majority. The task was not difficult, and their success was considerable.

Some Democratic senators, though convinced that the Sherman Act was dangerous to the gold reserve, wanted to see repeal coupled with a sop to the silver men. At least they wished to see repeal implemented in stages. Cleveland's insistence on unconditional and immediate repeal was, they believed, an invitation to party revolt and defection in the agricultural areas of the West and the South. Cleveland scorned these senators as "trimmers"; they saw themselves as political realists. Cleveland let it be known that he was prepared to use his patronage power in an effort to force their concurrence.[12] This, in turn, provided another source of resentment for senators who complained that the presidential appointment power had never before been used to command votes for a particular legislative measure.

Cleveland denounced, as mischievous and impractical, Senator

John Tyler Morgan's proposal to persuade all countries to accept United States silver dollars at face value by means of a tariff bribe—import duties on the products of obliging governments to be reduced by 20 percent. Cleveland was more incensed when certain silver senators began a long filibuster which the prorepeal senators appeared to be either unable or unwilling to end. The Republicans were happy to witness the Democratic disarray, and within the Democratic majority, there were many who hid their grievances against the adminstration under the cloak of the senatorial tradition of unrestricted debate.

The Democratic senators went into caucus in an effort to find an alternative to unconditional repeal. A compromise plan, hammered out by Arthur Pue Gorman, George Gray, and others, would have continued silver purchases until October 1894, although at a reduced rate, and would have authorized the coinage of all silver bullion that remained in the vaults of the Treasury. Supporters of the plan believed, or pretended to believe, that it had the support of Treasury Secretary Carlisle and therefore, most probably, of the president. Carlisle had met with various Democratic senators and perhaps had unintentionally given the impression of administration support.

Cleveland would have no part of the caucus's compromise plan. Only immediate repeal would provide an end to the stock-market panic and the general financial crisis. He let it be known that there would be no further patronage appointments until the Senate had passed the unconditional repeal bill. He had his way: on October 30 the Senate passed the repeal bill, 48 to 37, concluding a bitter two-month-long debate. Cleveland's obstinacy and patronage strategy had given him a victory that many observers had thought was beyond his power.[13] It was a dramatic example of presidential direction of the legislative process, but it would prove a costly triumph.

Edwin Godkin of the *Nation* was effusive in his praise of Cleveland's refusal to compromise and hailed him as the courageous statesman who had saved America from economic collapse and moral perfidy. There were few such encomiums, however, from Senate Democrats. Even some of Cleveland's supporters wondered if he had not made a serious tactical error in giving priority to the money question, which had long divided the Democratic party, instead of to tariff reform, around which the party had united in the last election. Would not the divisions that had been exacerbated in the bruising battle over repeal of the Sherman Silver Purchase Act now work against efforts to achieve party unity in behalf of tariff revision?

Other critics complained that Cleveland should have accompanied his demand for the immediate repeal of the Sherman Act with suggestions for a constructive alternative to the program of the silver inflationists. Cleveland offered no plan for a basic overhaul of the nation's banking-and-currency system. Although he would later endorse Secretary Carlisle's modest proposals to encourage an increased elasticity of the money supply, he failed to wage battle in their behalf. He had, moreover, seemingly adopted a defeatist attitude in regard to negotiations looking to international bimetallism. One can argue that Cleveland was correct in believing that there was no realistic chance for fashioning an international agreement to establish a two-metals currency standard, but his critics were not convinced. Their criticism sharpened when the repeal of the Sherman Act failed to produce the effects that its sponsors had too optimistically predicted.

In their determination to secure repeal, adminstration supporters in the House and the Senate had unwisely predicted that repeal would be followed by renewed business confidence and an end to the diminution of the gold reserve.[14] For a few weeks after the passage of the repeal bill, there was a reduction in gold export and an apparent stabilization of the gold reserve. It was soon apparent, however, that the gold-reserve crisis continued; by January 1894 the reserve had fallen to $65 million. As the gold-reserve problem continued, so did the labors of the silver congressmen. Their next effort was the seigniorage bill. Cleveland vetoed that bill and then proceeded to try to shore up the gold reserve by means of a series of bond issues that would widen the division within the Democratic party.

The seigniorage bill would have forced the Treasury Department to coin all silver bullion lying in its vaults. Under the Silver acts of 1878 and 1890, the Treasury Department had coined only enough silver dollars to match the amount of treasury notes issued to pay for the bullion. Because of the continuing decline in the market price of silver, there was a steady accumulation of surplus bullion in the vaults of the Treasury. The "seigniorage" represented the government's gain in its silver-purchase activities. Many Democrats in the House and the Senate believed that the coinage of the seigniorage would be a safe concession to the silverites. These Democrats were joined by Republicans from the silver states, and the Bland seigniorage bill quickly passed the two houses. It was vetoed by Cleveland with equal speed.

In his veto message of 29 March 1894, Cleveland made clear that he had no intention of moderating his opposition to silver coinage. Overvalued silver dollars were a dangerous form of monetary inflation, and the fact that the seigniorage bill would have introduced only $55 million of additional silver dollars was no reason to reopen the issue of silver coinage and thus risk destroying the reviving confidence of banking and commercial interests in the good faith of the government. Arguments of party unity were irrelevant when placed against the importance of a sound and stable currency. Cleveland made a telling argument against the quantity theory of money; but if his veto message demonstrated consistency, it also accentuated party division. In combination, the repeal bill and the seigniorage veto assured Cleveland the enmity of the more ardent silver Democrats, such as William Jennings Bryan. It would be the silver Democrats who would denounce Cleveland's efforts to sustain the gold reserve with new issues of government bonds and would charge that the Cleveland administration had sold out to Wall Street and J. P. Morgan.

When the repeal bill failed to end the financial crisis, Cleveland placed the blame on the continued reduction of the gold reserve. Repeal had not ended the presentation of treasury notes, greenbacks, and silver certificates for redemption in gold coin, and Cleveland attributed this fact to continued public uncertainty that the government would in the future make good its promise to maintain the gold standard. Because Congress had refused to enact Secretary Carlisle's proposal for the cancellation of greenbacks after first redemption, the only solution was the sale of government bonds in exchange for gold. If the gold reserve were increased to the level of $100 million, confidence would be restored, banks and private citizens would no longer hoard gold or send it abroad at a premium, and creditors would no longer be inspired to exchange governmental paper for gold specie. By an ingenious interpretation of an 1875 statute, Cleveland persuaded Secretary Carlisle of the need to float government bonds to compensate for declining federal revenues as well as to replenish the gold reserve. Cleveland proclaimed that he had full authority to approve bond issues, and he promised that "such authority will be utilized whenever and as often as it becomes necessary to maintain a sufficient gold reserve and in abundant time to save the credit of our country."[15]

In the two years between February 1894 and February 1896, Cleveland authorized four bond issues. Those of February and November 1894 each saw the sale of $50 million of 5 percent ten-year bonds. They proved to have little effect on the size of the gold reserve, because most of the bond purchasers had redeemed certificates and greenbacks for gold in order to buy the gold bonds. Peter paid Paul, and the gold reserve was not increased in the process. Indeed, by New Year's Day 1895 the reserve had reached a new low of $45 million. Cleveland feared that unless drastic action were taken, the government would soon be forced to default on its obligation to redeem all forms of currency in gold, with catastrophic effects for the financial market and American industry. Cleveland had agents of the Treasury make inquiries of the banking houses of Morgan and Belmont to ask their terms for a private sale of government bonds, with the condition that half of the gold for their purchase must come from abroad and half from the accumulated hoards of the syndicate and its customers. Morgan gave the required promise, but then he made his own demands. The Morgan-Belmont syndicate would purchase $62 million worth of 4 percent bonds at a markup to 104.25. After lengthy negotiations, a bargain was struck, which was in line with Morgan's terms. The February 1895 bond sale to the syndicate raised the level of the gold reserve to $107 million.

In the early days of 1896, however, the gold reserve was shrinking once again, and a fourth bond sale was arranged in February of that year. This was a bond issue for $100 million, and it was sold at popular subscription. By the spring of 1896 the level of the reserve had stabilized. In the process, Cleveland had floated gold bonds totaling a federal debt of $262 million.

The most criticized and controversial of the bond issues was, of course, the third, providing for private sale to the Morgan-Belmont syndicate. It was criticized on the grounds of the terms exacted by the syndicate and the gain reaped when the syndicate sold its bonds for a profit of better than $7 million. It was criticized even more for its connection with J. P. Morgan, the symbol of Wall Street financial power. Many thought it degrading that Cleveland had to go hat-in-hand to a private financier in order to assure the credit of the United States government.

Many years later, Cleveland wrote that the syndicate's "favorable bargain" was justified by its "labor, risk and expense"; but at the time he believed the terms of the third bond issue found justification only in the dire straits of the federal Treasury.[16] The government could not risk a popular subscription that might fail and start a new flood of legal-tender submissions requiring gold redemption by the Treasury. The immediate acquisition of gold from abroad or from the private hoards of Americans was essential if the government was not to suspend specie payments. Cleveland also insisted that had Congress agreed to his request for legislation authorizing 3 percent long-term gold bonds, the syndicate would have agreed to terms more favorable to the government.[17]

Cleveland's congressional opponents were quick to point out that the Morgan deal was contrary to Cleveland's professed wish to see a divorce of the federal government from the banking industry. Some of those opponents encouraged rumors to the effect that Grover Cleveland was in league with the money power of Wall Street and had derived personal profit from his negotiations with the syndicate. The charge was baseless, but there can be legitimate debate as to the necessity of the private sale of bonds to the Morgan group. In the final analysis, one's judgment rests largely on suppositions about what might have been. Would a public subscription have failed and incited another financial panic? Would the failure to redeem all legal tenders in gold have confined the circulating medium to paper, debased the currency, and halved the purchasing power of the U.S. dollar? Cleveland would have offered a loud affirmative to each question. He was convinced that he had saved the gold reserve and therefore the gold standard. He could not claim that he had ended the depression.

Bank failures and unemployment rose once again during the winter of 1895/96, while wages and prices declined. The depression appeared to be entering a second phase, and earlier reports that the economy had turned the corner were no longer heard. The country appeared to be no closer to recovery in the fall of 1896 than it had three years earlier.

To what extent was the continuation of the depression throughout his second term the fault of Grover Cleveland and his dogmatic allegiance to the gold standard? The answer would seem to be that Cleveland's overriding concern for the gold reserve was a major source of Democratic party division but had little relevance for the extent and severity of the depression. Cleveland might well have given more attention to reform of an outmoded banking system, and he might have fought harder for such currency reforms as the retirement of greenbacks after first redemption; but neither the repeal of the Sherman Silver Purchase Act nor the veto of the seigniorage bill contributed to the length of the depression. H. Wayne Morgan, a historian with little admiration for Grover Cleveland, has written: "Repeal of silver purchase was probably wise. The depression illustrated bimetallism's instability when paper money commanded endless redemption, and psychological fears eroded public and foreign confidence in the dollar."[18]

The depression had more fundamental causes than the volume of the nation's currency. It was primarily the product of problems in international markets of trade and finance, the overexpansion of the agricultural and transportation sectors of the U.S. economy, and a banking system that failed to provide a necessary measure of central authority and regional cooperation. Grover Cleveland entertained a narrow view of the responsibility of the federal government during a time of economic distress, but it was not to be expected that any presidential administration in the 1890s would have offered a New Deal program of "Relief, Recovery and Reform."

8

★ ★ ★ ★ ★

THE GREAT DISAPPOINTMENT: CLEVELAND AND THE TARIFF, 1894

Grover Cleveland's ambitions during the years of his second administration were to save the gold standard and reform the tariff. He was determined to accomplish both objectives, but he did not judge them to be of equal importance. To save the gold standard was a moral imperative; to lower the tariff would be a wise policy, helpful to American consumers and economic recovery. In his annual message of December 1893, Cleveland reminded congressional Democrats that the party was pledged to a united effort in behalf of tariff reform.

Economic conditions in the United States in December 1893 were very different from those in December 1887, when Cleveland had delivered his famous tariff message; but Cleveland's argument in behalf of tariff reduction had changed little. No longer did he speak about the problem of the surplus in the Treasury—now there was the threat of a deficit—but his major themes continued to be those of equity for the American consumer and the danger of governmental paternalism.

As noted in an earlier chapter, there are several historians who have associated Grover Cleveland, particularly during his second administration, with a diplomatic-economic strategy of market expansion. According to this interpretation, Cleveland, like his Republican predecessors, pursued a concerted foreign-policy strategy of promoting new markets abroad as a means of solving the crisis of overproduction. Tariff reduction was part of that strategy. Free raw materials would help the American manufacturer conquer markets in Latin America, Asia, and the Pacific; lower duties could serve to stimulate foreign commerce and force open new markets for our surplus industrial and agricultural goods.

The depressions of the 1890s did indeed encourage Cleveland to search for new auxiliary arguments in behalf of tariff reform, now that the Treasury-surplus argument had faded with the surplus. In the years 1893 and 1894, Cleveland made a few more references to the desirability of expanding our foreign export trade than he had six years earlier. Cleveland continued to emphasize, however, the stimulation of the domestic market, not the achievement of prosperity by opening new markets in Latin America and Asia. Cleveland naturally wished to broaden the base of political support for tariff reduction. When urging that raw materials be put on the free list, he spoke about the benefit that would be derived by American manufacturers, presently at a disadvantage to foreign competitors, and sought to associate tariff revision with the prosperity of the manufacturing community. On balance, however, Cleveland's advocacy of duty-free raw materials was more closely related to his concern for consumer prices at home than to foreign markets abroad. He believed, moreover, that it was as wrong for American producers of wool, coal, and iron to beg the federal government for excessive protection as it was for the producers of manufactured articles. In each instance, governmental paternalism encouraged dependence and displayed unjustified favoritism.[1]

Certain members of Cleveland's cabinet, particularly Secretary of State Walter Gresham, did write about glutted markets at home and the need to stimulate exports, but Gresham had little influence in determining Cleveland's rationale for tariff reduction.[2] Secretary Carlisle was an advocate of governmental promotion of the American merchant marine as a means of expanding trade, but there is little evidence that he persuaded Cleveland about its importance. The tariff reformers whose argument was most influenced by depression conditions were certain western agrarians. They did associate tariff reduction with the expansion of American exports, but the exports they had in mind were surplus wheat, corn, and cotton and the markets those of industrial Europe. Cleveland viewed these agrarians with suspicion, particularly in their insistence upon "radical reductions" in the tariff schedules.

It is surprising that Cleveland's rationale for tariff revision was not more influenced by the depression and that he did not give greater emphasis to the relationship between tariff reduction and international trade. One possible explanation is that it was difficult to speak about expanding exports without mentioning increasing imports, and Cleveland had an aversion toward mentioning the latter. He had been stung in 1888 by Republican charges that he was prepared to share the American home market with his British allies. Consequently, he was afraid to promote the argument that lower tariff barriers would help foreign nations to sell more to the United States and thereby gain the trade credits that would enable them to purchase an increasing amount of American exports. Only by indirection would Cleveland suggest that a reduction in tariff barriers would increase the custom revenue of the Treasury, revenue that had dropped sharply under the high protectionism of the McKinley Tariff of 1890, or suggest that there was a relationship between the level of imports and the stimulation of foreign trade. It was safer to emphasize the injuries inflicted on the American consumer by protectionism and the manner in which duties on raw materials increased the cost of production of American manufactures and lessened the opportunity for steady employment for American labor.[3]

If the depression conditions of 1893/94 did not significantly alter Cleveland's rationale for tariff reform, they did lessen its chance of success. In a time of depression, the argument that it was dangerous to "tinker with the tariff" was persuasive to some, and the argument that tariff reform was insufficient to the economic crisis was convincing to more. Would legislation revising the tariff system in behalf of the consumer public be of any immediate effect in stimulating industrial or agricultural recovery? For these doubts, Cleveland was in part responsible. By failing to explain the relationship between tariff reduction and foreign trade and by antagonizing the "agrarian radicals" with his calls for a cautious, sensible approach to tariff revision, Cleveland helped to transform a crusade for tariff reform into a confusing struggle over rates and schedules. In the process, the Wilson tariff bill became a battleground for the display of sectional economic interests and the disunity of the Democratic party.

Introduced into the House of Representatives on 19 December 1893, the Wilson tariff bill was authored jointly by Congressman William L. Wilson of West Virginia and Grover Cleveland. In contrast with his hands-off approach when the Ways and Means Committee had fashioned the Mills tariff bill in 1888, Cleveland was in frequent communication with Wilson during the winter of 1893/94, urging that emphasis be placed on free raw materials with only modest reductions in the general level of import duties. Wilson was informed that the president would make no patronage agreements with party members who failed to cooperate with Wilson and his committee.

Wilson, a man with a keen mind and a deceptively mild manner, believed that protection beyond the revenue needs of the government was unwise and unjust. Personally, he favored deep cuts in import duties, but he was prepared to accept Cleveland's leadership in the tariff struggle. Both men believed that the Republican system of high protectionism raised consumer prices, aided the trusts, and fostered governmental paternalism, and both men recognized that they were faced with a difficult task: trying to make good the pledge of the Democratic platform of 1892 while assuring increased revenue for the federal Treasury.[4] Many of the compromises engineered by Wilson in the Ways and Means Committee were the result of this difficult balancing act. A duty on sugar imports and a small tax on profits from corporate investments were examples of the perceived need to find revenue while expanding the free list.

When the Wilson bill was reported by the committee to the House, it was in nearly all respects a bill that matched Cleveland's demand for cautious and safe tariff revision. Less sectional in character than the Mills bill of 1888, it appeared to be secure from charges of southern dictation. Indeed, if it demonstrated any sectional bias, it was directed in favor of those New England manufacturers who imported most of their raw materials. Although a few Republicans in the House would claim that it was the first step toward the adoption of a system of free trade, the Wilson bill was, on the contrary, a modest effort at tariff revision. Coal, iron ore, wool, lumber, and copper were placed on the duty-free list, and while Cleveland considered this a significant move in behalf of tariff reform, agrarian-minded members of the House criticized the bill for its timidity. Jerry Simpson, a Kansas Populist leader, called it "a robber tariff in a little less degree than the McKinley Bill."[5] Simpson and others wanted to slash the duties on manufactured imports. A reduction in the duties on manfactured imports could best stimulate foreign demand for American wheat, cotton, and corn.

The agrarians sought to amend the Wilson bill on the floor of the House, but, for the most part, they failed. They were successful, however, in their effort to put sugar on the free list, and that success led to their major accomplishment, the income-tax amendment. They argued that with sugar on the free list, there was a need for compensatory revenue for the Treasury, and the most equitable source of revenue would be a 2 percent tax on personal incomes over $4,000. Corporate profits, gifts, and inheritances should be subject to the same 2 percent tax. In late January, the income-tax amendment was attached to the Wilson bill.

Cleveland had earlier approved a modest corporation tax, but he was critical of the income-tax amendment. It did not appear politically expedient, and it might produce the distraction and delay of a debate on the question of its constitutionality. Although Cleveland was irritated by the addition of the income-tax amendment, he agreed with Wilson that it would at least have the effect of assuring agrarian support for the bill when it came up for a final vote in the House. There would be time for making corrections when the bill went to the Senate. Cleveland sent Wilson a note of congratulations when the Wilson bill passed the House on February 1 by a surprisingly large majority, 204 to 140.

The framing of the tariff bill in the Ways and Means Committee and the bill's passage in the House represented the culmination of Cleveland's labors as a tariff reformer. By design, the Wilson bill was a cautious example of tariff revision, one that enlarged the free list with a number of major raw materials and lowered the general tariff level by roughly 15 percent. Compared with the McKinley Tariff Act, the Wilson bill was a tariff-reduction measure that took a modest step in the direction of tariff reform. After the Senate had added several hundred amendments to the Wilson bill, both its character and its direction were difficult to define. In the Senate battle, Grover Cleveland would give conflicting signals, display weak leadership, and finally suffer a humiliating defeat.

The tariff bill went from the House to the Finance Committee of the Senate. It would be five months before its mangled remains received senatorial approval.

In the Senate, the Democratic margin was slim. There were 44 Democrats, 38 Republicans, 3 Populists, and 3 vacancies. If the Wilson bill were to receive favorable consideration, the Democrats would have to stand united; but from the beginning, there were signs that this was unlikely. The Louisiana senators insisted that they would not vote for any tariff bill that did not include duties on imported sugar at specific rates; the Democratic senator from California, Stephen White, made the same threat if duties on imported fruit were not raised; the West Virginia senators and John Morgan of Alabama demanded that coal and iron ore be removed from the free list; Cleveland's old nemesis, David B. Hill, now a senator, declared he would not vote for any tariff bill that contained an income-tax amendment.[6] And then there were Democratic senators, such as Arthur Pue Gorman, who believed that it was a mistake for the party to promote tariff revision during a period of economic depression. In their eyes, it was yet another example of the political stupidity of Grover Cleveland. Irritated at Cleveland's obduracy during the battle over the repeal of the Sherman Silver Purchase Act, they placed cooperation with their party chieftain at a much lower priority than the wishes of economic interests within their state constituencies. They were, moreover, well aware that Cleveland had expended most of his patronage resources during the repeal fight and could no longer use his patronage power to whip them into line.

When the Senate Democrats held a three-day caucus in late February, it became apparent to such senators as James K. Jones of Arkansas and George Vest of Missouri that the Wilson bill in its present form had no chance of passage. During the first week of March, Jones and Vest made a pilgrimage to each Democratic senator who had expressed a demand or grievance at the caucus, and they asked for suggestions respecting alterations in the various schedules. As a result of their labor, a much-revised tariff bill was submitted to the Finance Committee on March 8. The free list was trimmed, and duties were raised on a long array of products from earthenware pottery to collars and cuffs. This revised tariff bill was approved by a majority of the Finance Committee and reported to the Senate on March 20.

After further squabbling and delay, the Senate finally began to debate the bill on April 2. More amendments were offered, the Republicans sought to send the bill back to committee, and such was the disarray of the Democrats that Senators Jones and Gorman issued a call for a new party caucus for May 3. At that time, Jones and Gorman offered a third version of the tariff bill, one that removed almost all raw materials from the free list and raised the Wilson duties on more than one hundred imports. Senator Jones informed the caucus that two days earlier he had held a conference with the president and had gained his assent to the changes. Jones later wrote a memorandum to this effect, but the evidence for Cleveland's concurrence is at best inconclusive. The only thing that is certain is that Jones and Cleveland did meet and that Cleveland expressed his hope that free coal and iron would be a part of any tariff bill that finally received the approval of both houses of Congress.[7]

By the time a final vote was scheduled, the Wilson bill—as originally sent to the Senate—had been amended more than six hundred times. The number of raw materials on the free list had been reduced to two—wool and copper; duties had been raised on iron, glass, chemicals, and woolen and cotton goods; additional products had been made dutiable at specific rates; and import duties had been assessed on both raw and refined sugar. The tariff bill was now referred to as the Wilson-Gorman bill, and it could lay no claim to tariff reform.[8] It passed the Senate on July 3, by a vote of 39 to 34, with 12 senators not voting. Senator Jones had urged the president to instruct the dwindling band of Cleveland loyalists to vote for the bill, and he believed that Cleveland had complied with his request. In all likelihood, Cleveland at this point only wanted to put an end to the five-month imbroglio and wished the House-Senate conference to begin its corrective labors as soon as possible.

More than the tariff act of 1883, the Wilson-Gorman bill was a "mongrel tariff." Some charged that in its protectionist character it was identical with the McKinley Tariff Act. There was a modest difference. On such products as metals, lumber, glassware, and chemicals, the Wilson-Gorman rates were lower than those of the McKinley Tariff by 7 to 19 percent, although approximately the same as those of the tariff law of 1883. If all rate schedules on dutiable goods are taken into account, those of the Wilson-Gorman bill averaged 42 percent; those of the McKinley Tariff Act, 49 percent. Cleveland and his loyal lieutenant, Congressman Wilson, hoped that the House-Senate conference would widen the difference between the Wilson-Gorman bill and the McKinley Tariff Act and, in the process, rescue victory for the cause of tariff reform.[9] The hope proved illusory.

Encouraged by Cleveland, the House conferees, led by Wilson, demanded that iron and coal be returned to the duty-free list and that the duties on raw and refined sugar be reduced. Gorman and the other Senate conferees refused to make any changes in the Senate tariff bill. On July 18 the conferees reported to their respective houses that they were deadlocked. Although Cleveland had made no attempt to consult with the Senate conferees—to offer either threats or concessions—he now authorized Wilson to make public in the

House a letter he had written some sixteen days earlier, when the Senate was about to approve the Wilson-Gorman bill.

It was late on the afternoon of July 19 when Wilson, a victim of neuralgia, with his face bandaged and his eyes covered, was led to the well of the House by a colleague.[10] In a voice weakened by pain, Wilson urged the House Democrats not to surrender or accept the Senate version of tariff revision. He assured them that in their steadfastness they would have the support of the president. The president's wishes had been expressed in a recent letter, which Wilson now read:

> Every true Democrat and every sincere tariff reformer knows that this bill in its present form . . . falls far short of the consummation for which we have long labored . . . which, in its anticipation, gave us a rallying cry in our day of triumph, and which, in its promise of accomplishment, is so interwoven with Democratic pledges and Democratic success that our abandonment of the cause of the principles upon which it rests means party perfidy and party dishonor.[11]

Cleveland can be faulted less for his insult to Senators Gorman and Jones than for his timing. The moment when Cleveland might have used such a letter as an encouragement to tariff reformers in the Senate was in late February, when the Democrats had held their first caucus. Mid July was too late for an appeal to public opinion that might have influence with Senate Democrats. The letter seemed less a rallying cry for tariff reform than a belated expression of personal anger.

Those senators who had urged the passage of the Wilson-Gorman bill were naturally resentful of the charge that they were guilty of "party perfidy and party dishonor." Gorman gave a bitter and emotional speech in the Senate, berating Cleveland for having attacked men who had long proven their loyalty to the Democratic party. Gorman received the congratulations of many of his colleagues, and relations between Cleveland and the Senate Democrats were further soured.

In the House, Wilson fought a gallant but losing battle to prevent the Democratic majority from accepting the Senate's version of tariff reduction. The heat of a Washington August had its effect in sapping the resolution of his colleagues, and at a Democratic party caucus, called over Wilson's objections, a majority instructed the House conferees to reconvene the conference and accept all 608 of the Senate amendments to the Wilson bill. The Wilson-Gorman tariff bill received final House passage on August 13 by a vote of 182 to 105.

It would not receive either Cleveland's signature or his veto. Cleveland considered the bill to be a defeat for "honest tariff reform" and wrote Wilson that he was "depressed and disappointed"; but he doubted that a better bill could pass the Senate and was convinced that the Wilson-Gorman bill, however unwise and illogical its provisions, was at least an improvement on the McKinley Tariff.[12] If he vetoed the bill, the McKinley Act probably would remain in force, with all its harmful impact upon governmental revenue. And yet he would not give his approval to a measure that saw Democratic principles sacrificed and tariff reform adopt the livery of Republican protectionism. There seemed to be no alternative but to let the bill become law without his signature. It was a lame stance, and Cleveland was aware of that fact. He did not, however, consider that he was in any way responsible for the failure of tariff reform.

His judgment was unduly generous. It is an exaggeration to say that Cleveland's failure to achieve a significant alteration of the protectionist system was a self-inflicted defeat, but Cleveland must bear a large measure of responsibility. If the major culprit was the Senate and the chief cause was the willingness of a majority of Democratic senators to identify their political future with regional economic interests, instead of with the success of the national administration, Cleveland's strategy during the tariff battle was marked by poor timing, false prediction, and a confusing mixture of obstinacy and timidity.

One can make a case to the effect that tariff reform lacked a sufficiently large constituency within the public or the Congress and that it was doomed in a time of economic depression, whatever Cleveland's strategy or timing. Certainly it is true that the apparent unity of the Democratic party during the election of 1892 in behalf of tariff reduction was more opportunistic than ideological and no president could easily have persuaded a majority of senators that they should ignore the demands of economic interest groups and their importance for financing party organization at the state level. With the passage of the Pendleton Civil Service Act, corporate contributions had become of increased significance for the state organizations of both parties. Cleveland, however, added to the difficulties of gaining legislative success for tariff reform by his decision to give priority to the repeal of the Sherman Silver Purchase Act and by expending too much of his patronage power in that earlier struggle. He can be faulted as well for his failure to emphasize the presumed identification of protection and industrial combination, thereby winning greater cooperation from the western agrarians, and for his reluctance to involve himself with the labors of the Senate Finance Committee in a manner similar to his supervision of the work of the House Ways and Means Committee. When Cleveland had his meeting with Senator James K. Jones, Senate opposition to the Wilson bill had developed a momentum that could only have been reversed by some dramatic expression of public opinion, and Cleveland had no talent or taste for inspiring popular protest. After the passage of the Wilson-Gorman Act, he wrote a letter to Congressman Thomas C. Catchings in which he sternly denounced lobbyists and trusts and the "communism of pelf"; but although this may have been helpful to his self-esteem, it was of little influence in determining the actions of Congress.[13]

Little excuse can be offered for Cleveland's failure to make a timely explanation to Democratic senators of his opposition to amendments that raised duties and whittled away at the duty-free list for industrial raw materials. That failure encouraged Jones and others to assume—with considerable self-deception—that Cleveland had been converted to the cause of compromise. Entertaining a personal distaste for Jones and Gorman, Cleveland failed to attempt to conciliate them by means of limited concessions and had finally to retreat to the vain hope of victory in the conference committee.

It was a sad conclusion for his lengthy battle against the protectionist system—a conclusion to which he had contributed by his inept tactics and wavering leadership. The lobbyists and their willing partners in the Senate deserve the chief blame, but they had an unintentional auxiliary in Grover Cleveland.

One of the most distinguished students of the Gilded Age has offered a more favorable judgment. According to Geoffrey Blodgett, Cleveland's effort to achieve tariff reform was perhaps "his most compelling protest against the untended sprawl of distributive politics." Cleveland was the first president to perceive the "widening rift between rich and poor fostered by government protection for corporate monopolies" and the first consistently to define American wage earners as "the consumers of the goods they produced." By his emphasis on the laborer as "consumer-citizen," he made a "prophetic contribution . . . to the public dialogue of his day."[14]

Blodgett is correct in saying that Cleveland wished to make such a contribution; it is less clear that he did so. The tariff bill that succeeded the Wilson-Gorman Act was the Dingley Tariff of 1900—a measure of high protectionism that demonstrated little concern for the "consumer-citizen." Cleveland's battle for tariff reform was too cautious in rationale and too unsuccessful in result to determine subsequent public dialogue on the relationships between tariff schedules, economic development, and consumer rights. Grover Cleveland had reason to believe he had failed and to share with Congressman Wilson a sense of "great disappointment."

9

LAW AND ORDER BY FEDERAL AUTHORITY: CLEVELAND AND BUSINESS AND LABOR, 1893–96

One of the most controversial actions of Cleveland's second administration was his dispatch of federal troops to Chicago in July 1894 to assure the free movement of rail traffic and to put an end to the Pullman strike. Many historians cite this as an example of Cleveland's increasing conservatism during his second term and his determination to preserve the status quo and protect the interests of corporate America.[1] Cleveland's actions during the Pullman strike were far from even-handed, and his tactics can be criticized on several counts, but he feared labor violence, not labor unions; his bias was toward federal executive and judicial authority, not toward George M. Pullman or the consortium of Chicago railroads.

During the depression winter of 1893/94, George Pullman decided to secure his high level of profit by making a series of wage cuts for all employees of the Pullman Car Company. Many of those employees lived in the much-publicized "model town" of Pullman, outside the city of Chicago. Though wage levels were cut by a fourth, the cost of company rents and utilities were not reduced by so much as a dime. Many workers' families discovered that after paying their rent, they had less than a dollar a day for food and clothing, and in May a delegation of workers begged for an interview with their employer and asked that either rents be reduced or wages be raised.

George Pullman's answer was to fire three members of the workers' delegation. This inspired 80 percent of the workers to go out on strike, and Pullman then ordered all shops closed until the crazy radicals came to their senses.

The Pullman strike generated national attention only when it ignited a sympathy strike by members of the American Railway Union (ARU). Some four thousand Pullman employees were members of the ARU, which had been founded a year earlier under the leadership of Eugene V. Debs. Debs, disgusted at the conservatism of the various railroad brotherhoods, had urged that there be a single union of all railroad workers, whatever their occupation or level of skill. By the spring of 1894 the ARU claimed 150,000 members in some 465 local unions. At the ARU convention in May, those of its members who were striking against the Pullman Company asked for the union's support. Debs first urged the strikers and the Pullman management to settle the strike by means of an impartial arbitration panel. When this suggestion was rebuffed by George Pullman, the ARU voted to boycott all Pullman cars, effective June 26: namely, to refuse to work on any train that carried a Pullman car. The Pullman strike now expanded into a general railroad strike that at its peak would affect rail traffic in twenty-seven states and territories. The General Managers Association (GMA), a consortium of the heads of twenty-four railroads that had terminals in Chicago, proclaimed the ARU to be an enemy of the public safety and resolved to destroy it. The railroad workers were equally determined to win their strike and increase their membership. By the early days of July, rail traffic to and from Chicago was at 10 percent of its usual volume, the federal mails were seriously obstructed, and the *Chicago Tribune* was denouncing Debs as an anarchist who had dictatorial ambitions. Attorney General Richard Olney obtained a sweeping court injunction, forbidding interference with rail traffic to and from Chicago; and President Cleveland ordered to Chicago a large number of federal troops with instructions to see that the federal injunction was observed. Incendiaries burned several of the buildings of the Chicago World's Fair; a pitched battle between soldiers and a mob of unemployed citizens, sympathetic to the railroad strikers, resulted in seven deaths; and Cleveland issued a presidential proclamation, promising punishment for all "unlawful assemblages." By July 10, Debs, with seventy other union members, had been indicted and arrested for violating the judicial injunction, and federal troops had secured the safe passage of rail traffic through Chicago. Strikes and disorders in states west of the Mississippi were ended by means of other injunctions and the dispatch of other units of the United States Army. Grover Cleveland received the congratulations of James J. Hill, the railroad builder, and the curses of agrarian politicians and John Peter Altgeld, the governor of Illinois.

The story of Cleveland's role in the Pullman strike is best examined by analyzing four relationships: those between Richard Olney and the General Managers Association; Olney and Cleveland; Cleveland and Altgeld; and Cleveland and Debs.

Richard Olney, a man who raised truculence to an art form, had the appearance of a rather ferocious terrier. Something of a tyrant at home—he had barred the door to his daughter when she had had the temerity to marry a dentist—he was, by his own lights, a man of unflinching courage who relished his reputation for blunt speech and unrestrained candor. Before joining Cleveland's second cabinet, he had made an excellent living as an attorney for various railroad corporations, such as the Boston and Maine, the New York Central, the Atchison, Topeka and Santa Fe, and the Chicago, Burlington and Quincy; he continued, indeed, to receive a retainer of $10 thousand a year from the Burlington after entering the cabinet. Olney's views during the Pullman strike were undoubtedly influenced by his background as a railroad lawyer, but it is doubtful that pecuniary advantage was an important factor. He was a man who believed devoutly in the sanctity of private property, identified the success of corporate America with national economic progress, and—together with a majority of the legal community—was convinced that sympathy strikes and labor boycotts were illegal. Olney was not a corrupt man, but as the nation's chief law officer, he demonstrated questionable legal ethics during the Pullman strike.

Olney worked in virtual alliance with the General Managers Association. He asked the consortium's advice when selecting a special counsel to assist the United States attorney in Chicago, he encouraged the United States attorney to attend conferences of the railroad lawyers and to call their attention to legal precedents in support of federal injunctions in labor disputes, and he saw nothing wrong in allowing the association to pay the salary of the hundreds of special deputies appointed by the chief federal marshal and the United States attorney. These temporary representatives of the national government were, in effect, privately paid strikebreakers. Convinced that the strike was a threat to interstate commerce and to the transport of the federal mail, Olney saw the General Managers Association, not as one side in a labor-management dispute, but as an ally in a fight between the forces of law and order and the proponents of anarchy and mob rule. This perception led Olney to work in collusion with a group of railroad managers who sought not only the resumption of rail traffic but also the destruction of the ARU. It was Olney who masterminded the issuance of perhaps the most sweeping injunction ever issued by a federal court in a labor-management dispute.

The injunction, issued by the district court in Chicago on July 2, forbade any person from interfering with a mail train or any train engaged in interstate commerce; from inducing "by threats, intimidation, persuasion, force, or violence any of the employees of said railroads not to perform any of their duties . . . [or] leave the service of said railroads"; or from doing any act "in furtherance of any conspiracy to interfere with the free and unhindered transportation of interstate commerce."[2] Olney had advised the special counsel on the terms of the injunction to be obtained from the federal judiciary, and he viewed the injunction as the first step toward persuading Cleveland to order the military to Chicago and, by a display of "overwhelming force," to awe the strikers and crush the strike.

Allan Nevins blames the "unfortunate influence" of Attorney General Olney for Cleveland's "precipitate" decision to order four thousand troops into Chicago. Olney undoubtedly arranged matters in a way that made more likely Cleveland's military intervention, but Cleveland was not in awe of Richard Olney or any other member of his cabinet. Olney understood that fact and was content to rely on the president's professional background and lifelong respect for the authority of the federal judiciary. Olney wished the strikers and their sympathizers to disobey the court injunction, appreciating that while Cleveland was reluctant to use military force to break the strike, he would most probably send troops to enforce an order of the Chicago district court and thereby uphold the authority and supremacy of the federal government.

A one-day riot in the town of Blue Island, south of Chicago, when a mob overturned rail cars and a deputy was stabbed, gave Olney his opportunity. He suggested that the United States attorney send a telegram to Washington, explaining that the deputies were unable to enforce the court injunction and that "no force less than the regular troops of the United States" could control the mob and protect property in the Chicago area. The special counsel, the chief United States marshal, and a federal judge should endorse the dispatch. These federal officials were quick to obey the attorney general's suggestion, and Olney took the telegram to the cabinet meeting of July 3. It inspired a unanimous decision by the cabinet officers that the emergency called for the intervention of the army. Cleveland, convinced that his constitutional duty demanded that he protect life and property and secure obedience to the orders of the federal courts, gave instructions to the secretary of war to send all available troops at Fort Sheridan to Chicago. In the early hours of the morning of July 4, federal troops took up their stations in the city, under orders to assure the free passage of interstate commerce and the United States mail and to enforce the decrees of the courts.[3]

The introduction of the military inspired renewed anger among the strikers and their sympathizers. During the four-day period from July 5 through July 8 there was a dramatic increase in the destruction of property. Olney believed this was ex post facto justification for Cleveland's action; the governor of Illinois insisted that it was further proof of the evil consequences of an unconstitutional usurpation of power by the federal government.

Cleveland was not the first American president to send federal troops to maintain law and order during a railroad strike; Hayes had done so during the "Great Strike" of 1877. Cleveland was, however, the first president to do so at his own initiative and not at the application of a state governor. Not only did the governor of Illinois not request the dispatch of federal troops, he objected publicly and often. Cleveland insisted that under Section 5298 of the Revised Statutes, he possessed the unrestricted authority to dispatch federal troops wherever there was a threat to life and property. Altgeld insisted that police powers were reserved exclusively for the states; in time of peace, federal troops could only intervene if invited to do so by a state legislature or governor. Altgeld wrote angry letters to the president and received equally angry replies. Cleveland argued that the troops had been sent only after he had received conclusive evidence from the judicial officers of the United States "that the process of the Federal courts could not be executed through the ordinary means, and upon competent proof that conspiracies existed against commerce between the States."[4]

Cleveland probably felt a greater personal distaste for Altgeld than for Eugene Debs. Cleveland saw Altgeld as the type of Democratic politician who would lead the Democratic party away from its true principles and down the path of agrarian radicalism, class antagonism, and disrespect for the constitutional restraints that kept popular passions in check. Debs was a demagogue, but he had never run for office under the banner of the Democratic party.

Debs saw Cleveland as a tool of the corporate interests, prepared to use the United States Army against the laboring class. For Cleveland, Debs was a man drunk with power who had received no sanction from the people. Years after the strike was over, Cleveland would tell a Princeton neighbor of his anxiety when deliberating the proper degree of federal intervention in the Chicago railroad strike and how he had resolved that anxiety: "I woke up one morning and as I got out of bed I asked myself: 'Did the people elect Eugene Debs or Grover Cleveland President?' And that settled it."[5]

Cleveland denied that the federal injunction that resulted in Debs's indictment and imprisonment was an unprecedented extension of the injunction powers of the federal judiciary. He argued that if a court could forbid an individual from committing a particular action, it could define in advance the nature of an offense and enjoin a group of individuals from encouraging others to commit that offense. If they dared to disobey, they could be charged with contempt of court and arrested. Confident that the Supreme Court would uphold the legality of the injunction, Cleveland considered Judge David J. Brewer's majority decision in the *Debs* case irrefutable. Actually, Brewer's opinion confined its attention to the power of the Chicago district court to issue the injunction; it did not discuss the breadth of the injunction's prohibitions or the details of Debs's "disobedience." The Court's decision in *Debs* v. *the United States* (27 May 1895) was sufficient, however, to keep Debs in jail and to allow him, at government expense, the opportunity to study the socialist doctrines of Karl Marx. Debs would leave prison as an avowed Socialist and would be the presidential candidate of the Socialist party in the election of 1900.

By his actions in the Pullman strike, Cleveland secured law and order in Chicago and the lasting animosity of John Altgeld and a majority of union leaders throughout the nation. Nor were they appeased when Cleveland appointed a commission to study the Pullman strike and to offer recommendations respecting the role of the federal government in future labor-management struggles that might threaten the peaceful conduct of the nation's business.

The three-man commission was chaired by Carroll D. Wright, and Cleveland probably did not find its report of 14 November 1894 completely to his taste. Consisting of 681 pages of testimony and a 42-page summary, the report concluded that Cleveland's dispatch of federal troops was justified, but it was highly critical of the General Managers Association. The association, it declared, was an example of "the persistent and shrewdly devised plans of corporations to override their limitations and usurp indirectly powers and rights not contemplated by their charters." Olney's accusations that officers of the American Railway Union purposely provoked violence were disputed, and the obduracy of George Pullman was sharply criticized.[6] Cleveland expressed his gratitude to the commission for its labors but offered no opinion as to the accuracy of its findings. Its recommendation for the establishment of a federal arbitral panel to which management and labor could appeal on a voluntary basis he found most satisfactory. He had made a similar recommendation to Congress eight years earlier.

For a student of the American presidency, the most interesting feature of Cleveland's actions during the Pullman strike is the witness they offer to his evolving conception of presidential authority. In the campaign of 1884, Cleveland had run on a Democratic platform calling for renewed respect for the rights and sovereignty of the individual states, and for many years thereafter he had given periodic warning against undue centralization of power in the federal government. In 1894 he claimed for the chief executive of the national government the authority to supersede the state of Illinois as the protector of law and order within its boundaries. Brushing aside the objections of Governor Altgeld, Cleveland assumed the police powers traditionally reserved to state and local governments as he authorized the use of federal military power in a labor-management dispute. Like his hero Andrew Jackson, Cleveland could simultaneously speak against the centralization of power in the federal government and expand the power of the federal executive. Cleveland's interpretation of the traditions of the Democratic party was, at the least, flexible. He quoted Jefferson when denouncing federal interference in local elections, but he acted like Jackson when he overrode Governor Altgeld and claimed supremacy for the federal government and its chief executive during the Chicago railroad strike.

As Robert Kelley has observed, Cleveland displayed "a bone-and-marrow instinct for the rightfulness and the transcendent necessity of authority."[7] It was yet another example of the victory of constitutional temperament over inherited dogma. Cleveland's psychological profile was that of the assertive leader. However much he worried over the effects of the centralization of political power, he had to see the expansion of his own authority as beneficial to the safety of the Republic.

There can be no question that during the years of his second administration, Grover Cleveland saw himself in the Jackson-Lincoln tradition of "the strong executive," clothed with power adequate to meet any crisis.[8] When years later he wrote a brief account of the Pullman strike, he spoke about the desire of his administration "to avoid extreme measures" and to confine its intervention to "purposes which were clearly within its constitutional competency and duty," but between the lines one can detect a note of pride in his display of prompt resolution in behalf of federal authority.[9] Shortly after the Pullman strike had ended, Cleveland received a newspaper clipping extolling that resolution. It was cast in poetic form, and Cleveland undoubtedly approved its praise, if not its versification:

> The railroad strike played merry hob,
>   The land was set aflame;
> Could Grover order out the troops
>   To block the striker's game?
> One Altgeld yelled excitedly,
>   "Such tactics I forbid;
> You can't trot out those soldiers," yet
>   That's just what Grover did.
>
> . . . .
>
> In after years when people talk
>   Of present stirring times,
> And of the action needful to
>   Sit down on public crimes,
> They'll all of them acknowledge then
>   (The fact cannot be hid)
> That whatever was the best to do
>   Is just what Grover did.[10]

Cleveland's handling of the Pullman strike demonstrated his expanded view of presidential authority, but his critics were quick to point out that such authority was being used against a labor union and not to fashion programs to assist victims of the depression. They refused to accept Cleveland's definition of "the public safety," and some labeled him the hired strikebreaker of the railroad corporations. The charge was understandable but wide of the mark.

Cleveland's tactics during the Pullman strike can be faulted on several counts: his failure to consult with state and local authorities; his failure to supervise Olney and prevent his collusion with the General Managers Association; his failure to instruct Olney to seek a more restricted injunction from the federal district court; his failure to suggest impartial investigation or some other means of settling the strike before resorting to the use of the United States Army. Cleveland permitted the judicial and the military force of the federal government to be used in a manner that was of exclusive benefit to one party in a labor-management dispute.[11]

The brief for the defense must rest on Cleveland's conviction that the railroad strike was not an ordinary labor-management dispute in the private sector. It represented, in his judgment, an illegal sympathy strike and a boycott that was paralyzing the nation's business, obstructing the free passage of the federal mails, and threatening the public safety in a large section of the country. As president, he had the responsibility to assure unhindered commerce among the several states, the unobstructed transit of the federal mails, and respect for judicial authority. The federal judiciary had the right to determine when local officials were unable to enforce the orders of the courts, and its judgment took precedence over the objections of mayors and governors.

Cleveland considered himself to be a friend of working people, however suspicious he frequently was of their self-appointed spokesmen and of the potential economic power of labor unions. Unlike Olney, Cleveland did not view the strikers and their sympathizers as anarchists; he did see them as men who posed a threat not only to property but also, and more importantly, to the American tradition of obedience to constituted authority. In the eyes of a conservative lawyer, that was an indictable offense.

Cleveland's self-assessment as a friend of working people was not a piece of hypocrisy. Having been the child of a family of straitened means and no stranger to physical labor, he was quick to see the hope of America in "the honest workingman," striving toward promotion and middle-class comforts. Cleveland, however, had little compassion for the indigent or the unlucky, and he had little sympathy for their requests for federal assistance. A self-righteous lack of understanding would characterize Cleveland's response to the Commonwealers and to Coxey's Army. Jacob S. Coxey was a foolish man who would encourage other Americans to believe that begging, not hard work, was the road to personal prosperity and improvement.

The widening depression of 1893/94 inspired the formation of bands of unemployed individuals who traversed the country in search of employment and local charity. Some of these bands coalesced into "industrial armies," the most publicized being the one led by "General" Jacob Coxey. Coxey, a short bespectacled man, was convinced that he had a cure for the nation's industrial unemployment and economic depression. He petitioned Congress to authorize the issue of $500 million in irredeemable paper money for highway construction and to allow local governments that wished to make public improvements to deposit with the Treasury Department non-interest-bearing twenty-five-year bonds and to receive treasury notes equal to their face value. Coxey's suggestions would receive partial legislative enactment with the Public Works Administration of the 1930's, but in the 1890s they were considered dangerously radical. "Made work" under governmental sponsorship was socialistic folly. When Coxey's petition was shelved by Congress, he determined to gather his followers and, "as a living petition," to march on Washington.

Coxey assembled his troops at Massillon, Ohio, on 25 March 1894. In the vanguard was the Coxey family: Jacob; his wife, Lucille; his son, "Legal Tender" Coxey; and his daughter, Mame, who on occasion assumed the costume of a goddess of peace. As the army trudged through Ohio, Pennsylvania, and Maryland, it generated great attention from the nation's press. Some eastern newspapers wrote about the Coxeyites in terms that outdid Dickens's fictional description of the French Revolution, predicting acts of bloody violence once the fearsome band had reached the nation's capital. In fact, Coxey's Army rapidly shrank in numbers as it wended its way east, and when in May it approached Pennsylvania Avenue, it boasted fewer than five hundred members. The bystanders and the police who were lining the avenue numbered several thousand. When the straggling band neared the Capitol, Coxey sought to break through the police cordon to read the Coxey Good Roads Bill petition and was arrested for trespassing on the grass. A week later, he was sentenced to twenty days in jail and a five-dollar fine. Coxey's followers fled the District of Columbia, and newspaper editors were soon reassuring their readers that Americans were too sensible a people to support mad revolutionaries.

Cleveland had approved Olney's orders to have Secret Service operatives trail Coxey's Army, but Cleveland at no time viewed the vagabond army as a threat to the safety of the Republic. The Coxeyites should, however, receive no recognition by the lawfully elected representatives of the people, and Coxey's Good Roads bill should be denounced as fiscal insanity. Hard times would never be cured by monetary inflation or government-sponsored work projects.

Local charity should be encouraged, but the unemployed could only receive permanent relief by redoubling their efforts to find work.

Many of Cleveland's opponents within and without the Democratic party believed that he was insensitive to the needs of the victims of the depression, but it was the "agrarian radicals" who were the most vociferous in their characterization of Cleveland as a tool of corporate interests, a front man for the moneyed power. Not only did they cite as evidence his intervention in the Pullman strike and the harsh treatment dealt the Coxeyites, but they blamed Cleveland for the decisions of the Supreme Court in the Sugar Trust case and in the income-tax case, and they insisted that Cleveland's "goldbug" cabinet was the agent of Wall Street financiers and railroad barons.

In the year 1895 the Supreme Court delivered a series of controversial decisions. Under the leadership of Chief Justice Melville W. Fuller, the Court appeared to be determined to enhance the injunction power of the federal judiciary, restrict the taxing and regulatory powers of the Congress, defend the legality of racial segregation in public schools, and interpret the Sherman Anti-Trust Act in a manner that would cripple the ability of the federal government to prosecute trusts or monopolies. In the last connection, the major case was *United States* v. *E. C. Knight Company*, in which the federal government sought to prosecute an instrument of the Sugar Trust that controlled better than 80 percent of the manufacture of refined sugar in the United States.

Cleveland had doubts about the clarity and intent of the Sherman Anti-Trust Act, and he considered state governments to be the most effective political agencies for restricting industrial combinations; but he believed that his administration had a duty to test the effectiveness of the law. His attorney general had little use for the Sherman Anti-Trust Act.[12] Olney agreed to prosecute the Sugar Trust, and he personally offered the government's argument before the Court; but Olney's legal effort in behalf of the applicability of the Sherman Act was less than half-hearted. Instead of emphasizing monopolistic practices in the interstate sale and distribution of sugar, he discussed only the degree of combination in the manufacture of sugar in Pennsylvania.

In a divided opinion the Court declared that the government had not proven the existence of a monopoly and decided that the Sherman Act only prohibited conspiracies in restraint of interstate trade and did not apply to combinations at the manufacturing stage.

Olney reported to a friend that the Court's decision justified his personal opinion respecting the flaws of a poorly drafted statute.[13] Cleveland's response to the *Knight* case was more constructive. In his annual message of December 1896 he denounced the trusts as creatures of special privilege and enemies of the nation's social and economic health and recommended that Congress pass a new anti-trust act.[14]

During Cleveland's second term, the Justice Department prose-cuted five cases against industrial combinations but was successful in only one. Its low percentage of success, however, was more the result of a Supreme Court that was bent on promoting a conserva-tive judicial revolution than of an adminstration that was reluctant to disturb the interests of capital during a time of economic depres-sion. For the judicial conservatism of the Court, Cleveland deserves some blame, but less than that of his predecessor. Four of the jus-tices were nominees of Benjamin Harrison, two of whom—David J. Brewer and George Shiras, Jr.—were outspoken opponents of any extension of the regulatory and tax powers of the government. It was Cleveland, however, who had nominated Melville W. Fuller as chief justice in April 1888. Fuller proved to be an excellent business manager for the Court and an undeviating judicial conservative, pledged to protect the economic liberty of the corporate individual against governmental restraint and regulation. He would serve as chief justice for twenty-two years, and his selection was one of the most important and unfortunate appointments of the Cleveland pres-idencies. Cleveland, a man who had a lifelong respect for the judi-ciary and its independence, was never known to utter a public word of criticism against Fuller or the Fuller Court.

The conservatism of that Court was made manifest in *Pollock v. Farmers' Loan & Trust Company*, the income-tax case. As noted in the preceding chapter, the Wilson-Gorman Tariff Act had included an income-tax provision, levying a 2 percent tax on all personal incomes over $4,000 and on all corporate profits above operating costs and expenses. It was warmly supported by southern and west-ern agrarians, who saw the income-tax provision as a step toward the equalization of tax burdens between classes and sections. In a 5 to 4 decision, the Fuller Court declared the income tax unconstitu-tional, despite the fact that a similar tax had been levied during the Civil War and had withstood all attacks on its legality. Ignoring earlier decisions, the Court decided that an income tax was not sim-ilar to an excise tax. It was a direct tax and could be levied only on a per capita basis.

Even more than the Court's opinion in the *Knight* case, this decision increased the unpopularity of the Cleveland administration with southern and western agrarians. They referred, not to the Fuller Court but to the "Cleveland Court"; and they saw the income-tax decision as yet another example of the Cleveland administration's reactionary determination to support the interests of capital and the creditor class against those of labor and the debtor class. They were convinced that Cleveland was surrounded by a cabinet of big-business agents who were determined to make the dollar ever dearer and the debts of the farmer ever heavier.

Cleveland's second cabinet was not composed of dyed-in-the-wool reactionaries, resolute in their protection of corporate interests. Such members as John Carlisle, Hilary Herbert, J. Sterling Morton, and Hoke Smith were "sound money men" who were unpopular in their home states among the advocates of free silver and monetary inflation; but they had few ties with big business or Wall Street. Together with Daniel Lamont, Wilson S. Bissell, and Richard Olney, they believed that the party would be best served by a continued alliance of eastern Democrats and sound-money, low-tariff southern Democrats, not by an alliance of southern and western "agrarian radicals." But they would have denied that they favored a party concerned only with protecting the interests of big business or a program characterized by governmental indifference to the nation's economic problems. Cleveland's cabinet was composed of men who believed that industrial progress and the general welfare were closely allied, but they did not see themselves as agents of the Sugar Trust or George Pullman. Secretary of War Daniel Lamont has been described as "the means of communication . . . between Cleveland and the big business men of the country," but that description is an exaggeration.[15] Lamont and the other members of Cleveland's official family self-consciously associated themselves with "the sound and sensible" element of the Democratic party, as distinguished from Altgeld and "Pitchfork Ben" Tillman. They wished the party to stand for governmental economy, honest money, law and order, and respect for the rights of private property. In holding such views, however, they reflected the common concerns of nineteenth-century liberalism.

Cleveland's first public address after leaving the presidency was to a convocation at Princeton University. He chose as his subject "The Self-made Man in American Life." It was one of his better addresses—avoiding the tangled sentence structure that often had marked his official messages—and it offers interesting insight respecting his attitude toward big business and material success. He informed the Princeton undergraduates that there was nothing wrong with striving for material success, but men who concentrated exclusively on the race for riches often stifled all feelings of civic and patriotic duty. The successful man who refused "to do something for humanity and the public good" did not deserve the praise of his neighbors. After expressing satisfaction with the nation's industrial progress since the Civil War, Cleveland warned against "the money craze" and told his listeners not to scorn the ideals of an earlier day, when frugality was a virtue; private charity, a duty; and economy of government, a common expectation.[16]

Cleveland praised people who had demonstrated their ability to rise from humble beginnings and achieve success in their profession or business. He always retained a certain suspicion of the very rich, however, particularly of those who had gained their wealth by means of sharp practice and speculation. He admired Andrew Carnegie and James J. Hill, but he disliked Jay Gould.

Cleveland frequently urged the successful businessman to enter politics, believing he could instill in government "a business character" and counter radical passions and "sudden gusts of excitement." The businessman-in-politics, however, must consider "the welfare of the public at large" and abjure the politics of special interests and "selfish benefits." Other groups should not be obliged "to feed from the crumbs which fall from the table of business," and no group should "attempt to appropriate the share of others."[17]

Paola E. Coletta, the author of an excellent three-volume biography of William Jennings Bryan, has written about Cleveland: "[He] was unwilling to tackle privilege; he sided with capital against labor, corporations against consumers, bankers against borrowers, entrenched political and judicial power against the common man."[18] This is an excellent summary of Bryan's view about his party enemy, but it is less than accurate. The president who broke the Pullman strike was the same man who denounced the lobbyists for high protectionism, abrogated the grass leases in Indian Territory, fought the western railroads in behalf of the homesteader, and extended the forest reserve against the wishes of timber and mineral corporations.

In Cleveland's judgment, the relations between government and business did not need to be antagonistic, but neither should they form an exclusive partnership. Government could properly investigate the operations of monopolies, railroads, and other businesses that directly affected the public welfare, but it should not interfere in the contractual relations between businessmen and their customers. As was so often the case with Cleveland's economic analysis, the distinction was more neat than practical, but it was the distinction of a man who was sincerely trying to meet the problems of a new economic era while only dimly perceiving its outlines.

10

★ ★ ★ ★ ★

CLEVELAND'S DIPLOMACY 1: BRITISH AND PACIFIC RELATIONS

Any analysis of Cleveland's diplomatic record must begin with two questions: Can it be treated separately from an analysis of the domestic politics of his administrations? Can the foreign policy of his two nonconsecutive terms be analyzed as the continuous diplomatic record of a single presidency? An affirmative answer to both questions provides the justification for reserving a discussion of Cleveland's diplomacy until now.

Cleveland's foreign policy was the subject of much criticism, but his diplomacy never determined the nature of his domestic policies or their measure of success. Similarly, although foreign-policy developments during his second term were more dramatic, and indeed more interesting, than those of his first administration, Cleveland's diplomatic objectives remained remarkably consistent throughout his years as the nation's chief executive. The depression of 1893-96 did not change those objectives; for Cleveland's foreign policy during his second administration was not characterized by a program of aggressive economic expansion and a determination to achieve recovery by finding new markets for the nation's industrial surplus. During both adminstrations, Cleveland's diplomacy was marked by inconsistencies, sporadic personal attention, and an uneasy mixture of anti-imperialism, moralism, and belligerent nationalism.

Together with other presidents of the Gilded Age, Cleveland gave only limited time to matters of foreign policy. His major interests were administrative reform, Indian and land policy, the currency and the tariff. Certain of those issues had obvious international ramifications, but Cleveland maintained a clear if somewhat artificial distinction between his domestic and foreign policies, and he found the former more interesting and more important. In part, this was because he had no wish to revise or redirect U.S. foreign policy but only to sustain the eternal verities enunciated by Washington, Jefferson, and Monroe. In his first Inaugural Address, he informed the American people that he contemplated no departure from "that foreign policy" which had been responsible for the safety and prosperity of the Republic over the past century: "It is a policy of independence, favored by our position and defended by our known love of justice and by our power. It is the policy of peace suitable to our interests. It is the policy of neutrality, rejecting any share in foreign broils and ambitions upon other continents and repelling their intrusions here."[1]

Cleveland's anti-imperialism was rooted in a conviction that U.S. diplomatic traditions required that the United States abjure overseas territorial expansion. Such expansion was forbidden not only by the admonitions of Washington but also by the doctrine of President Monroe. If we were to continue to insist that European nations not interfere in the affairs of the New World, we must not become involved in their colonial rivalries in other regions. As for commercial expansion, it occurred most safely and successfully if left to private entrepreneurs, without aggressive governmental direction that could embroil the United States in foreign quarrels. The federal government should protect the lives and property of its citizens overseas, but it must remain free of entangling responsibilities and commitments. It was right to promote trade and commerce, but the nation's primary emphasis must continue to be the development of its own resources. Cleveland wished to pursue a conservative, old-fashioned foreign policy or, as he would have said, a foreign policy marked by a respect for tradition. Tradition provided the sanction for anti-imperialism and for a qualified isolationism.

Cleveland's first foreign-policy decision was to withdraw from senatorial consideration the Frelinghuysen-Zavala treaty of December 1884, because he thought it violated the tradition of no entangling alliances. This treaty gave the United States the right to construct a transisthmian canal through Nicaragua, to be jointly owned by the two nations, and included a promise of permanent alliance and United States protection of Nicaraguan territory. Though Cleveland believed a transoceanic canal would be of value for the commerce of the United States and the world, he opposed the treaty on two counts: it made Nicaragua a protectorate of the United States, and it represented "an absolute and unlimited engagement" to defend the territorial integrity of a foreign state.[2]

Cleveland viewed with equal hostility the Berlin Convention, which the Arthur administration had endorsed during its last days in office. This convention presumably assured the perpetual neutrality of the Congo, and Cleveland considered that the United States had no business meddling with imperial rivalries in Central Africa. Believing that we should not have participated in the Berlin Conference and that the treaty represented a potentially entangling commitment and "responsibilities we are not in a position to assume," he ignored the requests of the Senate Foreign Relations Committee and buried the treaty.[3]

Opposition to territorial expansion and jingoism was reenforced by a wish to demonstrate the superior morality of U.S. foreign policy. Many years before Woodrow Wilson proclaimed the necessity of judging diplomatic options by moral as well as legal criteria, Cleveland demonstrated a determination—at least on occasion—to view foreign questions in a moral light. The United States could exhibit its superior morality by abjuring colonial adventures and by advocating the peaceful settlement of international disputes. As one trained in the law, Cleveland believed that the legal instrument of arbitration was well suited to that purpose.[4]

The Hawaiian diplomacy of Cleveland and Secretary of State Walter Gresham in 1893/94 had a strong moralistic element. Indeed, many would say that it was an excellent illustration of how a nation determined to teach moral lessons can lose sight of reality. Cleveland, however, sought to contrast, not moralism and realism, but moralism and "opportunism." It was opportunism that was best left to the Old World and its Bismarcks and Salisburys. The United States must be both powerful and just, and then its superiority to other nations would be clear to all the world.

Cleveland had little interest in other cultures and civilizations and was convinced of the political and cultural superiority of the United States. His diplomacy had as its final theme an element of nationalistic belligerence and ethnocentric patriotism. He had no wish to don the shining armor of the warrior chieftain, but he would have the United States recognized as a nation that was great as well as good. We would not allow any European nation to build and control an isthmian canal or undermine the independence of any republic in the Americas. The hegemony of the United States in the Western Hemisphere must be maintained in accordance with the declaration of President Monroe. Opposed to United States expansion, Cleveland was even more opposed to European expansion, particularly in "our hemisphere." His belligerent diplomacy toward Britain during the Venezuelan boundary dispute exemplified his conviction that not only must the United States abstain from aggression but it must also require a similar pledge from European monarchies when their ambitions impinged on the natural sphere of influence of the United States. With the Founding Fathers, Grover Cleveland pledged allegiance to the doctrine of the "two spheres."

Cleveland never offered a formal statement about the principles and objectives of his foreign policy. Had he done so, he might have listed them in the following order: the preservation of national security by adherence to the Monroe Doctrine and Washington's "Great Rule of Conduct"; abstention from colonial expansion, foreign adventures, and the power politics of Europe; strict neutrality in foreign wars; promotion of the peaceful settlement of international disputes by the legal instrument of arbitration and by the example of a nation whose diplomacy was characterized by justice to all nations.

Cleveland's diplomacy during his two presidential terms did not demonstrate undeviating allegiance to these principles or enjoy consistent success. It was marked frequently by ambiguity and a lack of foresight. He pursued no grand geopolitical strategy; instead, he reacted—or overreacted—to foreign-policy developments as they occurred. But there was no hypocrisy in Cleveland's convictions respecting rightful foreign-policy objectives; there was only considerable uncertainty as to how best to achieve them during a series of minor diplomatic crises.

Cleveland's secretaries of state were men of ability if of little previous diplomatic experience. Thomas F. Bayard served during the whole of Cleveland's first term; Walter Q. Gresham served for the first two years of the second term, dying in office; Gresham was succeeded by Richard Olney, who in June 1895 moved from the post of attorney general to that of secretary of state. Cleveland valued the advice of all three men, but he never permitted them to usurp his presidential prerogatives, and he took an active role in all important questions of foreign policy. If his secretaries were often the initiators of particular policy positions, it was Cleveland who gave or withheld approval for their implementation and who had the final word on all major diplomatic appointments.

Bayard, Gresham, and Olney were men of widely disparate personalities, and Cleveland formed a close bond with each of them. Bayard, the courtly scion of a family political dynasty in Delaware, was a man who abhorred jingoism and believed the United States could best achieve its foreign policy objectives by quiet and dignified diplomatic negotiation. Cleveland admired and praised Bayard's patient negotiations with Great Britain over the North Atlantic fisheries dispute. It was probably with Gresham that Cleveland developed the most affectionate personal relationship. Cleveland was attracted by Gresham's warm and open nature and his insistence that U.S. diplomacy should adhere to high moral standards. It was Richard Olney, however, who more than his predecessors achieved the position of a British-style foreign minister. At no point during the Venezuelan or Cuban crises of 1895/96 did Olney operate in contradiction to Cleveland's instructions, but Olney, a shrewd analyst of Cleveland's moods and temperament, had great influence in shaping those instructions.

Relations with Britain consumed a major share of the time and attention of the State Department during both of Cleveland's administrations. In Cleveland's first term there was the complex issue of the rights of U.S. fishermen in the North Atlantic fishing grounds off Canada and Newfoundland; the disputed boundary between Alaska and British Columbia; and the problem of the diminishing fur-seal population in the Bering Sea. In all of these issues, Canada and U.S.–Canadian relations played a central role.

The North Atlantic fisheries dispute may be traced back to the treaty that ended the War of the American Revolution, but for Grover Cleveland it began when Congress abrogated, as of 1 July 1885, certain articles of the Treaty of Washington (1871). Those articles had given New England fishermen generous rights to fish in the bays and the inshore waters of eastern Canada and—in compensation—had allowed Canada and Newfoundland to export fish to the United States free of duty. The latter feature had been a source of irritation to protectionist senators and congressmen.

With the spring of 1886, the Canadians, understandably angered at the unilateral action of the United States Congress, began to seize American fishing vessels that were exceeding their rights to fish in Canadian waters and dry their catch on Canadian soil under the ancient convention of 1818, which now provided the sole legal basis for Americans fishing the waters of British North America. The game of tit-for-tat provocation continued as Congress passed a harsh Retaliation Act in March 1887. This statute empowered the president to bar Canadian goods and ships from United States ports if, in his opinion, "American fishermen were being unjustly treated."[5] Republican senators who had sponsored the bill believed that the Canadians were harassing noble American seamen as a means of pressuring the Cleveland administration to establish a free-trade commercial union between the two countries.

Cleveland signed the Retaliation Act; but taking advantage of the discretion it allowed the president, he did not enforce it, while he continued to seek a diplomatic solution to a potentially dangerous quarrel. He decided to deal, not with the irritated Canadians, but with their mother country. Secretary Bayard, at Cleveland's suggestion, warned London that the Canadian officials were playing into the hands of an element in the United States that was "hostile to everything English and glad of any pretext to fan the flame of hatred and mischief."[6] Using the Retaliation Act both as a warning and as a bargaining chip, Cleveland and Bayard had the satisfaction of gaining British agreement in July 1887 to the formation of a six-member joint commission to meet in Washington. After long and arduous effort, this commission produced a solution that apparently was just to both sides, the Bayard-Chamberlain treaty of 15 February 1888.

The Bayard-Chamberlain treaty provided that a mixed commission would determine which Canadian bays and waters were and were not open to American fishermen, based on the agreed principles that the three-mile territorial limit should follow the sinuosities of the shoreline and that estuaries and bays that were entered by inlets more than six miles wide would be judged open waters. American fishing vessels were guaranteed the right to purchase supplies on their homeward voyages and could enter "reserved waters" to purchase bait and to transship catches upon purchase of a license. Section 15 of the treaty, which elicited the most debate, declared that whenever the United States removed the import duty on Canadian fish, these licenses would be free of charge, and American fishing vessels would be granted additional privileges when entering the inshore Atlantic waters of British North America. In an accompanying protocol the British described the terms of a modus vivendi that would be put into effect for a two-year period, pending the treaty's ratification.[7]

When submitting the treaty to the Senate, Cleveland wrote that it had been framed "in a spirit of liberal equity and reciprocal benefits" and bore witness that "mutual advantage and convenience" was the only "permanent foundation" of peace and friendship between nations.[8] The Republican majority in the Senate was not prepared to agree or to give Cleveland a diplomatic success in an election year. Republican senators complained that Cleveland had not submitted for senatorial approval the names of the three U.S. members of the joint commission and attacked section 15 as the opening wedge in an assault on the U.S. protectionist system. By tying Canadian concessions on license fees and inshore privileges to the abolition of duties on imported Canadian fish, the Cleveland administration was preparing to return to the discredited old agreement that linked free fishing with free fish. Senate patriots must repudiate this example of the Anglophilic subservience of the Cleveland administration. The treaty was rejected on 21 August 1888 by a vote of 27 in favor and 30 opposed.

The rejection of the treaty neither ended the northern voyages of Gloucester fishermen nor the political maneuvers of the Senate and Grover Cleveland. As to the former, the British sensibly put into effect the terms of the modus vivendi and then allowed its extension long after the stated two-year period had lapsed. Under its terms, United States fishing vessels could enter the bays and harbors of Canada and Newfoundland to buy bait and dry fish after purchasing an annual license at a fee of $1.50 per ship ton. On the domestic political front, the Senate demanded that Cleveland now enforce the Retaliation Act, and Cleveland responded by criticizing the law as being weak and insufficient. He requested that Congress pass new legislation that would empower the president to prohibit "the transit of goods, wares, and merchandise in bond across or over the territory of the United States to or from Canada."[9] Cleveland appeared ready to wage commercial war against Canada, in direct opposition to "a spirit of liberal equity"; but in fact, he had no such intention. He wanted an excuse for not implementing the Retaliation Act, and he wished to take a swipe at New England opponents of the Bayard-Chamberlain treaty. It was New England railroads that provided most of the "transit" of Canadian "goods, wares, and merchandise." In an election year, Cleveland also wished to counter Republican charges that his administration was the toady of Britain. Cleveland knew that the Senate would not act on his suggestion for broader retaliation, nor did it.

In supervising the negotiation of the Bayard-Chamberlain treaty, Cleveland was true to his self-image as a man of peace and an enemy of jingoism. In his suggestion of across-the-board commercial retaliation against Canada, he was as guilty of seeking political advantage at the expense of international good will as were the Republican partisans who rejected that treaty.[10]

Cleveland displayed a more conciliatory temper during the drawn-out negotiations over the disputed boundary between Alaska and British Columbia. When the United States had acquired Alaska from Russia in 1867, it had been understood that Alaska's southeastern boundary was the one described in a British-Russian convention of 1825. It was later determined that the description of this boundary line was a topographical impossibility. As Secretary Bayard explained in a letter to the United States minister in London, the line was "of uncertain if not impossible location for a good part of its length."[11] The British government was opposed to establishing an arbitral board to determine the boundary but did agree that each nation should make a scientific survey as a preliminary to further negotiation. The matter hung fire for many years, and then, toward the end of Cleveland's second term, Secretary of State Olney took up the matter, but with equal lack of success. Olney urged the British to allow "a joint delimitation of the 141 Meridian by an international commission of experts."[12] In November 1896, Olney fashioned a draft convention for the establishment of a joint commission, but the British were uninterested in pursuing the matter with a lame-duck administration. It would not be until the Klondike gold rush gave urgency to the question and Theodore Roosevelt offered a demonstration of carefully staged bellicosity that the Alaskan boundary dispute was finally settled by an arbitral panel in 1904.

Cleveland had demonstrated more interest in the issue of the fur seals of the Bering Sea, for here he believed was a question of morality as well as national honor and "sturdy Americanism."

The sealing industry in the Northern Pacific had for generations centered about the Pribilof Islands in the Bering Sea, where fur seals congregated to mate and bear their young. These islands were acknowledged to be a part of the Alaskan Purchase, and the United States possessed the sole right to hunt seals on the islands, a right that was monopolized by a California company, the North American Commercial Corporation. A dispute had arisen, however, over pelagic sealing—the killing of seals in the waters off the islands. Early in the nineteenth century, Russia had claimed that the Bering Sea was a mare clausum, a part of the territorial waters of Russian America, and Grover Cleveland now adopted this position for the United States. He was convinced that pelagic sealing was fast depleting the fur-seal herd, and Cleveland insisted on the right to regulate or prohibit pelagic sealing as necessary.

Canadian sealers insisted that the Bering Sea was an open sea and that pelagic sealing—unlike the land slaughter practiced by the North American Commercial Corporation—did not endanger the herd. The Canadian government made immediate protest when in the summer of 1886 United States revenue cutters began to seize Canadian and other foreign ships engaged in hunting fur seals in the Bering Sea. Authorization for these seizures had been given without the knowledge of Secretary Bayard, who disagreed with Cleveland's contention that the Bering Sea was a part of the territorial waters of Alaska. Bayard persuaded Cleveland to assure the British minister that pending proceedings against Canadian vessels would be canceled and that all persons arrested in connection with the seizures would be released. Cleveland, however, refused to promise that there would be no further seizures, and he instructed Bayard to try to negotiate an international agreement to end pelagic sealing "in Alaskan waters."[13] Other seizures then followed, accompanied by increasingly sharp protests from Ottawa and London.

While Bayard was seeking a diplomatic solution, Congress decided to enter the picture by passing a law on 2 March 1889, which instructed the president to issue an annual proclamation against the hunting of seals in the Bering Sea. United States naval vessels should cruise Alaskan waters and arrest all violators of the prohibition. On the day before he left office, Cleveland signed the bill.

Cleveland's position was not unlike the stand he later assumed in the Venezuelan boundary controversy. Convinced that the British were wrong in their support of illegal Canadian sealers, he believed that a posture of stern defiance was necessary in order that they be brought to reason and so agree to a diplomatic solution. He neither expected nor wanted a military confrontation, but he was determined to protect the interests of an important industry and the national honor. He had studied the matter and had decided that the Bering Sea was a part of the territorial waters of the United States. The British must be sensible, accept the validity of his judgment, and, in the process, save the seal herd. British talk of "the freedom of the seas" was only a cover for British arrogance and refusal to recognize the rightful claims and superior morality of the United States.

Cleveland was gratified when the British government later accepted a proposal by the Harrison administration to establish an international board of arbitration to settle the fur-seal-fisheries dispute. He was convinced that the arbitral panel would support his judgment respecting American claims to "all the waters of the Bering Sea." He was correspondingly angered when the arbitrators ruled against the United States on the mare-clausum question, limited the territorial waters of the United States to three miles off the shores of the Pribilof Islands, and ordered the United States to pay damages to Canada for ship seizures. Their recommendation that pelagic sealing be forbidden everywhere in the North Pacific for a three-month period each year provided little mollification.[14]

Never a man to accept the judgment of others as superior to his own, Cleveland sought in his second administration to reopen the issue and gain the agreement of Japan, Russia, and Great Britain to form a joint commission to investigate the continued threat to the seal herd and to fashion an international convention that would assure the "total cessation" of pelagic hunting in the Bering Sea.[15] The British government flatly rejected Secretary Gresham's proposal and thereby reenforced Cleveland's conviction that Great Britain had no intention of aspiring to the high moral standards of U.S. diplomacy.

Only two areas in the Pacific Ocean and its borderlands were of interest to Cleveland and the object of his attention: Samoa and Hawaii. During his first term he showed little interest in the struggle between China and Japan for the control of Korea, and during his second administration, he evinced only modest interest in the Sino-Japanese War. It was the government's duty to protect the lives and property of American citizens living and traveling in the Orient, but the expansion of Sino-American trade was the proper concern of American shippers and exporters. He gave no encouragement to U.S. minister Charles Denby, who wished to see the United States play a more active political and economic role in China.

Yet in the Samoan Islands—an area that was equally distant from Washington and of far less commercial importance—Cleveland demonstrated not only interest but also spurts of bellicosity.

Three nations—the United States, Germany, and Great

Britain—had signed treaties with the Samoan monarch during the 1870s. These treaties gave each nation trading rights and the right to establish a naval base in the islands, while acknowledging the independent sovereignty of the islands. The United States treaty had been negotiated in 1878, during the administration of Rutherford B. Hayes, and had passed virtually unnoticed except for a few American merchants, whalers, and naval officers. American trading interests in Samoa were small, and when Cleveland first took notice of the islands, it was from a desire, not to increase U.S. exports, but to block what he saw as the unjustified ambitions of the German government under Chancellor Otto von Bismarck.

Cleveland believed that the 1878 treaty required the United States not only to recognize the political independence of the Samoan people but also to protect that independence against the designs of others, and he was worried by reports that German officials in the islands planned to replace the Samoan king, Malietoa, with a claimant, Tamasese, more susceptible to German political influence. This represented both a threat to Samoan autonomy and disrespect to the United States. Once German interests were given "preferred status," the way would be paved for the islands to become a German protectorate. The United States had no wish to annex the islands, but neither did it intend to allow another power to do so.[16] Cleveland's position displayed a confusing mixture of moralism, ideological principle, and assertive nationalism; but it was little influenced by expansionist ambitions. When in May 1886 the United States consul accepted Malietoa's offer to put Samoa under United States protection, Cleveland recalled "the over-zealous official."[17]

German moves to install a puppet monarch inspired a formal protest by Secretary Bayard, which, in turn, led to a three-power conference in Washington in June and July 1887. The conference provided an opportunity to air mutual grievances but nothing more. A few months later, German naval vessels arrived at Samoa, and the German consul recognized Tamasese as the new king. Bayard's suggestion that there be an election to give the Samoan people the opportunity to indicate their monarchical preference was curtly rejected by the Germans. United States consular and naval officials were instructed not to recognize the authority of Tamasese, and those officials were soon openly encouraging the endeavors of a new claimant to the throne, Mataafa. Taking advantage of the unpopularity of Tamasese and his German patrons, Mataafa raised the flag of military rebellion and soon had gained control over a major portion of the islands. In the process, his warriors met and massacred a detachment of German naval guards, killing twenty and injuring thirty others.

Bismarck insisted that the honor of the Second Reich had been abused, and he threatened all-out war in Samoa, implying that the probable result would be a formal German protectorate of the islands. Cleveland responded by sending three warships to Samoan waters— the Pacific flagship, *Trenton*, the *Vandalia*, and the *Nipsic*. At the same time he instructed Bayard to inform Germany that the United States desired a diplomatic solution to the Samoan crisis. It was time to stand up to the arrogant German chancellor, but he should know that the United States had no wish to wage battle against the German navy.[18]

Faced with domestic problems and aware that Britain's previous toleration of German maneuvers in Samoa was eroding, Bismarck reversed course. He declared that Germany had no wish to destroy Samoan independence, and he called for another conference of the three Samoan powers. Cleveland was quick to agree. When Cleveland left office for the first time in March 1889, preparations were being made for a conference in Berlin, and German and American warships continued to confront each other in the harbor of Apia. Cleveland had seemingly scored a diplomatic victory, but the Samoan crisis continued.

Two weeks later, Samoa was hit by a major hurricane and accompanying tidal waves. Before the storm had passed, the warships of Germany and the United States had been sunk or damaged beyond repair. Fifty seamen of each country had lost their lives.

With tempers cooled by the tragedy of a natural disaster, the Berlin conference reached the rather unusual solution of a tripartite protectorate over the Samoan Islands. Cleveland was critical of the arrangement, believing that it represented an entangling alliance and that it lowered the position of the United States from moral champion of Samoan independence to that of a collaborator with imperial European monarchies. When he regained the presidency, he informed Congress of his dissatisfaction, but he took no positive action toward reaching an alternative solution. Secretary Gresham told the German minister to Washington that he personally favored American withdrawal from the tripartite arrangement, but neither Germany nor Britain wanted to aggravate their colonial rivalry by reconvening the Berlin conference. It was not until 1899 and the McKinley presidency that the tripartite protectorate was ended and the Samoan Islands were divided between Germany and the United

States, with Great Britain receiving territorial compensation elsewhere in the Pacific.

Cleveland's Samoan diplomacy was both a success and a failure. He helped to deter German ambition while avoiding war; but if his primary aim was to assure meaningful autonomy for the island government, he could only claim to have delayed its destruction. While Cleveland was sincere in his initial declarations in behalf of Samoan independence, his primary objective was German recognition of American rights. There is an obvious parallel with his diplomacy in the Alaskan fur-seals dispute. In both cases a supposedly moral cause was translated into a question of national pride.

Cleveland's determination to pursue a diplomacy of moral purpose had a longer duration when he sought to overturn a revolution and restore a monarch in the Central Pacific.

It was not a foregone conclusion that Cleveland would oppose the annexation of the Hawaiian Islands after the Hawaiian "revolution" of January 1893. In his first administration he had urged Congress to renew the commercial reciprocity agreement with the Hawaiian monarchy and had written that "those islands, in the highway of Oriental and Australasian traffic, are virtually an outpost of American commerce and a stepping-stone to the growing trade of the Pacific."[19] Secretary Bayard had negotiated a treaty of friendship and commerce with the kingdom of Hawaii, renewing for seven years the reciprocity agreement, and had included a proviso whereby the United States received permission to establish a naval base at Pearl Harbor on the island of Oahu. This treaty received Senate confirmation on 20 January 1887. A few months later, Cleveland and Bayard indicated to the Hawaiian monarch their opposition to a proposed loan by the British government to the Hawaiian royal treasury. To receive this loan, Hawaii would have to pledge governmental revenues as security, and such an arrangement might introduce an unwarranted element of "foreign" influence in the islands. The United States must maintain its paramount influence in Hawaii, and the kingdom of Hawaii must remain independent.

At no point did Cleveland express a wish that commercial predominance be followed by territorial annexation. To annex territory some two thousand miles from the North American continent was unwise and unnecessary. Cleveland favored a close commercial connection between the United States and Hawaii; a formal reciprocity agreement served to certify an economic bond forged by the free-enterprise operations of Hawaiian planters and United States mercantile interests. He was not, however, a closet annexationist. He wrote to Carl Schurz in March 1893 that he did not regard "annexation in all circumstances" as necessarily dangerous; but if ever the islands were to be annexed, it must be at the request of the Hawaiian people, without any indication of pressure or interference by officials of the United States government. Even were the Hawaiian people to request annexation, "we ought to stop and look and think."[20] From the beginning, Cleveland had strong doubts that the annexation treaty that was fashioned by the Harrison administration and the Provisional Government of the Hawaiian revolutionaries represented the will of the Hawaiian people or was innocent of collusion by agents of the United States government.

The Hawaiian revolution of January 1893 was not directed from Washington, and it came as a pleasant surprise to the administration of Benjamin Harrison, but there was undeniable collaboration between the rebel leaders and the U.S. minister to Hawaii, John L. Stevens. Less a revolution than a coup, the bloodless rebellion was planned by a group of American-born planters and their commercial allies, who feared that the Hawaiian monarch, Queen Liliuokalani, was preparing to abrogate the Hawaiian Constitution of 1887, reduce the political influence of the white minority, and return the islands to native rule. Forming a secret Committee of Safety, under the leadership of the wealthy planter Sanford B. Dole, these men laid plans to overthrow the monarchy and to seek annexation to the United States. In annexation they saw political safety and economic profit. The McKinley Tariff of 1890 had put an end to the preferred position of Hawaiian sugar in the American market and given domestic producers a subsidy of two cents a pound. Were the islands to be annexed to the United States, the Hawaiian sugar planters would enjoy that subsidy, while they and other propertied white men would continue to dominate the political and economic development of the islands. If their motives were selfish, their ambition was understandable. Although Americans in the islands represented less than 20 percent of the population, they controlled better than 80 percent of its wealth. In such a situation, friction between the native monarch and the white masters of the Hawaiian sugar economy was inevitable. The Committee of Safety only dared move from conspiracy to revolution, however, when its members were certain that they would receive the assistance of the United States minister in Honolulu.

John L. Stevens had made no secret of his wish to see the United

States acquire the Hawaiian Islands, and when Sanford Dole and his cohorts began their revolution, Stevens ordered naval marines from the U.S.S. *Boston* to land and occupy key governmental buildings in the capital, allegedly the better to protect the lives and property of United States citizens. The strategic placement of the marines paralyzed resistance by the queen's forces and was crucial to the success of the coup. Stevens, on behalf of the United States, recognized the legitimacy of Dole's Provisional Government and, on his own authority, he proclaimed Hawaii a United States protectorate and ordered the United States flag flown from all governmental buildings. Queen Liliuokalani, under virtual house arrest, declared she had been overthrown by the superior military power of the United States government.

Five days after the successful coup, commissioners of the Provisional Government set sail for Washington, reaching their destination on February 3. They were met with open arms by the Harrison administration, and in less than three weeks a treaty of annexation had been drawn up and submitted to the United States Senate with a request for immediate action. If Harrison wished to present Cleveland with a *fait accompli*, he was disappointed. When Grover Cleveland took the oath of office for a second time on 4 March 1893, the treaty was still in the Foreign Relations Committee. After consulting with Secretary Gresham, Cleveland recalled the treaty from the Senate on March 9. The momentum for United States annexation of the Hawaiian Islands ground to a halt.

Cleveland did not publicly announce his opposition to annexation for another nine months. But by his decision to withdraw the treaty, he indicated his doubts about its wisdom; and by his concurrent decision to send former Congressman James H. Blount of Georgia to Hawaii on a fact-finding mission, he indicated his suspicions respecting the popular origins of the Hawaiian revolution.[21] Grover Cleveland recognized that annexation had considerable popular support, and he would proceed with caution. From the beginning, however, there was a strong probability that Cleveland would oppose annexation unless Commissioner Blount discovered that Stevens had played no part in the overthrow of a government with which the United States had formal diplomatic relations and unless Blount found solid evidence that annexation to the United States was the wish of a large majority of the Hawaiian population. In selecting Blount as investigator and executive agent, Cleveland signaled his doubt that Blount's report would reach either conclusion. Blount, when a member of the House Foreign Affairs Committee, had opposed overseas territorial expansion as well as the construction of a transisthmian canal.

Once established in Hawaii, Blount made an honest effort to interview proannexationists as well as their opponents, but his voluminous report of July 25 came down hard against Minister Stevens and U.S. acquisition of Hawaii. He concluded that a large majority of native Hawaiians opposed annexation, that the revolutionary leaders sought annexation for their own economic gain, and that Stevens had been in collusion with the revolutionary leaders from beginning to end.[22]

Blount's report confirmed Cleveland's earlier suspicions respecting a treaty that he associated with the dangerous adventurism of the Harrison-Blaine administration. While Cleveland would appear to delay and hesitate during the fall of 1893, his uncertainty did not concern the issue of annexation but whether to insist upon the resignation of the Provisional Government and the restoration of the Hawaiian monarch. Always ready to find a moral component in a foreign-policy question, Cleveland was prepared to accept the judgment of Secretary Gresham that Stevens's conduct had been shameful and, insofar as he had acted in the name of the United States government, required the government to see that justice was done to Queen Liliuokalani. He also found persuasive, however, the opinion of Attorney General Olney, who in a memorandum to Gresham had made the point that the United States should be as concerned for "securing justice and fair play" for the members and adherents of the Provisional Government as for "the restoring to power of the Queen's constitutional government."[23]

Cleveland was convinced of the importance of ethics for international relations, but the conflicting advice of Gresham and Olney suggested that the moral issue was not as simple as he would have wished. He agreed with Gresham when the latter wrote: "Should not the great wrong done to a feeble but independent State by an abuse of the authority of the United States be undone by restoring the legitimate government?"[24] And yet he agreed as well with Olney's conviction that the United States government had the responsibility of assuring amnesty for the Hawaiian revolutionaries and preventing the despoliation of their property. Liliuokalani must receive justice, and she must promise to behave in a manner befitting a constitutional ruler. Nor would it be morally right to send troops to Hawaii to restore the queen by force of arms. This would exceed the authority of the executive, and the incitement of civil war in the islands would be of little service to the native population.[25]

Cleveland's initial answer to the dilemma was inspired by a large measure of wishful thinking. He instructed the new U.S. minister to Hawaii, Albert S. Willis, to obtain a promise from the queen that she would show clemency toward the Provisional Government and recognize their acts while in power. Willis should then request the Provisional Government and its president, Sanford Dole, to abdicate in favor of the queen and accept the restoration of the Hawaiian monarchy. As might have been predicted, Willis met with obstinacy on both sides. Liliuokalani spoke of a legal right to behead her enemies, and Sanford Dole declared that he would not accept the interference of the United States government in the internal affairs of Hawaii. Dole insisted that the only alternatives for the Cleveland administration were the annexation of the islands or the recognition of his government.

It was now that the influence of Olney overrode that of Gresham. Taking the advice of his attorney general, Cleveland decided to find a solution to the Hawaiian problem by submitting the problem to Congress.[26] It was an abdication of executive responsibility and, in the outcome, a mistake. Cleveland worked long and hard on his congressional message of 18 December 1893. One of his more interesting state papers, it concluded with an anticlimactic admission of failure.

Cleveland began his six-thousand-word message with a review of the history of the Hawaiian revolution, the part played by Secretary Stevens, and the administration's decision to reject the annexation request of the Provisional Government "under the circumstances disclosed." The Provisional Government owed its existence to armed intervention by the military forces of the United States. Annexation would be not only contrary to our tradition of restricting national expansion to the continent of North America but would also represent acquiescence in the wrongful collaboration of an agent of the U.S. government with an oligarchic council that did not represent the Hawaiian people. Injustice committed against the legitimate government of Queen Liliuokalani must be redressed:

> . . . the United States cannot be properly put in the position of countenancing a wrong after its commission any more than of consenting to it in advance. On that ground it cannot allow itself to refuse to redress an injury inflicted through an abuse of power by officers clothed with its authority and wearing its uniform; and on the same ground, if a feeble but friendly state is in danger of being robbed of its independence and its sovereignty by a mis-

> use of the name and power of the United States, the United States cannot fail to vindicate its honor and its sense of justice by an earnest effort to make all possible reparation.

Cleveland then offered a detailed description of the failure of his efforts to gain a promise of amnesty from the queen or an agreement by the Provisional Government to accept the reinstatement of the monarchy. He was obliged, he concluded, to refer the subject to "the extended powers and wide discretion of the Congress." He pledged the cooperation of his administration with any solution devised by Congress consistent with "American honor, integrity, and morality."[27]

By submitting the Hawaiian problem to Congress, Cleveland made likely continued debate within and between the major parties, but he did not ensure a solution that would demonstrate the superior morality of American diplomacy. John Morgan, the Democratic chairman of the Senate Foreign Relations Committee, an expansionist and a party enemy of Grover Cleveland, held lengthy hearings; but the committee's final report pleased neither Democrats nor Republicans. Various resolutions were introduced in the Senate and the House, but they found common ground only in their recommendation to let the Dole government remain in peace. The nearest that Cleveland's Hawaiian diplomacy came to receiving even limited congressional support was the passage in May 1894 of the Turpie resolution in the Senate. That resolution declared that no further move should be made to annex the Hawaiian Islands, no attempt should be made to restore the Hawaiian monarchy or disturb the existing government, and all foreign governments should be warned not to intervene in Hawaiian affairs. In effect, Congress advised the Cleveland administration to recognize the white minority government. Grover Cleveland reluctantly obeyed the advice.

In August 1894 the U.S.S. *Philadelphia* was recalled from Honolulu, and in that same month, Cleveland addressed Sanford Dole as "Great and Good Friend," acknowledged Dole's proclamation establishing the Republic of Hawaii, and offered best wishes "for your personal prosperity."[28] Cleveland's acquiescence was balanced, however, by a desire to have the last word. When Senator Morgan and others urged the construction of a cable between San Francisco and Honolulu, Cleveland expressed his determination to veto any such appropriation. He wrote to his friend Thomas Bayard: "I do not believe we should in the present circumstances boom the annexation craze by entering upon Government cable building."[29]

Cleveland's Hawaiian diplomacy offers a study in frustration, the frustration of a powerful country in which public opinion is divided. Does it also illustrate an administration misled by moralism to ignore the hard realities of the national interest?

Most students of American foreign policy would give Cleveland credit for honorable motives and a sincere determination to find a solution respectful of the nation's reputation and diplomatic traditions. But he is frequently accused of having pursued an impractical policy and of having confused moral scruples with a viable diplomatic option.[30] R. Hal Williams has characterized Cleveland's Hawaiian diplomacy as "a mixture of admirable principle and blundering naïveté."[31] Cleveland's failure, however, was only partial. Although he failed to restore the status quo ante in Honolulu, he did have the satisfaction of postponing the march of empire in the Pacific. "Political realism" has no single definition. Cleveland defined the term in relation to the American past, and the events of the following decade made such a definition appear old-fashioned if not reactionary. Cleveland cannot be held responsible, however, for having failed to predict the aftermath of the War of 1898. If his Hawaiian diplomacy in 1893/94 was guilty of hesitancy at points and wishful thinking quite often, it had a quality of knight-errantry that was agreeably free of national greed or personal ambition.

Cleveland's personality was one that encouraged the belief that U.S. diplomacy should focus on questions of justice and honor. He never saw diplomacy as a matter of conflicting rights, of differing shades of gray. For Cleveland there had to be—whether dealing with Britain in the fur-seals controversy, Germany in the Samoan tangle, or the Provisional Government in Hawaii—a right side and a wrong side. With little effort, he always saw himself monopolizing the former. That the right often matched the self-interest of the United States was but a pleasant coincidence. He insisted that he was concerned only with preserving the nation's honor and international respect for the authority of the American Republic. It was a position that could inspire charges of hypocrisy then and later, and never more than in Cleveland's diplomacy toward Latin America and his controversial interference in the Venezuelan boundary dispute.

11
★ ★ ★ ★ ★

CLEVELAND'S DIPLOMACY
2: RELATIONS WITH
LATIN AMERICA

While Cleveland and Secretary Bayard paid only fitful attention to Latin America during the first administration, that region
often appeared to dominate the diplomacy of the second administration, as Secretary of State Gresham and his successor, Richard Olney,
worried over events in Brazil, Nicaragua, Venezuela, and Cuba.
Cleveland's diplomatic objectives did not change, however, as a result
either of the depression crisis of the nineties or of the growing interest in foreign markets exhibited by editors, publicists, and the newly
formed National Association of Manufacturers. In neither administration did Cleveland pursue a policy of territorial or economic expan-
sionism in Latin America; in both administrations he expressed a
determination to prevent foreign interference in the Western Hemisphere and to sustain the diplomatic influence of the United States.
Events during the second administration offered more opportunities
to exhibit the latter aim, but it was not absent during the years of
Cleveland's first term.

During his first term, Cleveland's interest in Latin America was
confined to the Caribbean and Central America, and even there it
was sporadic, centering chiefly around the issues of a future isthmian canal and commercial reciprocity.

As noted in the previous chapter, Cleveland withdrew from Senate consideration the Frelinghuysen-Zavala treaty, which would have given the United States authority to build a canal in Nicaragua and promised that the United States would guarantee that nation's territorial integrity. Cleveland notified the Senate that he did not favor the "acquisition of new and distant territory or the incorporation of remote interests with our own." While "the general project of connecting the two oceans by means of a canal" was to be encouraged, it should never become "a point of invitation for hostilities or a prize for warlike ambition."[1]

Cleveland was not as articulate in explaining his objectives as in noting his objections. He wished no foreign nation—and especially Great Britain—to build a canal in Central America, and he wished no unilateral action by the United States that could incur diplomatic entanglement; but whether he wished to see an internationalized canal or a United States canal neutralized by international agreement was never made clear by either Cleveland or Secretary Bayard. They were prepared to give indirect warning to Britain that it not further extend its influence in areas around the United States; and they favored the modernization of the United States Navy for purposes of diplomatic as well as coastal defense; but both were men of peace who seem to have felt that it was only necessary for the United States to indicate its disapproval in order to prevent foreign aggression in the Caribbean area. In the relative diplomatic quiet of the 1880s, that belief was not tested.

Only on one occasion during Cleveland's first administration did he order military intervention. When a minor revolt broke out in the Colombian province of Panama in April 1885, Cleveland ordered that a small detachment of naval marines land to restore order and "assure the neutrality of the isthmus," under the vague authority of an old treaty of 1846 between the United States and New Granada, the parent state of Colombia. The naval officers, probably without Cleveland's knowledge, went well beyond their instructions and, in collusion with the Colombian officials, rounded up the rebels and helped assure their quick defeat.[2]

Cleveland's intervention in Panama did not demonstrate a wish to strengthen the ties of the United States and Colombia. The Arthur administration had, in its last days, fashioned a draft for a commercial reciprocity treaty with Colombia. It was allowed to gather dust, as was a similar draft treaty with El Salvador. Cleveland and Bayard rejected commercial reciprocity as an instrument of U.S. diplomatic policy in Caribbean America. Limited reciprocity treaties with the

Dominican Republic and the Spanish Antilles were withdrawn from the Senate, and a treaty with Mexico lapsed when no positive action was taken on the enabling legislation.[3] The Republican origin of these treaties and their possible negative effect on Democratic efforts for general tariff reduction were of influence in persuading Cleveland to bury them, but there was as well his fear that they represented the beginnings of a policy of establishing economic protectorates in the Caribbean. Increasing United States economic influence in that region was not to be discouraged, but it was best left to the natural laws of trade and the initiative of private capitalists and exporters.

Cleveland's sole effort during his first administration to promote that initiative by official diplomacy was his decision—at congressional urging—to issue a call for a Pan-American conference "to discuss sundry important monetary and commercial topics" and policies encouraging "freer mutual exchange of products."[4] This call was announced in Cleveland's annual message of December 1888; and by the time the delegates had assembled in Washington in the spring of 1889, the Harrison administration was in office.

Walter Quintin Gresham, Cleveland's secretary of state from March 1893 to May 1895, wrote on several occasions about the desirability of increasing United States exports to Latin America and elsewhere.[5] Together with Secretary of the Treasury Carlisle, Gresham apparently saw expanded markets abroad as a partial solution to economic depression at home. There was little correlation, however, between Gresham's economic analysis and the Latin American diplomacy of Gresham and Grover Cleveland.

During a brief rebellion by promonarchists in the Republic of Brazil, Gresham refused to recognize the belligerency of the rebels or to honor their blockade of Rio de Janeiro. Under Cleveland's instructions, he ordered U.S. naval vessels to the harbor of Rio to assure the right of American exporters to land goods and continue trade with agents of the Republican government. Although the dispatch of warships can be seen as the action of a government determined to safeguard its foreign markets, a more persuasive explanation is that Cleveland suspected that the British were encouraging the rebels and was opposed to the restoration of a monarchical government in diplomatic debt to Great Britain.[6] On two occasions Nicaragua created some small measure of concern for Cleveland and Gresham, first when the Nicaraguan government quarreled with Great

Britain over the Miskito Indian reservation, and then when the British briefly occupied the port of Corinto to punish the Nicaraguans for imprisoning several British citizens and refusing to pay the expected indemnity. In neither case did Cleveland and Gresham do more than indicate a passing worry that Britain might expand its territorial claims in Central America, and in neither case did Cleveland and Gresham indicate a wish to expand the negligible amount of exports that U.S. manufacturers shipped to Nicaragua. Only in Venezuela did Gresham suggest an association between diplomacy and commerce, when he protested an effort by that country to prevent smuggling by closing the mouth of the Orinoco River. A note of diplomatic protest was sufficient to reopen the river to foreign trade.

When complying with Gresham's request, Venezuela took the opportunity to remind the United States that Britain, were it ever to gain control of the Orinoco, might not prove as obliging. It was some months before Washington became convinced that the British entertained such ambitions and that they represented a threat not only to the few Americans with trading interests in Venezuela but also to the Monroe Doctrine and U.S. diplomatic authority in the Western Hemisphere. Such convictions inspired the most publicized and controversial episode of Latin American diplomacy during the Cleveland years: United States intervention in the British-Venezuelan boundary dispute.

The chronological narrative of the Venezuelan boundary dispute is easily described; more difficult are questions concerning the purpose and objectives of United States intervention and the significance of the Venezuelan Affair for the history of U.S. foreign policy.

At the end of the Napoleonic era, Great Britain acquired a portion of Guiana on the northern coast of South America. The boundary between British Guiana and its western neighbor, Venezuela, was in dispute throughout the nineteenth century, despite the effort in 1841 of a British subject, Sir Robert Schomburgk, to chart the boundary line through the jungle territory. The Venezuelans refused to accept the Schomburgk line and made claims to territory hundreds of miles to its east. The Venezuelans coupled their claims with offers to submit the matter to international arbitration. The British insisted that they would only consent to arbitrate certain disputed areas west of the Schomburgk line, where there had never been any British settlement. The Venezuelans on several occasions had asked the United States to take up their cause with the British and to serve as arbitrator. Convinced that any arbitral panel would take the easy path of "splitting the difference," the British refused all suggestions of United States mediation or arbitration. By the date of Cleveland's second inaugural, Venezuela and Great Britain had broken diplomatic relations and had extended their boundary claims. Feelings of injury on both sides were accentuated by the discovery of gold in a small section of the disputed territory.

Between March 1893 and June 1895, Cleveland gradually became convinced that the dispute embodied the danger of a war between Great Britain and Venezuela, that the British were aggressively extending their territorial claims to embrace the mouth of the Orinoco River, and that it was the duty of the United States, in defense of the Monroe Doctrine, to force Britain to submit the dispute to arbitration. Various factors encouraged Cleveland to adopt a personal interest in the Venezuelan question and to take umbrage at what he judged to be the unreasonable obstinacy of the British. Among those factors was a former United States minister to Caracas, William L. Scruggs. Scruggs, now a paid propagandist for the Republic of Venezuela, visited Cleveland in the winter and spring of 1895 and sought to convince him that the imperial ambitions of Britain in her quarrel with Venezuela were a threat to the noncolonization prohibition of the Monroe Doctrine. In his annual message of December 1894, Cleveland had been content to renew an earlier U.S. suggestion for international arbitration; but in March 1895, influenced by the warnings of Scruggs and anxious to head off the jingo agitation of certain Republican congressmen, Cleveland decided to hold a special cabinet meeting to discuss the Venezuelan boundary dispute. At this meeting, which was attended by Gresham, Carlisle, Lamont, and Olney, Cleveland raised for the first time the issue of whether British claims—if pursued by diplomatic pressure or military force— would represent a violation of the injunctions of President Monroe. Cleveland was as yet undecided on this point, but he instructed Gresham to prepare a detailed report on the history of the controversy and the best means for putting an end to a stubborn dispute that had festered for more than half a century.

Gresham began to prepare his report, but he soon fell ill with pleurisy and died on May 28. Eleven days later, Cleveland appointed Richard Olney as Gresham's successor and instructed him to complete and revise Gresham's report in the form of a diplomatic dispatch to London. Olney's objective was similar to that of Gresham, but his tactical approach and literary style were not. Although he pursued the diplomatic procedure of addressing the British government by means of a letter of instruction to Ambassador Bayard to be read to the British foreign minister, he cast his letter in the language of a prosecutor's brief.

As Olney prepared his draft, he was apparently unaware of its contradictions of purpose. He was determined simultaneously to persuade and to censure the British government. While insisting that the United States had no intention of prejudging the issue, he implied that the British claims were exaggerated and inspired by unworthy motives. Offering the services of the United States as an impartial arbitrator, he insisted that the national self-interest of the United States required its intervention and that U.S. intervention found full and sufficient justification in the Monroe Doctrine.[7]

Olney had some doubts as to whether Cleveland would accept his elastic interpretation of the Monroe Doctrine, but those doubts proved groundless. Cleveland and Olney had summer homes at Cape Cod, and it was there that Cleveland read Olney's draft and gave warm approval to what he called "your twenty-inch gun." Cleveland carefully revised Olney's draft but in no way did he moderate its insistence on the relevance of the Monroe Doctrine to a boundary dispute in South America.

As revised and approved by Cleveland, Olney's famous dispatch of 20 July 1895 began with a selective historical account of the boundary dispute which emphasized the "many earnest and persistent efforts of Venezuela" to reach an agreement and the continuing refusal of Great Britain to arbitrate "except upon the condition of a renunciation of a large part of the Venezuelan claim and of a concession to herself of a large part of the territory in controversy." He traced the readiness of the United States, over several administrations, to offer its good offices and to express its concern "whenever new alleged instances of British aggression upon Venezuelan territory" were brought to its notice. The United States had made known to Great Britain and the world that the controversy involved "both its honor and its interests." It was well known that under international law a third nation could "justly interpose in a controversy" to prevent a result that could menace "its own integrity, tranquility, or welfare"; and this justification was given specific substance by the prohibitions of the Monroe Doctrine.

The Monroe Doctrine of 1823 proclaimed that no European state should be allowed to "deprive an American state of the right . . . of self-government and of shaping for itself its own political fortunes and destinies." Threats against the territorial independence of any American state involved "the safety and welfare of the United States" and gave warrant for its interposition:

> The states of America, South as well as North, by geographic proximity, by natural sympathy, by similarity of governmental constitutions, are friends and allies, commercially and politically, of the United States. To allow the subjugation of any of them by an European power is . . . to completely reverse that situation and signifies the loss of all the advantages incident to their natural relation to us. . . .
>
> To-day the United States is practically sovereign on this continent, and its fiat is law upon the subjects to which it confines its interposition . . . its infinite resources combined with its isolated position render it master of the situation and practically invulnerable as against any or all the other powers.
>
> All the advantages of this superiority are at once imperiled if the principle be admitted that European powers may convert American states into colonies or provinces of their own.

Having proven the continuing vitality of the Monroe Doctrine, Olney declared that it only remained to demonstrate that the boundary dispute between Venezuela and Great Britain did represent a threat to Venezuelan territorial integrity and independence. The demonstration was easily made: "Though the dispute relates to a boundary line, yet, as it is between states, it necessarily imports political control to be lost by one party and gained by the other. The political control at stake, too, is of no mean importance, but concerns a domain of great extent."

Being entitled "to resent and resist any sequestration of Venezuelan soil by Great Britain," the United States had the right to know whether such sequestration had occurred. The only way that it could gain that satisfaction was to insist that the merits of the boundary question be determined by impartial arbitration. The United States must require "a definite decision" from Her Majesty's government, whether it "will consent or will decline to submit the Venezuelan boundary question in its entirety to impartial arbitration."[8]

Olney's dispatch was a strange mixture of national self-interest and braggadocio. Olney and his chief could have written a shorter and better message to the same purpose. Their aim was to persuade Britain to arbitrate its boundary dispute with Venezuela "in its entirety" and to inform Britain that the United States had a right to intervene in the dispute to secure that objective. There was no need to offer the judgment that "any permanent political union between an European and an American state" was "unnatural and inexpedient"; and the boast that the United States was "sovereign on this continent" and that its fiat was the equivalent of international law was foolish and self-defeating. To say that Olney wished to drape his message in patriotic rhetoric the better to end any threat of interference by congressional jingoes is to offer an explanation without an excuse. Cleveland, however, found such passages unexceptionable.

Olney's "twenty-inch gun" of July 20 met long delay and subsequent censure from the British government and Lord Salisbury. It was not until December 7 that Sir Julian Pauncefote, the British ambassador to Washington, delivered Salisbury's note to the secretary. Salisbury offered the opinion that the Monroe Doctrine had no standing in international law and no relevance to a boundary dispute in South America. Colonel Monroe had never thought to claim the "novel prerogative" of demanding that a boundary controversy between a European and an American state be submitted to arbitration at the fiat of the United States. Salisbury then proceeded to reiterate the longstanding British position that the boundary claims of Venezuela were without foundation and that it would be unjust to residents of British Guiana, who had long been accustomed to British law and justice, to place their fate in the hands of an international tribunal. Salisbury's tone was that of the peremptory schoolmaster trying—with fading patience—to correct the ignorance of dullards in Washington. If he had wished to write with the sole purpose of exciting the increased irritation of Grover Cleveland, he could not have written to greater effect.[9]

Cleveland decided to send to Congress a special message, while forwarding copies of Olney's note of July 20 and Salisbury's reply. He would seek a showdown and, in the process, play the dangerous game of trying to utilize the Anglophobia of his political enemies while blocking congressional interference and coercing the British to accept the peaceful path of international arbitration.

Cleveland's message to Congress of 17 December 1895 offered a lengthy account of the controversy and of earlier American efforts to seek its solution, and bluntly declared that British rejection of the Venezuelan request for an arbitral settlement of the entire disputed area represented a serious threat to the Monroe Doctrine:

> If a European power, by an extension of its boundaries, takes possession of the territory of one of our neighboring Republics against its will and in derogation of its rights, it is difficult to see why to that extent such European power does not thereby attempt

to extend its system of Government to that portion of this continent which is thus taken. This is the precise action which President Monroe declared to be "dangerous to our peace and safety," and it can make no difference whether the European system is extended by an advance of frontier or otherwise.

That being the case, the United States must insist on the right to determine the respective justice of the boundary claims of Great Britain and Venezuela. The president had decided to appoint a commission to "make the necessary investigation," and he was now requesting Congress to make "an adequate appropriation" for the commission's expenses. When the commission made its report,

> it will in my opinion be the duty of the United States to resist by every means in its power as a willful aggression upon its rights and interests the appropriation by Great Britain of any lands or the exercise of governmental jurisdiction over any territory which . . . we have determined of right belongs to Venezuela. . . . In making these recommendations I am fully alive to the responsibility incurred, and keenly realize all the consequences that may follow.
>
> I am, nevertheless, firm in my conviction that . . . there is no calamity which a great nation can invite which equals that which follows from a supine submission to wrong and injustice, and the consequent loss of national self-respect and honor, beneath which are shielded and defended a people's safety and greatness.[10]

Reaction to Cleveland's message was both widespread and predictable. It was applauded by Congress, and the appropriation for an investigating commission was passed with record speed. It caused a brief panic on Wall Street, however, and a run on gold, much to the consternation of Secretary of the Treasury Carlisle.[11] The financial community, more than the spokesmen for the nation's manufacturers, was worried by the possibility of war and its impact on the gold reserve and the national debt.[12] A majority of the nation's editors were ready to accept Cleveland's position respecting the relevance of the Monroe Doctrine, but such long-time Cleveland supporters as the editors of the *Springfield* (Mass.) *Republican* and the *Nation* chastised the president for his belligerence. For Edwin Godkin, Cleveland had joined the jingoes and was risking a war that could only bring comfort to Irish-Americans and free-silver men.

Cleveland was privately worried by the war fever that he had inspired, particularly because it was most apparent among such political enemies as "agrarian radicals" and Republican congressmen. He had no doubts as to the moral rightness of his message to Congress, but his wish for a quick and peaceful settlement was heightened by the commendation of political enemies and a brief Wall Street panic. He wanted to avoid further confrontation, but he would not back down.

After a spasm of self-righteous belligerence, the Salisbury ministry decided that there was little long-term profit in further controversy with the United States. Worried by the colonial adventures of the German kaiser and wary of global overcommitment, it had reason to avoid the possibility of a war with the United States over the distribution of jungle terrain in South America. Like Cleveland, however, the British were reluctant to retreat from their public position or to appear to sacrifice national honor. For the next few months, both sides sought ways to compromise substance while maintaining principle. They utilized various unofficial intermediaries as a way of testing the likelihood of discovering areas of flexibility. Although this informal diplomacy produced no solution, it provided a valuable cooling-off period; and by the time official negotiations resumed, both sides exhibited better temper.[13]

Initially, Salisbury sought to "reserve" from international arbitration all areas settled by British residents, but he finally declared his willingness to reserve only those areas that had been settled for over fifty years. Cleveland and Olney initially refused to allow any limitation on the authority of an arbitral panel, but finally accepted exclusion of areas settled for more than fifty years.[14] They wisely accepted an accommodation that allowed Britain to maintain diplomatic dignity while the United States achieved its main objective, a permanent settlement of the boundary dispute by the instrument of international arbitration.[15]

Once the British had agreed to arbitration and Cleveland to the fifty-year exclusion, all that remained was to block out a formal agreement between Pauncefote and Olney and then coerce the Republic of Venezuela to incorporate its terms in a treaty to be signed by representatives of Great Britain and Venezuela. On 12 November 1896, Olney and Pauncefote signed the "heads" of an arbitration treaty. There would be a tribunal of five members—two Americans, two Englishmen, and one other—and the tribunal would have final authority to determine the boundary between Venezuela and British Guiana. The Venezuelans made a small effort in behalf of national pride by insisting on the right to appoint one of the tribunal members. Once they had agreed not to select a citizen of Venezuela, the way was cleared for the ratification of the British-Venezuelan treaty of February 1897.[16]

The arbitral panel met in Paris and on 3 October 1899—thirty-one months after Cleveland's retirement from public life—submitted its report. It supported Venezuela's claim to the ownership of the mouth of the Orinoco River but otherwise largely confirmed the Schomburgk line. Britain did not receive territory to match its maximum claim, but it did receive an award that closely conformed to its minimum claim. It was an anticlimactic conclusion to a major crisis in Anglo-American diplomacy.

A description of the chronological sequence of events has, of necessity, alluded to questions of rationale, motives, and justification; but these questions deserve more extended analysis.

Cleveland's rationale for U.S. intervention in the Venezuelan boundary dispute was most succinctly expressed in a letter he wrote to Ambassador Thomas Bayard. Bayard had raised Olney's ire by appearing to soften the U.S. position in his interviews with the British foreign minister and had indicated to Cleveland his fear that the administration was taking too belligerent a position towards Great Britain. Cleveland had a real affection for Bayard and was anxious to convince him that the administration's course was right and just. His letter was written not for publication or to thwart the interference of congressional jingoes but to convince an old friend of the relevance of the Monroe Doctrine to a boundary dispute between an American state and a European power and the importance of upholding the Monroe Doctrine for the defense of the United States. Cleveland emphasized that he was pursuing American, not Venezuelan, objectives. The Monroe Doctrine was vital to the security of the United States and to its proper diplomatic hegemony in the New World: "In an application of the Monroe Doctrine, though another country may give the *occasion*, we are . . . not looking after *its* interests but *our own*. . . . I am entirely clear that the Doctrine is not obsolete, and it should be defended and maintained for its value and importance *to our government and welfare*."[17]

Historians of the Venezuelan controversy have agreed that Cleveland was primarily concerned, not with the "interests" of the Republic of Venezuela, "but *our own*." They have differed sharply, however, over what motivated Cleveland's determination to protect American interests and which particular interests he had in mind.

Three major interpretations have emerged, which can be classified by the adjectives *economic, political,* and *strategic.*

Currently, the most popular interpretation emphasizes Cleveland's concern for the economic interests of the United States. A simplistic paraphrase of this interpretation would run as follows: Cleveland's belligerent interposition into the Venezuelan boundary dispute was inspired primarily by his evaluation of U.S. economic needs and power. He appreciated the importance of the Orinoco River for the control of trade in a large area of South America and was convinced of the importance of foreign markets as a solution for the economic depression at home. Concerned that the British would gain control of the commerce of the Orinoco basin and thereby limit the necessary expansion of United States exports, he acted to prevent the threat of British commercial domination and to promote the commercial hegemony of the United States in Latin America. Venezuela must own the land at the river's mouth, and Latin America must acknowledge the United States as its protector if the natural role of Latin America as a market for United States goods was to be assured. It was not a coincidence that Cleveland revived the Monroe Doctrine during the worst year of the United States economic depression: the Monroe Doctrine was consciously used in support of the economic diplomacy of the Cleveland administration in Latin America.[18]

The economic interpretation is possibly more ingenious than persuasive. Cleveland and Olney undoubtedly defined the danger of aggressive British colonialism in economic as well as strategic terms, but Olney advocated overseas economic expansion only after he left office, and Cleveland was never convinced of the necessity or the propriety of government-directed trade expansion. Cleveland's primary concern was not Venezuelan ownership of the several tributaries that formed the principal mouth of the Orinoco but British acknowledgment that the United States had the right to require arbitration. The peremptory treatment that Cleveland and Olney accorded to the Venezuelans was not that of market experts anxious to gain the gratitude of Latin American customers. Nor could they have been so naïve as to believe that any particular boundary settlement would deny the British their commercial bases in the Caribbean area or inspire an explosion of trade between the United States and Latin America sufficient to cure the economic depression at home before the Cleveland administration left office.[19]

The "political interpretation" emphasizes Cleveland's desire to reestablish his political popularity by distracting his countrymen from domestic troubles with an exercise in flag waving and saber rattling. Determined to unify and regain control of his party and to prevent Republican success in 1896, Cleveland engineered the Venezuelan crisis as an election maneuver.[20] This interpretation can be attacked on several counts: those who most applauded Cleveland's special message to Congress were Republican expansionists and Democratic-Populist silverites, and they would provide no assistance to Cleveland either in reuniting his party or in reclaiming its leadership. Cleveland's timing was not that of a man who was plotting to gain victory for Cleveland Democracy in the election of 1896. Had partisan strategy provided his primary motive, he would have taken an earlier opportunity to whip up a diplomatic crisis and would not have suggested in his special message an investigating commission, for the time-consuming deliberations of the latter would undoubtedly extend past the election campaign.[21]

The "strategic interpretation" is chiefly associated with the writings of George Berkeley Young. Young believes that Cleveland's primary motive was to strengthen and extend the authority of the United States in the Western Hemisphere. In Young's opinion, the "Olney Corollary" was "the ultimate expression of determination by the strongest power in the American continents to maintain the inviolability of those continents."[22] This is both accurate and insufficient. Neither Cleveland nor Olney was a student of Capt. Alfred Thayer Mahan; and although both wished to promote United States diplomatic hegemony in the New World, neither thought in geopolitical terms or ever devised a hemispheric political strategy.

A satisfactory explanation of Cleveland's motives and intentions must take into consideration not only his fears respecting the expansion of British economic and strategic power in the New World and his association of U.S. national security and U.S. hemispheric predominance but also his personal temperament and his readiness to resent presumed slights against the national honor. Cleveland's Venezuelan policy was not an aberration; it was of a piece with his German diplomacy in Samoa and his British diplomacy in the waters off Alaska. Cleveland was not a jingo, but he frequently displayed the old-fashioned assertive nationalism of his hero Andrew Jackson. If Cleveland had no feeling of brotherhood for the Venezuelans, he was determined that both the Monroe Doctrine and Grover Cleveland would gain the respectful acknowledgment of Lord Salisbury. Britain and all of Europe must recognize the Monroe Doctrine, which Cleveland convinced himself was as embedded in the traditions of U.S. foreign policy as Jefferson's warnings against entangling alliances. Cleveland saw himself, not as the creator of a new version of that doctrine, but as a stalwart defender of diplomatic tradition. He was only reiterating the principles established by President Monroe in regard to the relations that the United States was to bear both to Europe and South America.

Blunt and impatient, Cleveland had little talent for the tactical intricacies of Old World diplomacy. He found no difficulty in becoming as irritable and suspicious with the British as with Tammany Hall or Senator Gorman and as convinced that he had a duty to win the day for justice and morality.[23] Cleveland's Venezuelan policy was inspired by apprehensions of British ambition in the Western Hemisphere and by moral self-righteousness. His innate talent to identify his personal judgment with righteousness and truth encouraged him to confuse compromise with surrender. He did compromise on the British demand for a fifty-year exclusion, but he refused to recognize that fact; and when, years later, he wrote an account of "The Venezuela Boundary Controversy," his laborious recital was cast in the form of a patriotic morality tale.[24]

As Cleveland's motivation has been a source of controversy, so has the accuracy of his judgments in respect to the applicability of the Monroe Doctrine and the necessity of demanding an arbitral settlement even at the risk of military confrontation. Dexter Perkins, generally acknowledged as the foremost historian of the Monroe Doctrine, concludes that Cleveland's interpretation of the doctrine was "a proposition far from fully established or accepted." Perkins doubts that either the disputed title to a jungle wilderness or "possible British possession of the mouth of the Orinoco" involved "the vital interests of the United States."[25] Thomas A. Bailey believes that the Cleveland-Olney corollary "seriously overstrained the original Monroe Doctrine" and faults Cleveland for threatening war while making no preparation for fighting a war. Charles C. Tansill suggests that Cleveland was misled by Venezuelan propagandists; and Allan Nevins, an admitted champion of the Cleveland presidencies, chides Cleveland for encouraging "a primary wave of warlike enthusiasm, followed by a secondary and vaguer wave of imperialist sentiment."[26]

Cleveland had his defenders, then and later, but his critics are the more persuasive. The Cleveland-Olney corollary was an unwarranted extension of the Monroe Doctrine, and the Venezuelan diplomacy of Grover Cleveland, despite its self-assessed peaceful intentions, risked a war for which neither Cleveland nor the nation was prepared. A war with Britain over the eastern boundary of Venezuela was neither necessary for the national honor nor helpful to the national interest. It would have damaged both. The end result of Cleveland's Venezuelan diplomacy was a peaceful settlement of a long-festering dispute and an indirect recognition by Great Britain of the Monroe Doctrine. To that extent Cleveland could claim a diplomatic victory, but he had taken unnecessary risks and was the fortunate beneficiary of the longer sight of his diplomatic adversary.

It is Cleveland who should be credited with the "victory" and blamed for the "unnecessary risks." Those students of the Venezuelan affair who have suggested that a bellicose Olney misled Cleveland and persuaded him to take a course of action contrary to his pacific nature have misjudged the relationship between the president and his secretary of state as well as the constitutional temperament of Grover Cleveland.[27] Cleveland was not a man to accept unthinkingly the advice of any man. As noted earlier, Cleveland endorsed and revised Olney's note of July 20 and proved the more determined and consistent in his conviction that the Monroe Doctrine required U.S. intervention.[28] If Cleveland was misled in his Venezuelan policy, it was by his own irritability and impatience and by a readiness to associate opposition with immorality.

What was the long-term significance of Cleveland's Venezuelan diplomacy? Did it mark the elevation of the Monroe Doctrine to the rank of secular scripture for the American public? Did it result in British and European acceptance of the diplomatic dominance of the United States in the Western Hemisphere and initiate a new era in the recognition accorded to American power and influence? Did Cleveland's successors accept his interpretation of the scope of the Monroe Doctrine and shape their Latin American policies according to its demands? Was Cleveland's intervention followed by an increase in U.S. exports to Latin America and the displacement of British economic influence?

The last question can be answered quantitatively; the others, only impressionistically. The percentage of U.S. exports to Latin America rose only very slowly in the period 1896 to 1910. Britain remained the largest supplier of manufactures and, indeed, increased its share of Latin American trade during the first decade of the twentieth century.[29] It would appear that few Latin American politicians or importers found reason to praise the United States as the savior of the sovereignty and territorial independence of Venezuela.

There is no solid evidence that Theodore Roosevelt's intervention in the Dominican Republic in 1905 was influenced by the Cleveland-Olney corollary, and subsequent adminstrations found no occasion to cite it in defense of American interventions in Central America and the Caribbean. If European nations during the two decades following the Cleveland presidency took greater cognizance of U.S. influence in the Western Hemisphere, this was the natural result of the increasing economic and naval power of the United States and bore no direct correlation to Cleveland's interposition in the Venezuelan boundary dispute. It was only with the Treaty of Versailles that the Monroe Doctrine was formally recognized by the powers of Europe.

The significance of Cleveland's Venezuelan diplomacy was largely confined to its influence on the American public. Not only did it encourage an initial spasm of militant nationalism; it also had the consequence of stimulating public acceptance of the Monroe Doctrine as an eternal principle of United States foreign policy. It would be many years before Mary Baker Eddy proclaimed that she believed "in the Monroe Doctrine, in our Constitution, and in the laws of God,"[30] and there were other events and episodes that encouraged popular identification of the doctrine with the national security of the United States, but the Venezuelan diplomacy of Grover Cleveland played a major role in that development. Cleveland inaugurated a new chapter in the elevation of the Monroe Doctrine to a position of virtual sanctity for the American public.[31]

Although the Venezuelan dispute dominated the diplomacy of Cleveland's second administration, there were two other foreign-policy issues in which he took a strong interest during his last year in office: the insurrection in Cuba against Spanish misrule and the attempt to fashion a general arbitration treaty with Great Britain.

Cleveland's determination to negotiate a general arbitration treaty with Great Britain in the last year of his presidency was the result in part of a wish to improve Anglo-American relations in the aftermath of the Venezuelan controversy. Cleveland, however, had indicated an interest in the diplomatic instrument of arbitration for many years. As a lawyer, he had frequently served as a court-appointed arbiter, and he saw no reason why the sensible arrangements of the Buffalo bar could not be transferred to the international arena. At several points during his first presidential term he had indicated his belief that international arbitration was the most logical way to settle disputes that did not readily yield to bilateral negotiation. If the issue was carefully defined and the authority of the arbitrators carefully fixed by the consent of both parties, international arbitration posed no threat to national honor and sovereignty. As his second term drew to a close and as thoughts about his place in history became more frequent, Cleveland paid increased attention to the labors of such peace groups as the Lake Mohonk Conference on International Arbitration, and he instructed Olney in the spring of 1896 to sound out Sir Julian Pauncefote on Great Britain's willingness to negotiate a treaty that would provide a mechanism for the settlement of future diplomatic controversies between the two major English-speaking nations. For all of his suspicion of British colonial ambitions in Central America and the Caribbean, Cleveland was no Anglophobe; indeed, he saw Britain as the nation best able to aspire to the high standards of justice and morality characteristic of U.S. diplomacy.[32] Great Britain and the United States could jointly offer the world a model of international peace keeping.

Cleveland took a strong personal interest in the drawn-out negotiations between Olney and Pauncefote. The Cleveland Papers in the Library of Congress contain Cleveland's copy of a note from Lord Salisbury to Pauncefote; and the margins of each page bear Cleveland's penciled comments. Alongside Salisbury's complaint that compulsory arbitration could occasionally result in a miscarriage of justice, Cleveland wrote, "So must every human expedient for adjusting conflicting interests." The chief issue in dispute during these negotiations was whether the parties must agree in advance of the arbitration to be bound by its results. Olney and Cleveland insisted that they must; Pauncefote and Salisbury initially wished both parties to have the option of rejecting an arbitral award.[33]

The Olney-Pauncefote treaty, signed in Washington on 11 January 1897, represented a victory for the U.S. position: the judgment of the arbitral panel, in most cases, would be final. For a five-year period, the two nations agreed to submit to arbitration "all questions in difference between them which they may fail to adjust by diplomatic negotiations." All questions, however, would not be subject to the same arbitral procedure. When the controversy involved pecuniary claims that did not exceed £100,000, an arbitral panel of three members would have the final decision. When the pecuniary claims exceeded £100,000, a similar arbitral panel would make the initial award; but if the decision of the tribunal was not unanimous, there could be an appeal to a second tribunal of five persons. For controversies involving the disposition of territory, there would be a tribunal of six members (three from each nation), and the tribunal's decision would not be final unless accepted by at least five of the arbiters.[34]

Despite its loopholes and complexity, the Olney-Pauncefote treaty represented a significant contribution to the legalist approach to the peaceful settlement of international disputes, and Cleveland sent it to the Senate with his strong personal endorsement. He proclaimed that the treaty would assure peace between the United States and Britain and set an example to all nations: "Its ultimate ensuing benefits are not likely to be limited to the two countries immediately concerned. . . . The example set and the lesson furnished by the successful operation of this treaty are sure to be felt and taken to heart sooner or later by other nations, and will thus mark the beginning of a new epoch in civilization."[35]

For many Republican senators, Cleveland's endorsement provided ample reason to cripple the treaty with amendments and then prevent its confirmation. The Senate majority finally allowed a formal vote on the skeletal remains of the treaty on 5 May 1897, two months after the inauguration of William McKinley. The vote was 43 yeas and 26 nays, 3 votes short of the necessary two-thirds majority.[36] In retirement, Cleveland expressed to Olney his anger and disappointment.

Cleveland's relationship to the Cuban insurrection is usually treated as an unimportant prologue to the Cuban policy of the McKinley administration. It is better analyzed as an illustration of the apprehensions and ethnocentric bias that characterized the Latin American diplomacy of Grover Cleveland.

The last in a series of rebellions against Spanish misgovernment, the Cuban insurrection erupted in the early spring of 1895, inspired by an economic depression that was the product of the misguided mercantilist practices of Spain as well as the 40 percent tariff duty imposed on Cuban sugar by the Wilson-Gorman Tariff. The insurrection soon developed the usual characteristics of a guerrilla war. Atrocities were committed by both sides, with those of the Spanish troops receiving increasing attention in the American press. The Spanish attempted to deny civilian support to the rebel warriors by instituting a *reconcentrado* policy, kenneling thousands of Cuban civilians in designated areas where disease and malnutrition took a heavy toll of life. The guerrillas attempted a scorched-earth policy in an effort to drive out the Spanish and win national independence.

As the war raged, sugar and tobacco plantations were destroyed; and American exporters and investors suffered financial loss. Before the insurrection, the United States had provided 40 percent of Cuban imports and had been the market for almost 90 percent of Cuban exports.[37] From many parts of the American public there came a growing clamor that the Cleveland administration put an end to the increasing loss of life and property on the island of Cuba.

Grover Cleveland was concerned with the sharp decline in U.S.–Cuban trade, but from beginning to end, his Cuban policy was dictated by his concern for the security of the United States. He wished an end to the insurrection not only because it required increased expenditure by the federal government to patrol the Atlantic Coast and frustrate filibustering expeditions that had been organized by a Cuban junta in New York City but also, and more importantly, because he feared that Spain might seek the military aid of some other European power if a rebel victory became likely.[38] Cleveland had little sympathy for the insurrectionists and little faith in their political intelligence. He worried that Cuban independence might well be followed by political anarchy and European intervention. A strong flavor of ethnic superiority characterized his attitude toward the Cuban rebels and helped to dictate the goals of his Cuban policy.

The primary objective of that policy was Spanish pacification of Cuba, and he believed this would best be assured if Spain were to promise economic reforms and a reasonable measure of home rule. Unlike many of his countrymen, Cleveland did not picture the insurrectionists as Cuban replicas of the Minutemen of Lexington and Concord. Although he had no taste for the Catholic monarchy of Spain, Cleveland believed that the national security of the United States would best be assured by the continued presence of Spain in Cuba.[39] He suspected that politicians and editors who were proclaiming their fraternal regard for the Cuban revolutionists and demanding that the United States recognize Cuban belligerence and independence were warmongers, hungering for United States military intervention.

When Cleveland issued the customary proclamation of neutrality on 12 June 1895, he acknowledged that there existed a state of rebellion in Cuba. He did not, however, recognize the belligerency of the insurgents, and he warned that every effort would be made to prevent filibustering expeditions from leaving the East Coast for Cuban waters. The Cuban junta in New York proved skillful in evading U.S. naval patrols, but over the next twenty months, Cleveland made a serious effort to capture filibusterers and thereby reduce Spanish complaints against the flow of American arms to Cuban rebels.

Cleveland found Congress more troublesome than the Cuban junta. He was determined to keep Cuban policy in his own hands, and Congress was equally determined to participate in its formation. Senators and congressmen from both parties saw the Cuban insurrection as a battle against monarchical tyranny and as a sturdy stick with which to beat the unpopular Cleveland administration. They sought to force Cleveland to abandon a policy of pro-Spanish neutrality in favor of a policy of open support for the insurgents. The Senate adopted a resolution in February 1896 urging the president to use his good offices to secure Cuban independence, and two months later, both houses passed a resolution reiterating this request and demanding that the president immediately recognize the belligerency of the Cuban insurgents. As this was a concurrent and not a joint resolution, it did not require executive acknowledgment. Cleveland dismissed it in silence. He did not publicly declare his derogatory opinion of the political ambitions of the insurgents, but it was widely suspected by his congressional enemies.

Cleveland's strategy for achieving Spanish concessions was consistently unsuccessful. Its tactical confusion was first displayed with Secretary Olney's note of 14 April 1896 to the Spanish minister, Enrique Dupuy De Lôme. Olney offered Spain a mixture of warning and assurance. He referred to the Cuban revolutionaries in uncomplimentary terms and implied his disappointment at the failure of Spain to crush the insurrection by military means. He then proceeded to inform Spain that if the war dragged on, Spain might be forced to abandon Cuba "to the heterogeneous combination of elements and of races now in arms against her." Spain should promise meaningful reforms and ask Cleveland to play the role of mediator.[40] The Spanish reply arrived two months later: it was, in effect, an unqualified rejection of the administration's warning and offer of mediation. Cleveland continued to search for ways to promote what he judged to be the only safe and reasonable solution—pacification with reform and without independence; but to no avail. By pinning his hopes on Spanish concessions while assuring Spain that he had no wish to see a rebel victory, he managed simultaneously to irritate the Spanish government and anger the Cuban insurgents.

Cleveland became increasingly exasperated with the U.S. consul general in Havana, Fitzhugh Lee, but failed to replace him. He suspected that Lee favored U.S. military intervention, and Lee's request for the dispatch of a U.S. man-of-war to Cuban waters met as little favor as did his suggestion that the United States purchase Cuba. It would be dangerous to incorporate Cuba into the "United States system," and it would "seem absurd for us to buy the Island and present it to the people now inhabiting it, and put its government and management in their hands."[41]

Several historians have suggested that had Cleveland remained in office for another year, he, like his successor, would have chosen the option of military intervention and would have waged war against the Spanish monarchy.[42] The hypothesis seems doubtful. Whereas McKinley later proclaimed a moral imperative to end the Cuban civil war by forcing Spain to grant Cuban independence, Cleveland considered that his primary duty was to prevent the dangerous consequences that might accompany a rebel victory. Passages from Cleveland's message to Congress of 7 December 1896 are often cited to support the judgment that Cleveland contemplated U.S. military intervention in Cuba. In that message, Cleveland did indeed sharpen his warning to Spain as he advocated "a measure of home rule" for the population of Cuba:

> When the inability of Spain to deal successfully with the insurrection has become manifest and it is demonstrated that her sovereignty is extinct in Cuba for all purposes of its rightful existence, and when a hopeless struggle for its re-establishment has degenerated into a strife which means nothing more than the useless sacrifice of human life and the utter destruction of the very subject-matter of the conflict, a situation will be presented in which our obligations to the sovereignty of Spain will be superseded by higher obligations, which we can hardly hesitate to recognize and discharge.

Cleveland, however, was seeking to hold back Congress, where there was a renewed effort to pass a joint resolution recognizing Cuban independence, and the passage quoted was immediately followed by this declaration: "Until we face the contingencies suggested or the situation is by other incidents imperatively changed we should continue in the line of conduct heretofore pursued."[43]

Cleveland remained convinced that the Cuban rebels had not proven their title to be recognized as the provisional government of an independent Cuba, and he instructed Olney to make a statement to the press that were Congress to pass a resolution recognizing Cuban independence, it would be an invasion of the authority of the executive branch of the federal government and would be disregarded by the president. Cleveland never seriously considered using United States military power in behalf of Cuban independence. When war was declared against Spain in April 1898, Cleveland wrote Olney of his unhappiness that the United States was "in alliance and cooperation with Cuban insurgents—the most inhuman and barbarous cutthroats in the world."[44]

Cleveland's Cuban policy was deeply flawed by an anti-Cuban bias. It is difficult to see how he could have thought that the Cubans would acknowledge him as mediator, even had they been willing to forego their aim of national independence and accept a measure of home rule. Because Cleveland had little leverage with the obdurate Spanish monarchy and no empathy with the Cuban insurgents, his offer of good offices, however well intended, could only meet failure.[45] Neither Cleveland nor Secretary Olney understood the sources and strength of Cuban nationalism, and this was perhaps the major weakness of their diplomacy in Cuba. Their boast during the Venezuelan controversy that the "fiat" of the United States was law in the Western Hemisphere rang hollow when the controversy pitted the pride of a fading European power against the nationalist aspirations of a colonial population.[46]

Neither of the Cleveland administrations provided a turning point in the history of United States foreign policy, and it is difficult to characterize Cleveland's diplomacy in a few neat sentences or to discover some all-connecting theme.

Cleveland displayed only sporadic interest in foreign policy, although insisting on the presidential prerogative of final arbiter. His chief concerns were domestic, and he thought primarily in terms of domestic legislative solutions for such problem issues as the tariff, the currency, and the gold reserve. His concern for governmental economy dictated his opposition to subsidies for shippers and exporters, and his fear of foreign entanglements tended to make him wary of commercial reciprocity agreements and other government-directed efforts at trade expansion. Cleveland was prepared to defend U.S. economic interests abroad from harassment or attack, but he had no desire to coordinate a governmental effort in their behalf. Grover Cleveland entertained no grand strategy of economic diplomacy, nor did he have a plan to solve the depression crisis at home by a concerted governmental effort to push U.S. exports into new markets in East Asia and Latin America.[47]

It is not enough to say that the major theme of Cleveland's diplomacy was its lack of a theme, but that judgment, however trite, does contain a measure of truth.[48] Cleveland did possess a set of vaguely defined principles respecting what was right and just for U.S. foreign policy, but his diplomacy was often marked by inconsistency, a lack of coordination, and a tendency to respond to foreign-policy problems on an ad hoc basis as they arose. In his responses, he usually sought to apply what he considered the traditional principles of American foreign policy: anti-imperialism, the avoidance of entanglement in foreign quarrels, the promotion of arbitration and other legal instruments of peace keeping, and a jealous concern for the national honor and safety. But the application provided no single pattern or design.

There were similarities in Cleveland's policies toward the Alaskan seal-fisheries dispute, the Samoan controversy, Hawaiian annexation, and the Venezuelan boundary crisis, but the connection was essentially one of personal temperament and psychology. In all four instances, Cleveland's response was dictated by his bulldog determination to settle matters in accordance with his own judgment as to what was morally right and best for the United States. Convinced that the nation's diplomatic traditions reflected a superior morality, he was impatient with diplomatic opponents and suspicious of their ulterior motives. Dexter Perkins admirably summarizes the personal qualities that directed Cleveland's response to diplomatic problems: "There is something at once admirable and forbidding in the intellectual processes of this President . . . so honest, so brave, so independent . . . but also so rigid and inflexible in his thinking, so unimaginative, so dogmatic."[49]

The Cleveland years are of some importance in the history of United States foreign policy for their transitional nature and for individual diplomatic episodes in Latin America and the Pacific; but Grover Cleveland, for all his earnest labor to thwart overseas expansion and to guard against perceived threats by European powers to expand their influence in the New World, does not rank high among American presidents as a successful diplomatist.

12

★ ★ ★ ★ ★

THE PARTY DIVIDES: CLEVELAND, BRYAN, AND THE ELECTION OF 1896

When Cleveland left office in March 1897, he believed he was one of the most hated men in America. His judgment was not without foundation. He had been called a Judas and a traitor by such Democrats as John Altgeld and Ben Tillman; his policies had been publicly repudiated at the Democratic Nominating Convention of July 1896, and a majority of the nation's press had declared his second administration a sorry failure. The Democratic party was deeply divided and was under the leadership of his sworn enemies, and the Republican party, having secured the allegiance of urban America, was prepared to enjoy a new period of national political dominance. The repudiation of Cleveland and Cleveland Democracy was a drama in three acts. The congressional elections of 1894 provided the first act and made likely, if not inevitable, the subsequent victories of William Jennings Bryan at the Democratic convention and of William McKinley in the presidential election of 1896.

The Republican party waged a skillful campaign in the congressional elections of 1894, damning the Cleveland administration for what it had and had not done. The Wilson-Gorman Tariff was blamed for the deepening depression—with chronological inaccuracy and persuasive effect; and the Cleveland administration was accused of callous indifference to the plight of the unemployed workman and the sore-oppressed businessman. For two years the Democratic party had been in control of both branches of the national government, and its reign had seen financial panic, bank failures, widening unemployment, farm-mortgage foreclosures, and a mounting national debt. Its record was one of unrelieved failure and incompetence. It was a party bereft of ideas and paralyzed by division.

The electioneering efforts of the Democrats in the fall of 1894 appeared to support the last charge. Democratic energies were expended primarily in castigating party enemies, instead of fighting Republican opponents. It was clear to most political observers that the Democrats would suffer a political defeat in the congressional elections, but the extent of that defeat exceeded all predictions. The Democrats lost 113 seats in the House and 5 in the Senate. Champ Clark, a Democratic congressman from Missouri, called it the greatest slaughter of the innocents since Herod. In the new House of Representatives, the Republicans would have 244 members and the Democrats 104. The latter were almost exclusively from the South. The Democrats failed to elect a single member of Congress in twenty-four states and elected only one congressman in each of six other states.[1] Republican gains represented the largest swing of any election since the Civil War.[2]

During his last two years in office, Grover Cleveland would face not only a Congress that had both houses under Republican control but also a Democratic minority that was dominated by southern agrarians who felt little loyalty and less obligation to his administration. The shrinking base of Democratic political power lay now in the South, and southern congressmen were alert to the growing popularity of free silver among their constituents and to the mounting criticism of Cleveland's efforts to sustain the gold standard. Such Democratic politicians as Benjamin Tillman were determined to outflank and outbid the Populists on the silver issue or, failing this, to join forces with them. During his first term, Cleveland had sought to forge a political alliance between "reform-minded" Democrats in the Northeast and sound-money, low-tariff conservative Democrats in the South. During the last years of his second term, Cleveland witnessed the dissolution of that alliance, as well as widening sectional division between East and West.

State and national Democratic politics in the years 1895 and 1896 was increasingly dominated by the battle of the standards. The fight over free-silver coinage became a symbol of the protest of agrarian regions against what they saw as their colonial subservience to the Northeast. Democratic silver congressmen gave the call to battle when, after an informal caucus, they issued a public statement in March 1895 denouncing the gold standard and proclaiming free silver as the new orthodoxy for the Democratic party. Cleveland quickly seized the opportunity to excoriate "silver monometallism" as heresy to the traditions of the party and damaging to "the common people of the land," for whose interests the party had fought throughout its history. He wrote a public letter to Henry S. Robbins, chairman of the Honest Money League of Chicago, in which he declared, "The line of battle is drawn between the forces of safe currency and those of silver monometallism":

> . . . it is time for the American people to reason together as members of a great nation which can promise them protection and safety only so long as its solvency is unsuspected, its honor unsullied, and the soundness of its money unquestioned. . . . An insidious attempt is made to create a prejudice against the advocates of a safe and sound currency by the insinuation . . . that they belong to financial and business classes, and are therefore not only out of sympathy with the common people of the land but for selfish and wicked purposes are willing to sacrifice the interests of those outside their circle. . . . If reckless discontent and wild experiment should sweep our currency from its safe support, the most defenceless of all who suffer in that time of distress and national discredit will be the poor, as they reckon the loss in their scanty support, and the laborer or workingman, as he sees the money he has received for his toil shrink and shrivel in his hand when he tenders it for the necessities to supply the humble home.[3]

Both the silver congressmen and Grover Cleveland were determined that their party opponents be driven into outer darkness. After their respective public declarations during the spring of 1895, the break was final, and compromise was impossible.

Cleveland judged that such western states as Kansas and Nebraska were beyond the call of reason and that such states as Missouri and Nevada were too in thrall to the silver producers to consider the national welfare, but he continued into the spring of 1896 to believe he could reclaim the South for sound money and true Democratic principles. In three consecutive presidential elections he had received the support of the South; how then could the region turn against such Cleveland Democrats as Hoke Smith and Hilary Herbert and pay heed to such Populist Democrats as Tom Watson and Ben Tillman?

Cleveland made a concerted effort to raise money among his friends in New York City for the distribution of "sound money" propaganda in the South; he wrote to southern editors and politicians, explaining how a depreciated currency would hurt the region's export trade; and he sent Treasury Secretary Carlisle on a tour of cities in the Border States to trumpet the economic and political wisdom of an "honest currency."[4] In October 1895, Cleveland took six members of his cabinet to the Cotton States Exposition in Atlanta, where, in a series of conversations with Democratic politicians, he sought to convince them that were the Democrats to abandon advocacy of the gold standard, the Republican party would claim the role of its sole champion and would make permanent their recent political gains. The effort gives the lie to those who picture Cleveland as a sulking sphinx during his last years in office, but it was without noticeable effect. Cleveland's veto of the silver-seigniorage bill and the "Morgan bond issue" proved to have more influence than did Cleveland's journey to Atlanta. Free silver continued to gain southern adherents at a growing rate, with corresponding unpopularity for Grover Cleveland and his administration. By the end of 1895 a majority of southern politicians saw the interests of their region as best served by an alliance with the agrarian West, not the creditor East.

Providing the essential context for the augmented influence of the silverites and "agrarian radicals" within the Democratic party was the continuing depression. Above all else, the length and severity of the depression weakened Cleveland's hold on his party and made certain the victory of Bryan, Altgeld, Bland, and Tillman at the Democratic National Convention of 1896. Hard times, economic grievances, and conflicting sectional interests splintered the Democratic party as a national political organization.

That judgment is not offered as an introduction to a stalwart defense of Grover Cleveland in his role as party leader. Cleveland was guilty of tactical blunders and errors of policy strategy, and he must share the blame for the division and defeat of the Democratic party. Before analyzing his weaknesses as a party leader, however, it should be reiterated that Cleveland—like all presidents who have the misfortune to serve during a period of economic depression— was as much victim as culprit. Granted the very rudimentary knowledge of the time respecting the cause and cure of business cycles, no administration could have provided more than limited measures of relief for the depression's victims or escaped a sharp loss of public favor. It is possible that had Cleveland adopted the subtreasury plan of the Populist party or urged the "good roads bill" of Jacob Coxey he would have lessened the discontent of southern and western agrarians. Neither proposal, however, possessed broad national support, and it is doubtful that either would have shortened the length of the depression. Cleveland had not inherited a united party, and even in the triumphal year of 1892 the national Democratic party was no more than a cooperative league of sectional, ideological, and economic factions. A more talented and flexible politician might have slowed the splintering of the party under the impact of hard times and agrarian discontent; it is doubtful that even a master of conciliation could have prevented some measure of rebellion.

The most determined defender of Cleveland must admit, however, that Grover Cleveland did better service for his country than for his party. Some of the very strengths of Cleveland as chief executive contained the seeds of failure in his role as party leader. The obverse of tenacity was obstinacy; of candor, rudeness; of consistency, intolerance; of integrity, self-righteousness. Cleveland's temperament required that he proclaim his independence of party even as he insisted that he never deviated from the true principles of Democracy. He would interpret those principles for himself, and he made few commitments to the organization of his party. His independence of Democratic-party managers has been exaggerated, but he was inclined to use them during presidential campaigns and then display little sense of obligation between elections. Cleveland envisaged his presidential position in two disparate ways: he was the nation's chief magistrate, above parties and factions, as intended by the Founding Fathers; he had been elected to the presidency on the Democratic ticket and consequently should receive the cooperation of all Democratic members of the House and the Senate. Cleveland never resolved the contradiction. He demanded recognition as party leader, yet he scorned the role of party manager. Prepared to instruct the Democratic members of Congress, he considered it beneath presidential dignity to cajole and conciliate them.

In his social relations with a small band of friends, Cleveland was a gregarious man who could generate lifelong admiration and loyalty, but in his relations with Democratic congressmen he was often tactless and rude. A man who prided himself on his own self-sufficiency when making policy decisions, he had little patience with those who insisted on an equal measure of independence. He confused the necessity for tact with the sin of weakness. Cleveland saw such Democratic senators as Arthur Pue Gorman as unprincipled wafflers, ready to abandon Democratic principles for the sake of superficial and meaningless party harmony. They increasingly viewed

Cleveland as arrogant and ungrateful, a man who ignored his obligations to the party that had rewarded him beyond his deserts.

The fact that Cleveland, throughout his second administration, lived under the shadow of a recurrence of cancer probably increased his tendencies to irritability, but at no time in his life was his the disposition of a successful conciliator. His temperament was essentially authoritarian, and he had never enjoyed currying favor or asking for advice. He reached policy decisions only after much deliberation; but once made, those decisions assumed an aura of moral righteousness and were seldom susceptible to alteration or compromise. His conviction in the rightness of his policies had been a source of Cleveland's strength with the rank and file of his party in three presidential elections, but it was a source of weakness for Cleveland's effort to direct his party during his second term. This was particularly true in its last two years, as Cleveland came increasingly to view party opponents as party heretics. Convinced that his own policies were right and principled, he saw his opponents as not only wrong but dishonorable. To make concessions to them was to betray the people's trust and to deny his God-given sense of public duty.[5]

Cleveland considered himself to be a man besieged, attacked by wrong-headed enemies and poorly defended by those who should have been outspoken in his defense. He informed Thomas Bayard, the U.S. ambassador to London, that there was "not a man in the Senate with whom I can be on terms of absolute confidence."[6] At times, Cleveland appeared to relish his self-characterization as the last brave champion of the principles of Cleveland Democracy, a man surrounded by socialistic demagogues, feeble allies, and selfish politicians engaged in internecine struggles. There was a measure of moral masochism in Cleveland's psychological constitution, but only a small measure. He was deeply hurt by what he considered to be the unwarranted enmity of most Democratic members of the Fifty-fourth Congress, and he grieved over the splintering of his party. Cleveland remained convinced, however, that this was the work of others. He saw no reason to fault his efforts as leader of the party, and he saw no reason to alter his political policies or tactics.

Those Democrats who were "Populists in all but name" could expect no patronage favors from his administration; nor did they receive any. When Ben Tillman wrote to Cleveland, requesting to be consulted on federal appointments in South Carolina, Cleveland made the letter public without answering it.[7] Applications from other Democratic critics received like treatment. He incurred the enmity of Senators John McPherson, Francis Cockrell, and George Vest by disregarding the tradition of "senatorial courtesy" when making patronage appointments in their states; and his relations with Senator David Hill reached a new low when Cleveland twice sought to fill a Supreme Court vacancy by appointing New York lawyers who were on Hill's list of personal enemies. Cleveland made no secret of his determination not to conciliate his party enemies; those who had proven traitor to honest tariff reform, as well as those who criticized the treasury-bond sales or his handling of the Pullman strike, deserved censure, not conciliation. Cleveland never knowingly appointed an incompetent or corrupt man to public office, but as his sense of isolation within his party grew, he was inclined to see political virtue in those who were the opponents of his party enemies.

For his enemies in the press as well as in Congress, this was but a further sign of his arrogant willingness to divide and weaken the Democratic party. By 1896, only a scattering of Democratic papers expressed support for Cleveland and his administration, and Cleveland was reaffirmed in his belief that the press was a source of scandal and persecution. He had always lacked what a later generation would call a "talent for public relations," and there was an element of tragedy in Cleveland's inability during his second administration to explain his motives and policy objectives to the press and the public.

R. Hal Williams has written that it was Cleveland's primary task "to unify and revitalize the aging Democratic party" and that Cleveland ignored his responsibility: "Instead, he adopted an individual approach to the presidency, which enhanced his own stature but did not cure his party's deep-seated ills."[8] The conclusion of this indictment is more accurate than its implications of intent. Cleveland did not split the Democratic party in an effort to promote his historical reputation as a one-man "Study in Courage." He believed that in his battle in behalf of an "honest currency," he was fighting for his country's honor and the purchasing power of wages, as well as the safety of investments. Sound money, tariff reduction, law and order, respect for constitutional limitations on government: these were eternal verities, not the coin of political debate.

Cleveland's personality, as well as his policies, must bear a share of the blame for the sharpening internal division of the Democratic party in the years 1895 and 1896. But so, too, must his party critics; and those historians who imply that a more flexible, innovative, and conciliatory president could have prevented party division have yet to prove their case. Ideological and programmatic divisions within the Democratic party ran deep, and no Democratic president—whatever his leadership skills—could have done more than reduce the level of animosity between the "Cleveland Democrats" and "Bryan the Democrats." The division of the Democratic party and the victory of the "Bryan Democrats" was, if not inevitable, highly probable.

By 1896, Cleveland saw Bryan as his arch enemy within the party, and Bryan was anxious to accept the designation. The two men came to represent the battle within the Democratic party between gold and silver, between a national currency based on the gold standard and a policy of bimetallism which would inflate the currency by the unlimited coinage of silver. The "battle over the standards" was neither a false nor an unimportant issue, but the struggle between Cleveland and Bryan for control of the Democratic party involved other issues as well and reflected a basic difference with respect to the role of government in a democratic Republic.

To say that Cleveland represented the industrial East and Bryan the agrarian West is an oversimplification and a partial truth. Bryan's animus toward Cleveland was rooted in his conviction that the Cleveland Democrats had done nothing for the depressed farmer except to make his debt burdens heavier by their repeal of the Sherman Silver Purchase Act and by their collusion with eastern bankers to save the gold reserve and the gold standard. Their warnings about the dangers of governmental paternalism and constitutional limitations on the regulatory powers of the federal government were but hypocritical justifications for their failure to meet the crisis of the depression with programs that would raise the price of farm staples, stop the robber practices of the railroads, restrict the political and financial power of the private bankers, curb the trusts, and provide easy credit for the agrarian sections of the nation. For Bryan, the demand for free silver represented both the economic panacea of monetary inflation and a wide range of popular grievances. The farmer symbolized the common man in America, and Bryan would be his spokesman against the manufacturing, banking, and mercantile interests which, he believed, controlled the Cleveland administration. Cleveland's policies were no better than those of the Republican protectionists: both were agents of an international conspiracy organized by parasitic bankers in support of the gold standard. Cleveland had demonstrated his enmity to the working classes by breaking the Pullman strike, begging the assistance of J. P. Morgan, and approving the Court's decision in the income-tax case. Cleveland represented the power of the moneyed East in the party and nation, and he had to be repudiated and driven into exile.

While Bryan accused Cleveland of inoculating the Democratic party "with Republican virus," his denunciations were not as inflammatory as were those of other Democratic critics. Perhaps no president has ever generated so much hatred among members of his own party as did Grover Cleveland. The crude and slanderous remarks of Senator Ben Tillman are often quoted, together with his promise to his constituents to stick his pitchfork into Cleveland's "fat ribs"; but a better illustration of the depth of hatred was Governor Altgeld's declaration at a banquet marking the anniversary of Thomas Jefferson's birth: "To laud Clevelandism on Jefferson's birthday is to sing a Te Deum in honor of Judas Iscariot on a Christmas morning!"[9]

Cleveland's denunciations of his party enemies were less colorful but no less sincere. He wrote about Bryan: "His mind, training and imagination all combine to make of him a Populist, pure and simple. He has not even the remotest notion of the principles of Democracy."[10] Not only was Bryan not a Democrat, he was a false spokesman of "the common man." It was the Cleveland Democrats, not the radicals, who were the true friends of the consumer, the factory hand, the widow with her mite. In a letter to a New York editor, Cleveland argued that as the market ratio of silver to gold was now 32 to 1, the free coinage of silver at 16 to 1 would halve the value of the dollar, generate price inflation, and reduce the purchasing power of wages, pensions, and savings. "None of our fellow-citizens, rich or poor, great or humble [can escape] the consequences of a degeneration of our currency." For the Democratic party to remain "the party of the people," it must avoid dangerous monetary schemes "born of discontent . . . and re-enforced by the insidious aid of private selfishness and cupidity" and recognize that a sound currency was as essential to the American consumer as to the national honor.[11]

In a very real sense the battle of the standards was a battle between the agrarian producer and the urban consumer; and for a majority of the nation's Democrats, Bryan was a more effective propagandist for the one than was Cleveland for the other.

Cleveland kept a close watch on the actions of various state Democratic conventions during the spring of 1896 and was aware of the growing strength of "the Silver craze" within the party; yet he continued to believe, until the opening day of the Democratic National Convention, that the party would avoid the shame of a silver platform and candidate.[12] But by failing to give the lie to rumors that he desired a third term and by failing to rally the shrinking band of Cleveland Democrats in support of another sound-money candidate, Cleveland made all the more likely the victory of William Jennings Bryan.

Grover Cleveland had no wish or expectation to receive a fourth nomination from the Democratic party in 1896. He had grown perceptibly older during his second term, had lost sixty pounds, and was a man tired in mind and body. Unlike similar sentiments expressed in 1888, Cleveland's declaration to friends that he looked forward to retirement from political life was completely sincere.[13] Why, then, did he not make a public statement denying rumors that he was covertly seeking a third presidential term? Why did he not indicate his support for a Democratic "loyalist" such as John Carlisle, William Whitney, William Vilas, or Massachusetts Governor William E. Russell?

Cleveland apparently thought it beneath his dignity to deny rumors of third-term ambitions, and he was afraid to appear ridiculous by insisting that he was not a candidate when every day saw fresh denunciations of his presidential performance. Nor could he make up his mind as to who among the Cleveland loyalists would make the strongest candidate. Like many men of authoritarian personality, he could find no one who would be completely satisfactory as his successor. He had great admiration for John Carlisle's intelligence but doubts about his will power and understandable worries over Carlisle's periodic drinking bouts. Whitney was too closely associated with Wall Street; Vilas was strong only with Cleveland Democrats in the Old Northwest; Russell would not have support outside the New England Democracy.[14] Cleveland worried and deliberated but did nothing to rally his supporters behind an alternative to a Silver Democrat as the party's nominee. His silence inhibited efforts by his lieutenants, and the result was a sense of disenchantment with their leader and a measure of mutual suspicion among themselves.[15] The opponents of the "radical agrarians" had demonstrated political paralysis before the Democratic Convention formally convened in Chicago on July 6.

The report of the convention's Platform Committee made clear that a majority of the delegates were prepared to repudiate the Cleveland administration and its policies. Not only did the platform call for the free and unlimited coinage of silver and more effective federal regulation of the trusts and railroads, but it specifically condemned "trafficking with banking syndicates," the use of judicial injunctions in labor strikes, and "Federal interference in local affairs"—the last being a clear reference to Cleveland's introduction of federal troops in the Pullman strike over the objections of Governor Altgeld. Repudiation was followed by insult, as Senator Tillman took the floor in defense of the platform. Tillman elicited applause as he denounced the Cleveland administration as undemocratic and tyrannical and proclaimed Cleveland a traitor to the party, a man "faithful unto death, the death of the Democratic party."[16]

Although many of the southern and western delegates had initially favored the veteran champion of silver coinage, Senator Richard Bland, as the party's nominee, Bryan's "Cross of Gold" speech generated such enthusiasm that Bland was pushed aside in favor of the young orator from Nebraska. On July 9, Bryan was nominated as the presidential candidate and new leader of the Democratic party. Having won one battle against the gold men, Bryan would now engage the Republican nominee, William McKinley, in a new battle in behalf of silver and the grievances and values of agrarian America.

Cleveland was surprised and angered by the results of the Democratic convention. He expressed bitterness not only toward the victorious Silver men but also against the sound-money men who had failed to defend his policies with force and courage. Only his enemies had dared mention his name.[17] He insisted that he found a measure of comfort in the reflection that no one could blame his administration for the discredit and disaster that awaited the party in the forthcoming election, but it was a cold comfort.[18]

In the presidential election of 1896, Cleveland voted neither for Bryan nor for McKinley but for Senator John M. Palmer. Here, perhaps, he could be indicted for party recusancy, if not treason. Cleveland, however, believed that the Democratic party under Bryan was no longer the party of Jefferson and Jackson. The Bryan Democrats were Populists, and the Gold Democrats who were running as a third party were the true heirs of the Founding Fathers of the Democracy.

A small band of Democratic national committeemen who stood firm for the gold standard held a conference in the first days of August. At its conclusion, they issued a call for a new Democratic party and convention to meet in Indianapolis on September 2.

Cleveland never publicly endorsed this call, nor did he ever publicly support the third-party slate of Palmer and Simon B. Buckner. Cleveland did, however, encourage his cabinet officers to speak in its behalf; he forced the resignation of Secretary of the Interior Hoke Smith when Smith's Atlanta paper came out for Bryan; and he made it clear to his personal correspondents that while he would vote for the Palmer ticket, his primary objective was the defeat of William Jennings Bryan.[19] When McKinley won the election, Cleveland made no attempt to hide his satisfaction. Bryanism was populism, and even a protectionist president was to be preferred to one who sought the ruin of the national honor and who included among his followers men who were little better than anarchists.[20]

The presidential election of November 1896 reaffirmed the Republican gains in the congressional elections of 1894. By consolidating their support in the industrial cities and towns, the Republicans had gained their objective, a seemingly permanent national electoral majority. Bryan received the votes of the South and the Plains West but lost the election by an electoral count of 271 to 176. A majority of the citizens of the East and the Midwest voted for McKinley and "honest money," as did the bulk of the Catholic immigrant vote.[21]

Bryan blamed the unpopularity of the Cleveland administration for his defeat, but one can argue that it was the capture of the Democratic party by a coalition of western and southern agrarians that solidified the Republican allegiance of industrial towns and cities from Minneapolis to Baltimore. Cleveland's second administration severely damaged the national political popularity of the Democratic party, but McKinley's victory was the result as well of urban suspicion of William Jennings Bryan.

Cleveland attributed sole blame for Democratic division and Republican victory to Bryan and the "agrarian radicals." When Cleveland left office in March 1897, he was embittered by the reversal of the political fortunes of his party, but he took solace in his own sense of virtue. As he dressed for McKinley's inaugural, he was not conscious of having deviated from duty by a hair's breadth. If he had it all to do over again, there would be not a single change of presidential policy. The day would come—he was sure—when the American people would understand how he had saved the nation's financial credit, and, on that day, the Democratic party would be rescued from the heretics and his historical reputation gain redemption.

13

★ ★ ★ ★ ★

THE POLITICAL LEADERSHIP
OF GROVER CLEVELAND

Any student of the Cleveland presidencies is faced with a difficult requirement: to explain Cleveland's domination of the American political scene in the years 1884 to 1896. Cleveland's growing unpopularity in the last years of his second administration does not alter the fact that Grover Cleveland, a man of little charisma, less eloquence, and limited imaginative and intellectual powers, was the dominant figure in United States politics for more than a decade. Cleveland authored no laws; he often failed to gain congressional acceptance for his legislative proposals, but he had an undoubted hold on the public imagination and was seen by friend and foe alike as "a strong president." How is one to explain his personal force and attraction for the American public?

The answer given by his foremost biographer, Allan Nevins, is that Cleveland achieved greatness through strength of character. If his personal qualities of candor, courage, and independence were characteristic of many of his countrymen, Grover Cleveland possessed them to an extraordinary degree, and this was understood and admired by the American public.[1] Such an answer appears to oversimplify Cleveland's personality while suggesting that the post–Civil War generation had such a paucity of courageous politicians that Cleveland shone as a single beacon in a dark and naughty world. Cleveland was a public man who sought earnestly to do his duty, but it does him little service to paint him as an overweight

George Washington. On a few occasions he shaded his political courage to curry public favor, as in his encouragement of the Chinese immigration bill and the dismissal of Lord Sackville; and he was prepared to accept the assistance of such political managers as Daniel Manning and William Whitney, even while pretending to scorn the arts of political management and the machinations of political machines. Cleveland was a good man and an ambitious man. He wanted to do what was right, and he wished to command and be obeyed. For all his distaste for campaigning, he successfully sought the Democratic nomination in 1884, 1888, and 1892 and enjoyed the authority of the presidential office. Cleveland was not power hungry, but neither was he without a strong ego and sense of self-worth.

Although Cleveland's public persona of the courageous statesman who gave no heed to considerations of party or personal advantage was not a fabrication, it was carefully and consciously embroidered. It was a public posture that matched his temperament while increasing his self-esteem, and Cleveland well understood its appeal for the American electorate. He wished to be seen as a president like Andrew Jackson, a man who was the tribune of the people. He appreciated that the American public was wearied of the personal quarrels and bickering that had characterized American politics since the Civil War and would look with favor upon a candidate and a president who appeared to stand tall and independent, an example of rugged individualism and political courage. Lacking the eloquence of a Blaine or the conciliatory temper of a Gorman or a Hill, Cleveland wisely portrayed himself as a public servant who was too conscientious to be brilliant, too honest to be eloquent, too independent to be conciliatory. He saw himself as a man of unshakable rectitude, forthright and fearless, concerned only for his own honor and that of the nation; and he understood that such a man would have appeal to a public disgusted with factional politics. His self-image and public posture became one, and in their unity there was no hypocrisy, only consistent effort.

The success of that effort was due in part to fortunate timing, but it was due as well to the political intelligence and the psychological constitution of Grover Cleveland. Cleveland was not a latter-day Cincinnatus, swept into office by an irresistible public demand; he was a man who understood that what was natural to his temperament was politically astute. Cleveland played to strength and made a virtue of his limitations. As a plain man of the people, a man of blunt candor and seeming simplicity, Cleveland could be easily comprehended by the average voter, and comprehension is the first step toward empathy and confidence. Honest Grover, portly and dignified, cautious and industrious, upright and solemn, painstaking and commonsensical, was held in the same regard as a respected small-town bank president. Not beloved or wildly applauded, he was admired.

This explanation of the political appeal of Cleveland leaves unanswered important questions respecting his political leadership and his dominance of the national political scene. How should one evaluate his performance as party leader and as chief executive? Did his presidential tenure mark a significant change in the institution of the presidency and in the relations between the executive and the legislative branches of the federal government? What was the direction of his political leadership? Does that direction demonstrate a conservative antipathy toward innovation and change?

As noted in an earlier chapter, Cleveland both succeeded and failed as leader of the Democratic party. In 1884 and again in 1892 he led the party to victory, its only two presidential victories in the years from 1860 to 1912. He linked the Democratic party to civil-service reform and tariff reduction; he helped to lessen the popular perception of the Democratic party as the party of negativism and obstruction; he gained support for the party from the Mugwumps and their academic cohorts; he succeeded, for a time, in lessening the division between northern and southern Democrats, but by his obdurate enmity toward the silverites and "agrarian radicals," he contributed to the party's division and defeat in 1896.

Grover Cleveland never reconciled his partisan allegiance to the Democratic party and his determination to stand apart from party politics as the nation's chief magistrate and tribune. He demanded total loyalty from party lieutenants during his three presidential campaigns, while continuing to insist that the president had a special relationship with the people that superseded any obligation to party workers and managers. He was not as independent of party managers and considerations of party advantage as he liked to think, but he did have a conception of the presidency that if not imperial, was vaguely monarchical. Convinced that the president was the sole officer of the national government who was elected by "all the people," he felt an obligation jealously to safeguard and protect the prerogatives of the presidential office for his successors. By the same token, he viewed the cabinet as his privy council, not as a party council representative of the diversity and leadership of the Democratic party. Cleveland never selected a cabinet member solely on the ground of personal friendship, but his refusal to use cabinet posts as a means of conciliating or coopting party rivals furnishes another example of his lack of skill as a mediator. Cleveland wanted a united party, but he increasingly appeared to believe that this could only be achieved through the obedience of congressional leaders to presidential directives.

Where Cleveland best demonstrated a talent for political leadership was in his role as head of the executive branch of the government and in his efforts to increase the authority of the presidency in its relations with Congress.

Cleveland received and retained the loyalty of cabinet officers and other appointees with remarkable unanimity during both of his administrations. Cleveland allowed his cabinet officers a fair degree of autonomy in their day-to-day operations, but it was Cleveland who set the broad outlines for administrative reform and kept watch on its implementation. If those reforms were of a piecemeal variety, they represented needed improvements in the efficiency of the federal government. The Treasury and Navy departments, the Pension Bureau, and the Bureau of Indian Affairs were more effective agencies in 1896 than they had been twelve years earlier, and the improvement was partially the result of Cleveland's determination that his administration be admired for its business efficiency as well as its economy and probity.

Cleveland was by no means a model administrator. He wasted too much time on detail and frequently confused the important and the peripheral. The workings of the presidential office under Cleveland represented little change or innovation from the days of Hayes, Garfield, and Arthur; and they were clearly inferior to those of the McKinley presidency, judged by the criteria of organizational and administrative efficiency. Grover Cleveland talked often of efficiency, but always in terms of individual diligence, not organizational reform. Presidential demands would presumably assure improved individual performance; there was no need to devise new administrative divisions or to refine reporting procedures.

There was a modest but perceptible improvement in the level of competence of federal officials during the Cleveland years. Much of the improvement was a result of the Pendleton Civil Service Act of 1883, but Cleveland sought to appoint qualified Democrats who were untainted by corruption, and he significantly increased the classified list. Not the unflinching champion of civil-service reform that his Mugwump supporters had predicted, Grover Cleveland nevertheless encouraged improved standards of honesty and efficiency among federal officeholders.

There can be little dispute that Cleveland dominated the executive branch of the government during both of his administrations. It is equally true that during both terms he frequently quarreled with the Senate and not infrequently met defeat at the hands of Congress. The student who seeks to evaluate Cleveland's impact on the office of the presidency is faced with the conundrum of a strong president who, although he was often successful in blocking congressional action, was usually unsuccessful in obtaining congressional agreement for his domestic and diplomatic policies.

Some historians who have acknowledged Cleveland's success in blocking congressional attempts to increase the pension rolls, enact pork-barrel legislation, and expand the silver currency have seen this as additional evidence that his was a negative and reactive presidency. Cleveland's readiness to use his veto and patronage powers to deter certain congressional actions is better seen as an illustration of his determination to promote the autonomy of the executive branch of the government. Cleveland believed that the balance between the branches of the federal government had been tilted in the direction of congressional domination during the presidencies of Andrew Johnson and Ulysses S. Grant and that the efforts of Hayes, Garfield, and Arthur had failed to right that balance. Cleveland's battle with the Senate over his power to appoint and remove federal officials can only be understood in relation to his determination to assert the independence of the executive branch in its relations with Congress. It was during that struggle that Cleveland made the most extreme assertion of executive privilege by any peacetime president prior to Richard M. Nixon, when he declared that department files were presidential property to be disposed of as the president wished. Subsequently, Cleveland urged the House of Representatives to pass the Morrison tariff bill, as he came to the conclusion that the presidency was both an administrative and a political office and that the independence of the executive branch was best assured if the president attempted to exert leadership in certain areas of legislative policy.

By using his powers of veto and appointment, Cleveland was successful in reestablishing an equilibrium between the executive and legislative branches of the federal government, and in the context of the post–Civil War generation, this was a needful and significant accomplishment.

Cleveland's frequent failure to secure the cooperation of Congress—for tariff reduction, revision of the Treasury banking system, ratification of an Anglo-American fisheries treaty, or restoration of the monarchy in Hawaii—was the result, at least in part, of political animosities beyond his control. For six of the eight years of Cleveland's presidencies, one or both branches of Congress had a Republican majority, and the growing division within the Democratic membership of Congress during his second administration was as much the consequence of the policy ambitions of the "agrarian radicals" as of the tactless obstinacy of Grover Cleveland. It is equally true, however, that the sporadic quality of Cleveland's efforts to shape legislative policy made more likely his failure to gain congressional concurrence. Cleveland appeared to oscillate between his initial notion that both branches must respect the independence one of the other and the conviction that the president must lead if Congress was to do right.

Cleveland's major struggles with Congress centered about tariff reduction and sound money. He failed in his efforts during both administrations to obtain a meaningful revision of the protective-tariff system; during his second administration, he gained a Pyrrhic victory in his struggle to repeal the Sherman Silver Purchase Act and preserve the gold reserve. The latter battle was primarily a defensive one, and here his patronage power was effective. In his battle with the Senate over tariff reform, Cleveland was seeking change, and here the power of the president to reward and punish proved insufficient. Cleveland's was not a "negative presidency," but Cleveland was always more comfortable when fighting to defend than when battling for change.

On those occasions when Grover Cleveland made a concerted effort to shape congressional policy, he was more likely to exhort than to consult Democratic leaders in the House and the Senate. Frequently in Cleveland's messages to Congress there was a judgmental, if not an authoritarian, tone and, not infrequently, a suggestion of the moral inferiority of Congress when it came to determining what was best for the American people. Democratic as well as Republican senators and congressmen found this offensive and were prepared to challenge what they saw as Cleveland's unwarranted assumption of the role of public censor. Republican cartoons often portrayed Cleveland in the toga of a Roman emperor, and there was a general belief that Cleveland was exerting the authority of the presidential office and intervening in legislative policy in an unprecedented manner. Cleveland's frequent failures to gain congressional obedience do not deny the accuracy of the judgment.

The contemporary perception of Cleveland as a strong, even domineering, president was furthered by his efforts to play "the national sheriff of public law and order," to use the descriptive phrase of Geoffrey Blodgett.[2] This was an area in which Cleveland was frequently able to by-pass or preempt the Congress, as in his actions during the Pullman strike. In his assertion of executive authority during that strike, Cleveland expanded presidential power as well as the scope of federal judicial injunctions. That expansion was accepted by a majority of the American people largely because he portrayed the use of federal troops as being necessary for the public safety. Cleveland had an innate ability to present complex issues in simplistic terms. The fight against Tammany was a fight against foul corruption; the fight against Debs was a fight against lawless anarchy; the fight against the British in the Venezuelan boundary dispute was a fight for the Monroe Doctrine and national honor. Cleveland tended to think in black-and-white terms of Right and Wrong, and in this fact lay much of his appeal to the electorate, as well as many of his difficulties with congressional and diplomatic opponents.

Grover Cleveland was successful in asserting the autonomy of the presidency, and he was unsuccessful in achieving executive-legislative collaboration. One can argue that both his success and his failure were inevitable, given his temperamental constitution. Self-confident and self-willed, Cleveland tended to decide policy positions on the basis of personal conviction, instead of from some broad set of philosophical or intellectual values. His restricted educational background and his provincial legal career encouraged a distaste for abstract thinking and theory, while his temperament encouraged a readiness to see policy opponents as enemies of righteousness and to view compromise as surrender. It was natural to his personal psychology to play the role of the combative and assertive chief executive; it was contrary to his temperament and self-image to mollify his political opponents or to gain his objectives by making timely compromises or devising clever stratagems. Cleveland had no talent for conciliation and indirection, and so decided that they were undignified, if not immoral. His self-deception was understandable and, for the legislative accomplishments of the Cleveland administrations, unfortunate.

Yet Grover Cleveland, for all his failures and failings, significantly reinvigorated the American presidency. Hayes had tried to do so, but it was Cleveland who was the more persistent and successful and who consequently gained "more lasting autonomy from congressional restraints and . . . more power for his office."[3]

Some historians who agree that Cleveland reinvigorated the American presidency would qualify that acknowledgment by criticizing the political direction of his two administrations. In their view, Grover Cleveland was a defender of the status quo, a bred-in-the-bone conservative. He exercised his presidential leadership to frustrate change and innovation and to fight a last-ditch battle in behalf of a laissez-faire government that was aidful alone to the rights and interests of the propertied.

Cleveland and the Cleveland Democrats had only limited reform aims, but these men were neither reactionaries nor tools of the moneyed classes. Their efforts, when trying to cope with the problems of an expanding urban industrial economy, were frequently uncertain, and their achievements modest; but the fact and sincerity of their efforts should not be denied. They were conservative in the sense that they sought to reclaim the civic virtues of a romanticized past and did not advocate fundamental changes in society or politics. They were convinced of the superiority of free enterprise to any other economic system; they defined "reform" in terms of improvements in public morality and administrative efficiency; they advocated "sound money" and the preservation of the gold standard— but these convictions were shared by a majority of middle-class Americans. It is false to the historical context of Gilded Age America to see such concerns as indicative of collusion with big business.

Grover Cleveland was not a stubborn foe of all forms of governmental regulation. He signed the Interstate Commerce Act, he warned against the growing power of industrial combinations, he sought to prevent the monopolization of western lands by railroad and timber corporations, and he favored a permanent federal instrumentality for the voluntary arbitration of labor-management disputes. He was anxious that federal intervention remain within strict constitutional limits, and he did not wish to see the federal government become an active participant in the operations of the national economy; but he was not an undeviating subscriber to laissez-faire dogma. He is vulnerable to criticism for his lack of sensitivity to the victims of the economic crisis of the mid nineties and for his failure to offer an answer to agricultural depression and industrial unemployment that would encompass more than tariff revision and an "honest dollar." But to portray Cleveland as a callous reactionary who was concerned only with the profit margin of his Wall Street companions is to paint a false portrait. His primary limitation was not a lack of compassion but of imagination.

Sincerely troubled by the growth of trusts and their ability to pervert the "natural operations" of a free-market economy, Cleveland continued to associate economic progress with industrial expansion. Undue interference by the federal government in the operations of the economy would be unwise as well as unconstitutional. The safest policy was to denounce the erosion of moral standards in business and in government and to demand that men of large property remember their civic duty and join a crusade for honesty in business as in government. Only so could there be economic progress without greed, social harmony without class envy.

Cleveland was not a deep thinker; neither was he inclined toward long-range planning. In domestic as in foreign affairs, he tended to deal with problems as they arose, and he took pride in being a practical man. Faced with a problem, he worried, not about primary causes, but about present consequences. In none of his public addresses did he project a view of America's future, although in many he offered a remembrance of its Jacksonian past. Cleveland was consistently susceptible to the appeal of nostalgia and the authority of the past, and in this fact lay the core of his conservatism. It is inaccurate to portray Cleveland as the slave of old Democratic dogmas of states' rights, limited government, and decentralization. It is more accurate to see him as a president who was troubled by the social implications of the post–Civil War economic revolution and who sought to convince himself that the solution lay in a revival of moral virtue and a measure of cautious governmental action. Not a standpatter, Cleveland's apprehensions and limitations helped to ensure that he was more successful in resistance than innovation, in prevention than construction.

Several scholars have seen in that fact conclusive evidence for a judgment that Grover Cleveland failed to meet the test of political leadership. Rexford G. Tugwell, a member of Franklin Roosevelt's "Brain Trust," offers an unvarnished version of that judgment in his biography of Cleveland: "He would never be other than a narrow conservative . . . nothing could cause him to lift his eyes to a larger future for the nation and use the government to make the promise a reality; nothing could make him a charming and persuasive party leader who formulated programs and plans and persuaded his party to adopt them willingly."[4] Tugwell's censure appears to be not only harsh but essentially ahistorical. If Cleveland is to be damned, it cannot be for his failure to imitate Franklin Delano Roosevelt. Cleveland's record of presidential leadership must be evaluated within the context of the last decades of the nineteenth century, not by the criteria and expectations of the 1930s.

One may regret Cleveland's failure to modernize the federal government or to attempt to make changes in the institutional structure of the presidential office, but the electorate in the Gilded Age made no demands that he do so. Grover Cleveland believed that there was little need for basic change in the institutions of American politics. He advocated the reform of personal behavior, not the reform of governmental structure.

The most telling indictment against Cleveland's political leadership would focus, not on his conservatism, his inability to engage in long-range planning, or his disinterest in institutional reform, but on his lack of leadership skills. He had little talent for diplomacy when dealing with Republican partisans, Democratic senators, or "western radicals"; and herein lay his primary failure as a political leader and constructive statesman.

By the end of his second administration, Cleveland had alienated not only the dirt farmers of the South and the West but also the Democratic organization in New York state, a majority of Democratic congressmen, and a number of his long-time supporters. Much of his unpopularity could be attributed to the ambitions of his political enemies, but much was also due to his self-righteous conviction that it was his duty to command and not to conciliate. Grover Cleveland failed as a political leader because of his personal limitations as well as his misfortune to be in office during a time of economic crisis and social distress. No president could have failed to suffer some loss of public confidence in the years 1893 to 1896, but Cleveland's inability to gain the cooperation of Congress, together with his increasingly poor relations with the press, helped to accelerate his alienation from important sections of the party and the nation. His "party perfidy" letter after the Senate Democrats had revised the Wilson tariff bill was but one example of his readiness to confuse opposition with iniquity, as was his characterization of inquisitive reporters as "ghouls of the press." In the final analysis, Cleveland refused to see that for a president to lead as well as command, it was necessary that he be party chieftain as well as chief executive. Cleveland lacked the ability to combine those roles, and in his failure there was an element of pathos. Few presidents have tried more earnestly to perform their presidential duties according to their judgment of what was best for the American people.

Contemporary assessments of Grover Cleveland's historical legacy changed dramatically between 4 March 1897, when he left Washington and public office, and 24 June 1908, when he died at his home in Princeton, New Jersey. When Cleveland retired from public life, he was one of the most unpopular political figures in the country. Several Republican editors suggested that historians of the future would rank his presidential tenure with that of Franklin Pierce or James Buchanan. Although a few papers dared to suggest that he would be remembered for his efforts to save the nation's financial credit, a majority of the press concentrated on the fact that he left office with the Democratic party divided and discredited.

Political reputations are susceptible, however, to dramatic changes, and death often serves as a solvent for partisan enmities. When Cleveland died, every newspaper in the United States, as well as the major ones in Great Britain, printed long obituaries; and better than 75 percent of these suggested that Cleveland would go down in history as one of America's great presidents.[5] Cleveland had given the nation an example of a man "who could speak the everlasting No," when such had been necessary for the safety and honor of the country. His integrity and sterling character would serve as "a shining beacon to which far-off ages may fondly and often turn their retrospective eyes."[6]

Time has not vindicated that prophecy. The legacy of personal example is vulnerable to the devaluation of time. With the possible exception of Washington and Lincoln, there have been no American presidents who are primarily remembered for their character. The student who would discover the historical legacy of Grover Cleveland must evaluate his impact on the office of the presidency and on the policy directions of the federal government.

Cleveland's legacy for the office of the presidency was both substantial and positive. Cleveland's presidential tenure serves as an essential introduction to the development of the modern presidency and to the identification of executive power in the person of the president. Cleveland's erratic efforts to shift policy-making initiative from the Capitol to the White House fell victim to his lack of leadership skills and his growing unpopularity as a "depression president," but the Cleveland presidencies provide an interesting chapter in the evolution from congressional to presidential government.

The historical importance of a president, however, resides primarily in his influence on the future direction of federal legislative policy, and it is here that Cleveland's legacy is found wanting. Some of his policy efforts did have lasting influence. His labors to save the gold standard had relevance to national policy, at least until 1933; he contributed modestly to the increased professionalism of the federal bureaucracy. His efforts to save millions of acres of western land from the greed of railroad corporations and cattle and timber barons and to enlarge the national forest reserve may justly be compared to the later and more publicized efforts of Theodore Roosevelt, and his Venezuelan policy had the effect of encouraging Americans in later generations to view the Monroe Doctrine as secular writ. But the Cleveland years were not a turning point in American political history. The reforms urged by Cleveland would have meager relevance for twentieth-century liberalism. The regulatory state of twentieth-century America owes little to Cleveland's imprecations against the trusts or to his worried approval of the Interstate Commerce Act. Not a standpat president, neither was Cleveland the initiator of any great movement for change. He saw his task as one of applying "elementary ethics to a number of discrete executive problems," and he saw no reason to attempt to make fundamental changes in the polity to match the economic and social changes that were being effected by the Second Industrial Revolution.[7]

Grover Cleveland's tenure provides the essential preface to the evolution of the modern presidency in the McKinley-Roosevelt administrations, but it would be a brave idolator who would claim for Cleveland a place on Mount Rushmore. Cleveland was not a great president, nor was he a man for all seasons. Nevertheless, he remains one of the more interesting presidents, and this largely because of the continuing conflict between his personal temperament and his inherited opinions. Fearing the consequences of governmental paternalism, his assertive personality encouraged him to dominate the executive branch of the government as no president had since Lincoln and, in his role as "the national sheriff of public law and order," to extend the authority of the federal government, despite his repeated warnings against the evils of undue centralization of power.

NOTES

In the notes, CP will stand for Cleveland Papers; LC for Library of Congress; and GC for Grover Cleveland in citations of his correspondence.

CHAPTER 1
INTRODUCTION

1. Morton Keller, *Affairs of State: Public Life in Late Nineteenth Century America* (Cambridge, Mass.: Harvard University Press, 1977), p. viii.

2. H. Wayne Morgan, "Toward National Unity," in *The Gilded Age: A Reappraisal*, ed. H. Wayne Morgan, rev. ed. (Syracuse, N.Y.: Syracuse University Press, 1970), p. 12.

3. Lewis L. Gould, "The Republican Search for a National Majority," in *The Gilded Age: A Reappraisal*, p. 171.

4. *Letters of Grover Cleveland, 1850–1908*, ed. Allan Nevins (Boston, Mass.: Houghton Mifflin, 1933), p. xi; Allan Nevins, *Grover Cleveland: A Study in Courage* (New York: Dodd, Mead, 1933), p. 766.

5. Samuel Eliot Morison and Henry Steele Commager, *Growth of the American Republic*, 4th ed., 2 vols. (New York: Oxford University Press, 1970), 2:227.

6. Richard Hofstadter, *The American Political Tradition and the Men Who Made It* (New York: Knopf, 1948), pp. 177, 182.

7. *Life*, 1 Nov. 1948, pp. 65–66, 68, 73–74.

8. Robert K. Murray and Tim H. Blessing, "The Presidential Performance Study: A Progress Report," *Journal of American History* 70 (Dec.

1983): 535–55.

9. Horace Samuel Merrill, *Bourbon Leader: Grover Cleveland and the Democratic Party* (Boston, Mass.: Little, Brown, 1957), pp. 44, 70.

10. Horace Samuel Merrill, *Bourbon Democracy of the Middle West, 1865–1896* (Baton Rouge: Louisiana State University Press, 1953), p. 180.

11. Vincent P. De Santis, "Grover Cleveland," in *America's Ten Greatest Presidents*, ed. Morton Borden (Chicago: Rand McNally, 1961), pp. 158–59, 162–64.

12. Keller, *Affairs of State*, pp. 557–58; Walter T. K. Nugent, "Politics from Reconstruction to 1900," in *The Reinterpretation of American History and Culture*, ed. William H. Cartwright and Richard L. Watson, Jr. (Washington, D.C.: National Council for the Social Studies, 1973), p. 387.

13. Robert F. Wesser, "Election of 1888," in *History of American Presidential Elections, 1789–1968*, ed. Arthur M. Schlesinger, Jr., and Fred L. Israel, 4 vols. (New York: Chelsea House/McGraw-Hill, 1971), 2:1615–16; John G. Sproat, *"The Best Men": Liberal Reformers in the Gilded Age* (New York: Oxford University Press, 1968), p. 147; Arthur M. Schlesinger, Jr., "Who Needs Grover Cleveland?" *New Republic* 181 (1979): 14–16.

14. Merrill, *Bourbon Democracy of the Middle West*, pp. vii–viii, and *William Freeman Vilas* (Madison: State Historical Society of Wisconsin, 1954), p. 203.

15. Wesser, "Election of 1888," p. 1615.

16. John M. Dobson, *Politics in the Gilded Age: A New Perspective on Reform* (New York: Praeger, 1972), p. 122; R. Hal Williams, " 'Dry Bones and Dead Language': The Democratic Party," in *The Gilded Age: A Reappraisal*, p. 131; Keller, *Affairs of State*, pp. 554–56.

CHAPTER 2

THE CONTRADICTIONS
OF PHILOSOPHY AND PERSONALITY

1. Woodrow Wilson, "Mr. Cleveland as President," *Atlantic Monthly*, Mar. 1897, p. 292; Leonard D. White, *The Republican Era, 1869–1901: A Study in Administrative History* (New York: Macmillan, 1958), p. 25; Allan Nevins, *Grover Cleveland: A Study in Courage* (New York: Dodd, Mead, 1933), p. 342.

2. *Public Papers of Grover Cleveland, Twenty-second President of the United States, 1885–1889* (Washington, D.C.: U.S. Government Printing Office, 1889), p. 261; see also "Remarks Delivered before Merchants' Association, Milwaukee," 6 Oct. 1887, Daniel S. Lamont Papers, LC.

3. Pearl L. Robertson, "Grover Cleveland as a Political Leader" (Ph.D. diss., University of Chicago, 1937), pp. 249, 268.

4. *The Writings and Speeches of Grover Cleveland*, ed. George F. Parker (New York: Cassell, 1892), pp. 97–98.

5. *Public Papers*, p. 238.

6. Orville T. Payne, "The Administrative Theory and Practice of Grover Cleveland" (Ph.D. diss., University of Chicago, 1951), pp. 295–96.

7. Geoffrey Blodgett, "Reform Thought and the Genteel Tradition," in *The Gilded Age: A Reappraisal*, ed. H. Wayne Morgan, rev. ed. (Syracuse, N.Y.: Syracuse University Press, 1970), p. 69.

8. See, e.g., Robert Kelley, *The Transatlantic Persuasion: The Liberal-Democratic Mind in the Age of Gladstone* (New York: Knopf, 1969), pp. 317, 323, and "Presbyterianism, Jacksonianism and Grover Cleveland," *American Quarterly* 18 (1966): 623, 629.

9. Adopting Freudian terminology, Pearl L. Robertson has written that for Cleveland, religion "proceeded on a conscience level (super ego) and involved habit and conviction rather than emotional experience" (*Grover Cleveland as a Political Leader* [Chicago: University of Chicago Press, 1938], p. 54).

10. See Cleveland's "Remarks before the Northern and Southern Presbyterian Assemblies at Philadelphia," 23 May 1888, in *Public Papers*, p. 334.

11. See Cleveland's "Address before the Business Men's Democratic Association of New York," 8 Jan. 1892, *Letters and Addresses of Grover Cleveland*, ed. Albert Ellery Bergh (New York: Unit Publishing Co., 1909), pp. 314–16.

12. *Public Papers*, pp. 438–40.

13. Ibid., p. 287.

14. Bergh, *Letters and Addresses*, pp. 318–28.

CHAPTER 3
"CLEVELAND LUCK":
THE ROAD TO THE WHITE HOUSE

1. Richard Hofstadter attributes Cleveland's political success to "a series of improbabilities" (*The American Political Tradition and the Men Who Made It* [New York: Knopf, 1948], p. 179); and Henry Jones Ford offers the opinion that "the rapid and fortuitous rise of Grover Cleveland to political eminence is without a parallel in the records of American statesmanship" (*The Cleveland Era* [New Haven, Conn.: Yale University Press, 1919], p. 42). Cleveland told a friend that when he was about to deliver his Inaugural Address in March 1885, he was struck by the fact that when four years earlier James Garfield had performed the same task, Garfield had never heard Cleveland's name (*London Daily Telegraph*, 25 June 1908).

2. Robert McElroy, *Grover Cleveland: The Man and the Statesman*, 2 vols. (New York: Harper & Bros., 1923), 1:3–18; Allan Nevins, *Grover Cleveland: A Study in Courage* (New York: Dodd, Mead, 1933), pp. 27–43.

3. E. Jay Edwards, "The Personal Force of Cleveland," *McClure's*

Magazine, Nov. 1893, p. 493.

4. Eastman Johnson's portrait of Cleveland, painted during his gubernatorial years, is a very flattering likeness.

5. Nevins, *Grover Cleveland*, pp. 111–24.

6. Interview in *New York Herald*, 10 Dec. 1883; Cleveland's second message to the New York Legislature, 1 Jan. 1884; *The Writings and Speeches of Grover Cleveland*, ed. George F. Parker (New York: Cassell, 1892), pp. 63–65.

7. GC to Fairchild, 17 Mar. 1884, in *Letters of Grover Cleveland, 1850–1908*, ed. Allan Nevins (Boston: Houghton Mifflin, 1933), pp. 30–31.

8. GC to Manning, 30 June 1884, in Nevins, *Letters*, p. 35.

9. The term *Mugwump* was first used by John Eliot in his Indian Bible. Charles Dana, editor of the *New York Sun*, was primarily responsible for its revival and its association with political dissidence.

10. Geoffrey Blodgett, "The Mind of the Boston Mugwump," *Mississippi Valley Historical Review* 48 (Mar. 1962): 614.

11. Quoted in H. Wayne Morgan, *From Hayes to McKinley: National Party Politics, 1877–1896* (Syracuse, N.Y.: Syracuse University Press, 1969), p. 211.

12. *Harper's Weekly*, 5 July 1884, p. 426.

13. Kirk H. Porter, comp., *National Party Platforms* (New York: Macmillan, 1924), pp. 116–23, 132–36.

14. *New York Times*, 15 Sept. and 7 Oct. 1884.

15. Marvin Rosenberg and Dorothy Rosenberg, "The Dirtiest Election," *American Heritage*, Aug. 1962, p. 99.

16. GC to Lamont, 14 Aug. 1884, in Nevins, *Letters*, p. 41.

17. *Public Papers of Grover Cleveland, Twenty-second President of the United States, 1885–1889* (Washington, D.C.: U.S. Government Printing Office, 1899), pp. 3–5.

18. *Letters and Addresses of Grover Cleveland*, ed. Albert Ellery Bergh (New York: Unit Publishing Co., 1909), p. 58.

19. GC to Curtis, 24 Oct. 1884, in Nevins, *Letters*, pp. 46–47.

20. See GC to Wilson S. Bissell, 11 Sept. 1884; GC to Carter H. Harrison, 21 July 1884; GC to Daniel S. Lamont, 11 Aug. 1884; GC to George F. Dege, 24 Oct. 1884—all in Nevins, *Letters*, pp. 37–47.

21. In later years, Cleveland became the guardian and then the husband of Folsom's daughter, Frances, a circle of coincidence that would have impressed Thomas Hardy.

22. Rosenberg and Rosenberg, "The Dirtiest Election," pp. 4, 7.

23. Nevins, *Grover Cleveland*, p. 165.

24. Quoted by Matthew Josephson in *The Politicos, 1865–1896* (New York: Harcourt, Brace, 1938), p. 366.

25. See GC to Charles W. Goodyear, 23 July 1884; GC to Wilson S. Bissell, 11 Sept., 5 and 9 Oct. 1884; GC to Mrs. Henry Ward Beecher, 20 Oct. 1884—all in Nevins, *Letters*, pp. 37–45.

26. Lee Benson, "Research Problems in American Political Historiography," in *Common Frontiers of the Social Sciences*, ed. Mirra Komarovsky (Glencoe, Ill.: Free Press, 1947), p. 131.

27. Thomas J. Osborne, "What Was the Main Reason for Cleveland's Election Victory in 1884?" *Northwest Ohio Quarterly* 45 (Spring 1973): 69.

28. See GC to Wilson S. Bissell, 13 Nov. 1884, in Nevins, *Letters*, pp. 47–48.

CHAPTER 4
THE CAUTIOUS REFORMER:
CLEVELAND'S FIRST ADMINISTRATION

1. Harry Thurston Peck, *Twenty Years of the Republic, 1885–1905* (New York: Dodd, Mead, 1906), p. 39.

2. In the last days of the first Cleveland administration, Norman J. Colman joined the cabinet as secretary of agriculture. In February 1889, Congress passed the Hatch Act, which raised the Bureau of Agriculture to departmental rank with cabinet representation. Colman, editor of *Colman's Rural World*, had previously served as commissioner of agriculture within the Interior Department.

3. Cleveland seldom found reason to consult Vice-president Thomas A. Hendricks during the early months of his administration. Cleveland considered Hendricks to be an example of the lifelong professional politician who was more interested in patronage than in efficient government. Hendricks's death late in 1885 left the administration without a vice-president and helped to inspire the Presidential Succession Act of 1886, which provided that upon the death of an incumbent, the presidential office would be filled by the vice-president or, were he to predecease the president, by the ranking member of the cabinet in order of the seniority of the department (secretary of state, secretary of the Treasury, secretary of war, etc.).

4. Vincent P. De Santis, "Grover Cleveland: Another Look," *Hayes Historical Journal* 3 (Winter 1983): 46.

5. Cleveland's First Annual Message to Congress, 8 Dec. 1885, *Public Papers of Grover Cleveland, Twenty-second President of the United States, 1885–1889* (Washington, D.C.: U.S. Government Printing Office, 1889), pp. 41–42.

6. Allan Nevins, *Grover Cleveland: A Study in Courage* (New York: Dodd, Mead, 1933), p. 270.

7. *Public Papers*, pp. 59–67; Louis Fisher, "Grover Cleveland against the Senate," *Congressional Studies* 7 (Winter 1979): 17–19.

8. Schurz to GC, 16 Jan. 1896, CP, LC.

9. Leonard D. White, *The Republican Era, 1869–1901: A Study in Administrative History* (New York: Macmillan, 1958), p. 31.

10. H. Wayne Morgan, *From Hayes to McKinley: National Party Pol-

itics, 1877–1896 (Syracuse, N.Y.: Syracuse University Press, 1969), pp. 249, 254; John G. Sproat, *"The Best Men": Liberal Reformers in the Gilded Age* (New York: Oxford University Press, 1968), p. 265.

11. *Letters of Grover Cleveland, 1850–1908*, ed. Allan Nevins (Boston, Mass.: Houghton Mifflin, 1933), pp. 52–53.

12. Henry Jones Ford, *The Cleveland Era* (New Haven, Conn.: Yale University Press, 1919), p. 111, citing *Harper's Weekly*, 21 Apr. 1888.

13. GC to Dorman B. Eaton, 11 Sept. 1885, in Nevins, *Letters*, pp. 74–75.

14. Geoffrey Blodgett, "A New Look at the Gilded Age: Politics in a Cultural Context," in *Victorian America*, ed. Daniel Walker Howe (Philadelphia: University of Pennsylvania Press, 1976), p. 104. For contrasting views of the importance of civil-service reform see Ari Hoogenboom, "Civil Service Reform and Public Morality," in *The Gilded Age: A Reappraisal*, ed. H. Wayne Morgan, rev. ed. (Syracuse, N.Y.: Syracuse University Press, 1970), p. 86; Horace Samuel Merrill, *Bourbon Leader: Grover Cleveland and the Democratic Party* (Boston, Mass.: Little, Brown, 1957), p. 38; John A. Garraty, *The New Commonwealth, 1877–1900* (New York: Harper & Row, 1968), p. 289; Morton Keller, *Affairs of State: Public Life in Late Nineteenth Century America* (Cambridge, Mass.: Harvard University Press, 1977), p. 314.

15. See, e.g., GC to A. Bush, 1 Aug. 1885, CP.

16. Nevins, *Grover Cleveland*, p. 235.

17. *Public Papers*, p. 157.

18. Ibid., pp. 229–37. In 1876 the federal government had spent only 10 percent of its budget on veterans' pensions; by Feb. 1887, it was spending 25 percent.

19. Ibid., pp. 257–59.

20. Ibid., p. 9.

21. Philip Foner, *The Life and Writings of Frederick Douglass* (New York: International Publishers, 1964), pp. 4, 417.

22. George Sinkler, *The Racial Attitudes of American Presidents: From Abraham Lincoln to Theodore Roosevelt* (Garden City, N.Y.: Doubleday, 1971), p. 223; *Public Papers*, pp. 216–17.

23. James Jefferson to GC, 22 July 1893, CP; Richard Olney to GC, 26 Feb. and 23 Nov. 1896, Olney Papers, LC.

24. See drafts of Cleveland's addresses at Atlanta, Ga., and Montgomery, Ala., Daniel S. Lamont Papers, LC.

25. Nevins, *Letters*, p. 413.

26. *The Writings and Speeches of Grover Cleveland*, ed. George F. Parker (New York: Cassell, 1892), pp. 344–45.

27. GC to G. A. Sullivan, 27 Aug. 1887, CP.

28. Sinkler, *Racial Attitudes of American Presidents*, pp. 229–30.

29. *Public Papers*, pp. 47–49.

30. See Cleveland's Second Annual Message, *Public Papers*, pp. 205–9.

31. Cleveland's Fourth Annual Message, in *Writings and Speeches*, p. 420; GC to the Reverend James Morrow, 29 Mar. 1888, CP.

32. GC to Hoke Smith, 4 May 1895, in Nevins, Letters, p. 390.

33. *Public Papers*, pp. 18-19.

34. Ibid., pp. 132-33.

35. GC to Bayard, 18 Dec. 1887, Bayard Papers, LC.

36. *Public Papers*, pp. 414-19. Cleveland also suggested that Congress pass legislation appropriating the sum of $276,619 "payable to the Chinese minister in this capital."

37. GC to Richard Olney, 4 July 1896, Olney Papers, LC.

38. *Public Papers*, pp. 176-77.

39. James D. Richardson, comp., *A Compilation of the Messages and Papers of the Presidents, 1789-1897*, 10 vols. (Washington, D.C.: U.S. Government Printing Office, 1897-1907), 9:758-60. See also Cleveland's Address at the Annual Banquet of the New England Society, 21 Dec. 1891, in *Letters and Addresses of Grover Cleveland*, ed. Albert Ellery Bergh (New York: Unit Publishing Co., 1909), p. 312.

40. See *Public Papers*, p. 53, for Cleveland's recommendation for a law to prohibit "the importation of Mormons into the country." An act of 3 Mar. 1887 authorized the federal government to seize and administer the property of the Mormon Church until it made a formal promise to abandon polygamy.

41. *Public Papers*, pp. 208-9.

42. GC to the Secretary of the Interior, 25 Apr. 1887, *Public Papers*, pp. 253-55.

43. Ibid., p. 461.

44. Geoffrey Blodgett, "The Political Leadership of Grover Cleveland," *South Atlantic Quarterly* 82 (Summer 1983): 295.

CHAPTER 5
LABOR, SILVER, AND TARIFF REFORM
DURING CLEVELAND'S FIRST ADMINISTRATION

1. *Public Papers of Grover Cleveland, Twenty-second President of the United States, 1885-1889* (Washington, D.C.: U.S. Government Printing Office, 1889), pp. 78-79.

2. Ibid., p. 212.

3. Ibid., p. 238.

4. Ibid., pp. 464-65.

5. GC to the Hon. A. J. Warner et al., 24 Feb. 1885, in *The Writings and Speeches of Grover Cleveland*, ed. George F. Parker (New York: Cassell, 1892), pp. 363-64.

6. *Public Papers*, pp. 32-36; see also ibid., p. 198.

7. GC to Samuel J. Randall, 14 July 1886, in *Letters of Grover Cleve-*

land, *1850–1908*, ed. Allan Nevins (Boston, Mass.: Houghton Mifflin, 1933), p. 115.

8. *Public Papers*, p. 31.

9. Ibid., pp. 194–97.

10. See Tom E. Terrill, *The Tariff, Politics, and American Foreign Policy, 1874–1901* (Westport, Conn.: Greenwood Press, 1973), pp. 10–11, 58–59, 96–97, 111–20, and "David A. Wells, the Democracy, and Tariff Reduction, 1877–1894," *Journal of American History* 56 (Dec. 1969): 540–55; Walter LaFeber, *The New Empire: An Interpretation of American Expansion, 1860–1898* (Ithaca, N.Y.: Cornell University Press, 1963), pp. 159–72.

11. For an effective rebuttal of the thesis of Cleveland as an exponent of government-directed market expansion see Paul S. Holbo, "Economics, Emotion, and Expansion: An Emerging Foreign Policy," in *The Gilded Age: A Reappraisal*, ed. H. Wayne Morgan, rev. ed. (Syracuse, N.Y.: Syracuse University Press, 1970), pp. 203–5.

12. See Terrill, *Tariff, Politics, and American Foreign Policy*, pp. 102–12; H. Wayne Morgan, *From Hayes to McKinley: National Party Politics, 1877–1896* (Syracuse, N.Y.: Syracuse University Press, 1969), p. 271, and *Unity and Culture: The United States, 1877–1900* (London: Penguin, 1971), p. 67; Robert F. Wesser, "Election of 1888," in *History of American Presidential Elections, 1789–1968*, ed. Arthur M. Schlesinger, Jr., and Fred L. Israel, 4 vols. (New York: Chelsea House/McGraw-Hill, 1971), 2:1620.

13. *Public Papers*, pp. 269–79.

14. Terrill, *Tariff, Politics, and American Foreign Policy*, p. 10n.

15. Fourth Annual Message, 3 Dec. 1888, in *Public Papers*, p. 442.

CHAPTER 6
DEFEAT, EXILE, AND VICTORY, 1888–92

1. "The Beast of Buffalo," pamphlet, Lamont Papers, LC; Pearl Louise Robertson, "Grover Cleveland as a Political Leader" (Ph.D. diss., University of Chicago, 1937), p. 124.

2. Kirk H. Porter, comp., *National Party Platforms* (New York: Macmillan, 1924), pp. 140–44.

3. Ibid., pp. 146–52.

4. Allan Nevins, *Grover Cleveland: A Study in Courage* (New York: Dodd, Mead, 1933), p. 416.

5. *Letters and Addresses of Grover Cleveland*, ed. Albert Ellery Bergh (New York: Unit Publishing Co., 1909), pp. 140–51.

6. GC to C. F. Black, 14 Sept. 1888, in *Letters of Grover Cleveland, 1850–1908*, ed. Allan Nevins (Boston, Mass.: Houghton Mifflin, 1933), p. 189.

7. Richard E. Welch, Jr., *George Frisbie Hoar and the Half-Breed*

Republicans (Cambridge, Mass.: Harvard University Press, 1971), pp. 141–42.

8. James L. Baumgardner, "The 1888 Presidential Election: How Corrupt?" *Presidential Studies Quarterly* 14 (Summer 1984): 416–27.

9. Charles S. Campbell, Jr., "The Dismissal of Lord Sackville," *Mississippi Valley Historical Review* 44 (Mar. 1958): 635–48; Robert Wesser, "Election of 1888," in *History of American Presidential Elections, 1789–1968,* ed. Arthur M. Schlesinger, Jr., and Fred L. Israel, 4 vols. (New York: Chelsea House/McGraw-Hill, 1971), 2:1645.

10. Harry Thurston Peck, *Twenty Years of the Republic, 1885–1905* (New York: Dodd, Mead, 1906), p. 165.

11. *The Writings and Speeches of Grover Cleveland,* ed. George F. Parker (New York: Cassell, 1892), pp. 91–98.

12. GC to Bissell, 21 Oct. 1891; GC to Dr. S. B. Ward, 21 June 1891, CP.

13. The McKinley Tariff Act, signed into law by President Harrison on 1 Oct. 1890, represented a victory for the forces of high protectionism. It placed certain imported agricultural products, such as sugar, on the free list; but such industries as tin-plate manufacture were virtually immunized from foreign competition, and the average rate of custom duties was raised to 49.5 percent, the highest in the nation's history. The most interesting feature of this act was a provision providing for a negative, or blackmail, version of tariff reciprocity. The president was granted the authority to reimpose a tariff duty on certain agricultural imports if the exporting nation would not make tariff concessions to United States products.

14. Richard E. Welch, Jr., "The Federal Elections Bill of 1890: Postscripts and Prelude," *Journal of American History* 52 (Dec. 1965): 511–26.

15. See, e.g., Cleveland's letters to the Indiana Tariff Reform League, 15 Feb. 1890, and to the Tariff Reform Club of Hagerstown, Md., 29 Apr. 1890, in *Writings and Speeches,* pp. 100–102.

16. Samuel P. Hays, "Political Parties and the Community-Society Continuum," in *The American Party System: Stages of Political Development,* ed. William N. Chambers and Walter Dean Burnham (New York: Oxford University Press, 1967), pp. 152–58; see also Paul Kleppner, *The Cross of Culture: A Social Analysis of Midwestern Politics, 1850–1890* (New York: Free Press, 1970), pp. 131–43; Richard Jensen, *The Winning of the Midwest: Social and Political Conflict, 1888–1896* (Chicago: University of Chicago Press, 1971), pp. 122–53; Hays, "The Social Analysis of American Political History, 1880–1920," *Political Science Quarterly* 80 (1965): 387.

17. See, e.g., Cleveland's address at the New York City Reform Club dinner, 23 Dec. 1890, and his Jackson Day Address to the Young Men's Democratic Association of Philadelphia, 3 Jan. 1891, in Bergh, *Letters and Addresses,* pp. 271–77, 279–85; GC, letter to the Indiana Tariff Reform League, 10 Mar. 1891, in *Writings and Speeches,* pp. 104–5.

18. Nevins, *Letters*, pp. 231–32, 248–49.

19. GC to R. W. Gilder, 18 Aug. 1891, Cleveland Papers; Charles Hamlin, diary for 22 and 26 Feb. 1892, Charles Hamlin Papers, LC.

20. GC to E. Ellery Anderson, 10 Feb. 1891, in Nevins, *Letters*, pp. 245–46.

21. See Cleveland's explanatory letter to William F. Vilas, 18 Feb. 1891, in Nevins, *Letters*, p. 246.

22. GC to W. H. Black, 20 Feb. 1892, CP; Charles Hamlin, diary for 30 Apr. 1892, Hamlin Papers.

23. See GC to Wilson S. Bissell, 1 Mar. 1892, in Nevins, *Letters*, pp. 278–79.

24. Bergh, *Letters and Addresses*, pp. 330–38.

25. *Washington Post*, 16 Mar. and 21 Apr. 1890, cited in H. Wayne Morgan, *From Hayes to McKinley: National Party Politics, 1877–1896* (Syracuse, N.Y.: Syracuse University Press, 1969), p. 404.

26. Peck, *Twenty Years*, p. 264.

27. See GC to Whitney, 28 May and 6 June 1892, William C. Whitney Papers, LC.

28. See letter draft of 3 June 1892, Whitney Papers.

29. GC to Whitney, 10 and 13 June 1892, Whitney Papers.

30. Charles Hamlin, diary for 18 June 1892, Hamlin Papers.

31. Henry Adams, *Education of Henry Adams* (Boston: Houghton Mifflin, 1918), p. 320.

32. Porter, *National Party Platforms*, pp. 159–65.

33. Festus P. Summers, *William L. Wilson and Tariff Reform* (New Brunswick, N.J.: Rutgers University Press, 1953), pp. 141–44; GC to Whitney, 9 July 1892, Whitney Papers; GC to William E. Russell, 13 July 1892, in Nevins, *Letters*, p. 292.

34. Harry J. Sievers, S.J., *Benjamin Harrison, Hoosier President* (Indianapolis, Ind.: Bobbs-Merrill, 1961), p. 243; Summers, *William L. Wilson*, p. 147.

35. Democratic National Committee, *Campaign Textbook of the Democratic Party* (New York, 1892), p. 17.

36. GC to R. W. Gilder, 25 Sept. 1892, CP.

37. GC to Whitney, 23 Aug. 1892, Whitney Papers.

38. GC to Whitney, 9 July and 23 Aug. 1892, Whitney Papers.

39. GC to Mrs. Mary Frost Ormsby, 6 July 1892, CP.

40. George Harmon Knoles, *The Presidential Campaign and Election of 1892* (Stanford, Calif.: Stanford University Press, 1942), p. 207.

41. See, e.g., GC to Indiana Senator Daniel W. Vorhees, 11 July 1892, GC to R. R. Bowker, 15 July 1892, GC to Clark Howell, 16 July 1892—all in Nevins, *Letters*, pp. 292–94; GC to Whitney, 9 July 1892, Whitney Papers.

42. Charles Hamlin, diary for 1 Aug. 1892, Hamlin Papers; GC to Wilson S. Bissell, 24 July 1892, in Nevins, *Letters*, pp. 295–96.

43. Whitney to GC, 30 Aug. 1892, in Nevins, *Letters*, p. 304.

44. Knoles, *Presidential Campaign and Election of 1892*, p. 246.

45. Woodrow Wilson, "Mr. Cleveland's Cabinet," *Review of Reviews*, Apr. 1893, p. 289.

CHAPTER 7
PANIC, DEPRESSION, AND THE CRUSADE
AGAINST SILVER MONOMETALLISM

1. *Letters and Addresses of Grover Cleveland*, ed. Albert Ellery Bergh (New York: Unit Publishing Co., 1909), pp. 347–50.

2. Daniel S. Lamont, memoranda of 7 Dec. 1892, 4 and 16 Jan. and 19 Feb. 1893, Lamont Papers, LC.

3. R. Hal Williams, *Years of Decision: American Politics in the 1890s* (New York: John Wiley, 1978), p. 77.

4. Walter T. K. Nugent, *From Centennial to World War: American Society, 1876–1917* (Indianapolis, Ind.: Bobbs-Merrill, 1977), p. 104.

5. For contrary assessments see John A. Garraty, *The New Commonwealth, 1877–1900* (New York: Harper & Row, 1968), p. 251; Milton Friedman and Anna Jacobson Schwartz, *A Monetary History of the United States, 1867– 1960* (Princeton, N.J.: Princeton University Press, 1963), p. 111.

6. See GC, letter to the annual banquet of the Democratic Editorial Association of New York, 24 May 1895, in Bergh, *Letters and Addresses*, pp. 369–71; Robert Kelley, "Presbyterianism, Jacksonianism and Grover Cleveland," *American Quarterly* 18 (1966): 627–28, and *The Transatlantic Persuasion: The Liberal-Democratic Mind in the Age of Gladstone* (New York: Knopf, 1969), p. 335.

7. James A. Barnes, *John G. Carlisle: Financial Statesman* (New York: Dodd, Mead, 1931), p. 271.

8. William W. Keen, *The Surgical Operations on President Cleveland in 1893* (Philadelphia: G. W. Jacobs, 1917), pp. 58–59. Microscopic examination later determined that the gelatinous mass was a carcinoma.

9. Ibid., pp. 58–63; Wilbur Cross and John Moses, "My God, Sir, I Think the President Is Doomed!" *American History Illustrated* 17 (Nov. 1982): 40–45; Robert Scott Stevenson, *Famous Illnesses in History* (London: Eyre & Spottiswoode, 1962), pp. 44–51.

10. GC to Bayard, 11 Sept. 1893, in *Letters of Grover Cleveland, 1850–1908*, ed. Allan Nevins (Boston, Mass.: Houghton Mifflin, 1933), p. 334.

11. Pearl L. Robertson, "Grover Cleveland as a Political Leader" (Ph.D. diss., University of Chicago, 1937), p. 256.

12. GC to Henry T. Thurber, 20 Aug. 1893, and GC to L. Clarke Davis, 25 Feb. 1894, in Nevins, *Letters*, pp. 331, 348.

13. See Charles S. Hamlin, diary for 1 Nov. 1893, Hamlin Papers.

14. Williams, *Years of Decision*, p. 83.

15. Barnes, *John G. Carlisle*, p. 360.

16. Grover Cleveland, *Presidential Problems* (New York: Century Co., 1904), p. 168.

17. Barnes, *John G. Carlisle*, pp. 390–91.

18. H. Wayne Morgan, *From Hayes to McKinley: National Party Politics, 1877–1896* (Syracuse, N.Y.: Syracuse University Press, 1969), p. 459.

CHAPTER 8

THE GREAT DISAPPOINTMENT:
CLEVELAND AND THE TARIFF, 1894

1. Paul S. Holbo, "Economics, Emotion, and Expansion: An Emerging Foreign Policy," in *The Gilded Age: A Reappraisal*, ed. H. Wayne Morgan, rev. ed. (Syracuse, N.Y.: Syracuse University Press, 1970), pp. 207–8.

2. See Walter LaFeber, *The New Empire: An Interpretation of American Expansion, 1860–1898* (Ithaca, N.Y.: Cornell University Press, 1963), pp. 160–68, 200–201.

3. Warren Hamill Wilson, "Grover Cleveland and the Wilson-Gorman Tariff" (Master's thesis, University of Texas, Austin, 1977), pp. 55–57.

4. See Wilson's speech of 8/9 Jan. 1894, *Congressional Record*, vol. 26, app., pp. 193–201.

5. H. Wayne Morgan, *From Hayes to McKinley: National Party Politics, 1877–1896* (Syracuse, N.Y.: Syracuse University Press, 1969), p. 462.

6. Wilson, "Grover Cleveland and the Wilson-Gorman Tariff," pp. 101–9.

7. Allan Nevins, *Grover Cleveland: A Study in Courage* (New York: Dodd, Mead, 1933), p. 573.

8. Wilson later referred to Gorman as "a crafty, unprincipled, debasing leader without the education of a lawmaker or statesman" (William L. Wilson, diary for 30 Oct. 1897, cited by Festus P. Summers in *William L. Wilson and Tariff Reform* [New Brunswick, N.J.: Rutgers University Press, 1953], p. 135).

9. GC to Wilson, 2 July 1894, CP.

10. Summers, *William L. Wilson*, p. 195.

11. GC to Wilson, 2 July 1894, in *Letters of Grover Cleveland, 1850–1908*, ed. Allan Nevins (Boston, Mass.: Houghton Mifflin, 1933), pp. 354–57.

12. GC to Wilson, 13 Aug. 1894, in Nevins, *Letters*, p. 363.

13. GC to Catchings, 27 Aug. 1894, in Nevins, *Letters*, pp. 364–66.

14. Geoffrey Blodgett, "The Political Leadership of Grover Cleveland," *South Atlantic Quarterly* 82 (Summer 1983): 295–96.

CHAPTER 9
LAW AND ORDER BY FEDERAL AUTHORITY:
CLEVELAND AND BUSINESS AND LABOR,
1893–96

1. Richard Hofstadter offers the opinion that "Cleveland fell quietly and naturally into an implicit partnership with the interests during the crisis of the nineties" (*The American Political Tradition and the Men Who Made It* [New York: Knopf, 1948], p. 181); while Horace Samuel Merrill insists that Cleveland held the conviction that "to serve business was to serve the nation as a whole" (*Bourbon Leader: Grover Cleveland and the Democratic Party* [Boston, Mass.: Little, Brown, 1957], p. 70).

2. Arnold M. Paul, *Conservative Crisis and the Rule of Law: Attitudes of Bar and Bench, 1887–1895* (Ithaca, N.Y.: Cornell University Press, 1960), p. 140. This injunction is also analyzed in detail by the biographers of Altgeld, Debs, and Olney, which are cited in the Bibliographical Essay.

3. Ibid., p. 140.

4. GC to Altgeld, 5 July 1894, in *Letters of Grover Cleveland, 1850–1908*, ed. Allan Nevins (Boston, Mass.: Houghton Mifflin, 1933), p. 360.

5. Paul Van Dyke, "My Neighbor: Grover Cleveland," *Scribner's Magazine*, Apr. 1927, p. 350.

6. Allan Nevins, *Grover Cleveland: A Study in Courage* (New York: Dodd, Mead, 1933), pp. 626–27.

7. Robert Kelley, *The Transatlantic Persuasion: The Liberal-Democratic Mind in the Age of Gladstone* (New York: Knopf, 1969), p. 320.

8. Orville T. Payne, "The Administrative Theory and Practice of Grover Cleveland" (Ph.D. diss., University of Chicago, 1951), p. 255.

9. Grover Cleveland, *Presidential Problems* (New York: Century Co., 1904), p. 109.

10. Quoted by Henry Jones Ford in *The Cleveland Era* (New Haven, Conn.: Yale University Press, 1919), p. 211.

11. Bennett M. Rich, *The Presidents and Civil Disorder* (Washington, D.C.: Brookings Institution, 1941), p. 109.

12. See Olney memorandum prepared for Cleveland's fourth annual message of Dec. 1896; Olney to C. S. Hamlin, 24 Oct. 1902, Olney Papers, LC.

13. Olney to "A.M.S.," 22 Jan. 1895, Olney Papers.

14. James P. Richardson, comp., *A Compilation of the Messages and Papers of the Presidents, 1789–1897*, 10 vols. (Washington, D.C.: U.S. Government Printing Office, 1897–1907), 9:714–45; GC to E. C. Benedict, 1 Jan. 1897, in Nevins, *Letters*, p. 466.

15. Matthew Josephson, *The Politicos, 1865–1896* (New York: Harcourt, Brace, 1938), p. 522.

16. Grover Cleveland, *The Self-made Man in American Life* (New York: T. Y. Crowell, 1897), p. 23.

17. GC to the New York Chamber of Commerce, 4 Nov. 1887, in *Public Papers of Grover Cleveland, Twenty-second President of the United States, 1885– 1889* (Washington, D.C.: U.S. Government Printing Office, 1889), p. 268; Address to the Banquet of the New York Chamber of Commerce, 15 Nov. 1892, in *Letters and Addresses of Grover Cleveland*, ed. Albert Ellery Bergh (New York: Unit Publishing Co., 1909), pp. 341–42.

18. Paolo E. Coletta, "Bryan, Cleveland, and the Disrupted Democracy, 1890– 1896," *Nebraska History* 41 (Mar. 1960): 26.

CHAPTER 10
CLEVELAND'S DIPLOMACY 1:
BRITISH AND PACIFIC RELATIONS

1. James D. Richardson, comp., *A Compilation of the Messages and Papers of the Presidents, 1789-1897*, 10 vols. (Washington, D.C.: U.S. Government Printing Office, 1897-1907), 8:301.

2. *Public Papers of Grover Cleveland, Twenty–second President of the United States, 1885-1889* (Washington, D.C.: U.S. Government Printing Office, 1889), pp. 16–17.

3. Ibid., p. 20.

4. See GC to Charles N. Plummer, 3 May 1893, in *Letters of Grover Cleveland, 1850-1908*, ed. Allan Nevins (Boston, Mass.: Houghton Mifflin, 1933), p. 324.

5. Charles S. Campbell, Jr., "American Tariff Interests and the Northeastern Fisheries, 1883-1888," *Canadian Historical Review* 45 (1964): 212–28.

6. Charles C. Tansill, *Canadian-American Relations, 1875-1911* (Toronto: Ryerson Press, 1943), p. 43.

7. Campbell, "American Tariff Interests," p. 220; Allan Nevins, *Grover Cleveland: A Study in Courage* (New York: Dodd, Mead, 1933), pp. 409–10; *Public Papers*, pp. 288–90.

8. *Public Papers*, pp. 290–92.

9. Ibid., pp. 394–97.

10. For a more complimentary view of Cleveland's strategy in his duel with the Senate see Campbell, "American Tariff Interests,"pp. 226–28; George Roscoe Dulebohn, *Principles of Foreign Policy under the Cleveland Administrations* (Philadelphia: University of Pennyslvania Press, 1941), pp. 71–73; Nevins, *Grover Cleveland*, pp. 406–13.

11. Tansill, *Canadian-American Relations*, p. 141.

12. Olney to GC, 23 Nov. 1896, Olney Papers, LC.

13. Tansill, *Canadian-American Relations*, pp. 270–75.

14. Robert L. Beisner, *From the Old Diplomacy to the New, 1865-1900*, rev. ed. (Arlington Heights, Ill.: Harlan Davidson, 1986), p. 63.

15. Charles Hamlin, diary for 21 Jan. 1895, Hamlin Papers, LC.

16. Paul M. Kennedy, *The Samoan Tangle: A Study in Anglo-German-*

American Relations, 1878–1900 (New York: Barnes & Noble, 1974), pp. 52–53.

17. *Public Papers*, p. 189.

18. GC to Bayard, 4 Dec. 1888, Bayard Papers, LC; GC to Rear Adm. Lewis A. Kimberly, 10 Jan. 1889, in Nevins, *Letters*, p. 196; "Message Relative to Samoan Question," 16 Jan. 1889, in *Public Papers*, pp. 470–72.

19. Richardson, *Messages*, 8:800–801; *Papers Relating to the Foreign Relations of the United States, 1886*, p. vi.

20. GC to Schurz, 19 Mar. 1893, Papers of Carl Schurz, LC; see also Thomas J. Osborne, *"Empire Can Wait": American Opposition to Hawaiian Annexation, 1893–1898* (Kent, Ohio: Kent State University Press, 1981), p. 63.

21. For a somewhat contrary view see Osborne, *"Empire Can Wait,"* p. 15; Tennant S. McWilliams, "James H. Blount, Paramount Defender of Hawaii," paper read at the convention of the Organization of American Historians, New York City, 11 Apr. 1896.

22. *Foreign Relations of the United States, 1894*, app. 2, pp. 567–605.

23. Olney to Gresham, 9 Oct. 1893, Olney Papers, LC.

24. Gresham to GC, 18 Oct. 1893, cited by Matilda Gresham in *Life of Walter Quintin Gresham, 1832–1895* (Chicago: Rand, McNally, 1919), p. 752.

25. Olney to Gresham, 9 Oct. 1893, Olney Papers.

26. See Olney draft for "President's Message to Congress," Dec. 1893, Olney Papers.

27. Robert McElroy, *Grover Cleveland: The Man and the Statesman*, 2 vols. (New York: Harper & Bros., 1923), 2:66; Nevins, *Grover Cleveland*, p. 560.

28. GC to Dole, 17 Aug. 1894, in Nevins, *Letters*, pp. 363–64.

29. GC to Bayard, 13 Feb. 1895, in Nevins, *Letters*, pp. 377–78.

30. William A. Russ, Jr., *The Hawaiian Revolution, 1893–94* (Selinsgrove, Pa.: Susquehanna University Press, 1959), pp. 350–51; Osborne, *"Empire Can Wait,"* p. 67.

31. R. Hal Williams, *The Democratic Party and California Politics, 1880–1896* (Stanford, Calif.: Stanford University Press, 1973), p. 192.

CHAPTER 11
CLEVELAND'S DIPLOMACY 2:
RELATIONS WITH LATIN AMERICA

1. Dexter Perkins, *The Monroe Doctrine, 1867–1907* (Baltimore, Md.: Johns Hopkins University Press, 1937), p. 104.

2. Robert L. Beisner, *From the Old Diplomacy to the New*, rev. ed. (Arlington Heights, Ill.: Harlan Davidson, 1986), p. 70.

3. Tom E. Terrill, *The Tariff, Politics, and American Foreign Policy,*

1874–1901 (Westport, Conn.: Greenwood Press, 1973), p. 91.

4. *Public Papers of Grover Cleveland, Twenty-second President of the United States, 1885–1889* (Washington, D.C.: U.S. Government Printing Office, 1889), p. 451.

5. Walter LaFeber, "The Background of Cleveland's Venezuelan Policy: A Reinterpretation," *American Historical Review* 66 (July 1961): 956 n.

6. For contrasting interpretations see Beisner, *From the Old Diplomacy to the New*, pp. 107–8; LaFeber, "Background of Cleveland's Venezuelan Policy," p. 956.

7. George Berkeley Young, "Intervention under the Monroe Doctrine: The Olney Corollary," *Political Science Quarterly* 57 (1942): 253.

8. *Papers Relating to the Foreign Relations of the United States, 1895,* pt. 1, pp. 545–62.

9. Perkins, *Monroe Doctrine,* pp. 173–77.

10. *Foreign Relations of the United States, 1895,* pt. 1, pp. 542–45.

11. Charles Hamlin, diary for 17 Dec. 1895, Hamlin Papers, LC; James A. Barnes, *John G. Carlisle: Financial Statesman* (New York: Dodd, Mead, 1931), pp. 409–10.

12. Walter LaFeber, "The American Business Community and Cleveland's Venezuelan Message," *Business History Review* 34 (Winter 1960): 393–402.

13. Joseph J. Mathews, "Informal Diplomacy in the Venezuelan Crisis of 1896," *Mississippi Valley Historical Review* 50 (Sept. 1963): 195–212.

14. Olney to GC, 25 Mar. 1896, Olney Papers, LC.

15. Gerald G. Eggert, *Richard Olney: Evolution of a Statesman* (University Park: Pennsylvania State University Press, 1974), p. 247.

16. Olney to GC, 28 Dec. 1896, Olney Papers.

17. GC to Bayard, 29 Dec. 1895, in *Letters of Grover Cleveland, 1850–1908,* ed. Allan Nevins (Boston, Mass.: Houghton Mifflin, 1933), pp. 417–18.

18. LaFeber, "Background of Cleveland's Venezuelan Policy," pp. 947–62, and *The New Empire* (Ithaca, N.Y.: Cornell University Press, 1963), pp. 242–83.

19. For an excellent analysis of the "economic interpretation" see Eggert, *Richard Olney,* pp. 245–46.

20. A qualified version of this interpretation can be found in Nelson M. Blake, "Background of Cleveland's Venezuelan Policy," *American Historical Review* 47 (Jan. 1942): 259–77.

21. Beisner, *From the Old Diplomacy to the New,* p. 113; Alexander E. Campbell, *Great Britain and the United States, 1895–1903* (London: Longmans, 1960), p. 16.

22. Young, "Intervention under the Monroe Doctrine," p. 280.

23. Charles Hamlin, diary for 28 Dec. 1895, Hamlin Papers.

24. Grover Cleveland, *Presidential Problems* (New York: Century Co., 1904), pp. 173–281.

25. Perkins, *Monroe Doctrine,* pp. 155, 163–66, 201.

26. Thomas A. Bailey, *Presidential Greatness: The Image and the Man from George Washington to the Present* (New York: Appleton-Century, 1966), p. 300; Charles C. Tansill, *The Foreign Policy of Thomas F. Bayard, 1885–1897* (New York: Fordham University Press, 1940), p. 603; Nevins, *Grover Cleveland*, p. 641.

27. See Horace Samuel Merrill, *Bourbon Leader: Grover Cleveland and the Democratic Party* (Boston, Mass.: Little, Brown, 1957), p. 202; Tansill, *Foreign Policy of Thomas F. Bayard*, p. 701.

28. Eggert, *Richard Olney*, pp. 219–21; George Roscoe Dulebohn, *Principles of Foreign Policy under the Cleveland Administrations* (Philadelphia: University of Pennsylvania Press, 1941), p. 20.

29. Eggert, *Richard Olney*, p. 245.

30. Dexter Perkins, *Hands Off!: A History of the Monroe Doctrine* (Boston, Mass.: Little, Brown, 1941), p. ix.

31. Perkins, *Monroe Doctrine*, p. 253.

32. GC to George F. Parker, 31 Mar. 1896, in Nevins, *Letters*, pp. 435–36.

33. Nelson M. Blake, "The Olney–Pauncefote Treaty of 1897," *American Historical Review* 50 (Jan. 1945): 228–43; Olney to Pauncefote, 22 June 1896, in *Foreign Relations of the United States, 1896*, p. 234.

34. Blake, "Olney Pauncefote Treaty of 1897," pp. 233 34.

35. Robert McElroy, *Grover Cleveland: The Man and the Statesman*, 2 vols. (New York: Harper & Bros., 1923), 2:243.

36. Blake, "Olney-Pauncefote Treaty of 1897," pp. 235–40.

37. Beisner, *From the Old Diplomacy to the New*, pp. 115–16.

38. Annual Message, 2 Dec. 1895, in *Letters and Addresses of Grover Cleveland*, ed. Albert Ellery Bergh (New York: Unit Publishing Co., 1909), p. 374.

39. John A. S. Greenville and George Berkeley Young, *Politics, Strategy and American Diplomacy: Studies in Foreign Policy, 1873–1917* (New Haven, Conn.: Yale University Press, 1966), p. 180.

40. Ibid, pp. 190–92.

41. Olney to GC, 14 July 1896, and GC to Olney, 16 July 1896, Olney Papers.

42. See Beisner, *From the Old Diplomacy to the New*, pp. 87, 116.

43. James D. Richardson, comp., *A Compilation of the Messages and Papers of the Presidents, 1789–1897*, 10 vols. (Washington, D.C.: U.S. Government Printing Office, 1897–1907), 9:720–22.

44. GC to Olney, 26 Apr. 1898, Olney Papers.

45. Greenville and Young, *Politics, Strategy and American Diplomacy*, pp. 193, 200.

46. Ibid., p. 200; Eggert, *Richard Olney*, p. 254.

47. Eggert, *Richard Olney*, p. 181.

48. Greenville and Young, *Politics, Strategy and American Diplomacy*, pp. 159–60.

49. Perkins, *Monroe Doctrine*, p. 189.

CHAPTER 12
THE PARTY DIVIDES:
CLEVELAND, BRYAN, AND THE ELECTION OF
1896

1. Morton Keller, *Affairs of State: Public Life in Late Nineteenth Century America* (Cambridge, Mass.: Harvard University Press, 1977), p. 571.

2. Walter Dean Burnham, *Presidential Ballots, 1836–1892* (Baltimore, Md.: Johns Hopkins University Press, 1955), p. 155.

3. GC to Henry S. Robbins, 13 Apr. 1895, CP.

4. See, e.g., GC to Mississippi Governor J. M. Stone, 26 Apr. 1895, in *Letters of Grover Cleveland, 1850–1908*, ed. Allan Nevins (Boston, Mass.: Houghton Mifflin, 1933), pp. 388–89.

5. GC to Richard W. Gilder, 26 Dec. 1894, and GC to E. C. Benedict, 25 Feb. 1895, CP.

6. GC to Bayard, 13 Feb. 1895, in Nevins, *Letters*, p. 377.

7. Francis B. Simkins, *Pitchfork Ben Tillman, South Carolinian* (Baton Rouge: Louisiana State University Press, 1944), pp. 312–13.

8. R. Hal Williams, " 'Dry Bones and Dead Language': The Democratic Party," in *The Gilded Age: A Reappraisal*, ed. H. Wayne Morgan, rev. ed. (Syracuse, N.Y.: Syracuse University Press, 1970), p. 136.

9. Horace Samuel Merrill, *Bourbon Leader: Grover Cleveland and the Democratic Party* (Boston, Mass.: Little, Brown, 1957), p. 168.

10. George F. Parker, *Recollections of Grover Cleveland* (New York: Century Co., 1909), p. 209; see also GC to Don M. Dickinson, 31 July 1895, in Nevins, *Letters*, p. 402.

11. GC to John S. Mason, 20 May 1895, in Nevins, *Letters*, pp. 394–95.

12. GC to Don M. Dickinson, 19 Mar. and 10 June 1896, CP; GC, "Letter to the Democratic Voters," 16 June 1896, *New York Herald*, 18 June 1896.

13. Richard W. Gilder "Notes," CP.

14. Charles Hamlin, diary for 3 Mar. and 28 Dec. 1896, Hamlin Papers, LC; GC to William C. Whitney, 18 June 1896, Whitney Papers, LC.

15. Geoffrey Blodgett, *Gentle Reformers: Massachusetts Democrats in the Cleveland Era* (Cambridge, Mass.: Harvard University Press, 1966), p. 206.

16. Allan Nevins, *Grover Cleveland: A Study in Courage* (New York: Dodd, Mead, 1933), p. 701.

17. GC to Lamont, 15 July 1896, in Nevins, *Letters*, pp. 446–47.

18. GC to Olney, 13 July 1896, Olney Papers, LC.

19. GC telegram to the *New York Evening Post*, 7 Aug. 1896; GC to D. B. Griffin, 2 Sept. 1896, GC to Hoke Smith, 4 Aug. 1896, GC to Wil-

liam F. Vilas, 5 Sept. 1896, GC to Daniel S. Lamont, 6 Sept. 1896—all in Nevins, *Letters*, pp. 451–58.

20. GC to E. C. Benedict, 28 Oct. 1896, in Nevins, *Letters*, p. 460. Cleveland invited McKinley to an informal dinner at the White House on the eve of the latter's inauguration. As earlier with President-elect Benjamin Harrison, Cleveland made every effort to observe customary courtesies and to make smooth the presidential transition for his Republican successor.

21. Carl Degler, "Political Parties and the Rise of the City: An Interpretation," *Journal of American History* 51 (1964): 41–59.

CHAPTER 13
THE POLITICAL LEADERSHIP
OF GROVER CLEVELAND

1. Allan Nevins, *Grover Cleveland: A Study in Courage* (New York: Dodd, Mead, 1933), pp. 4–5.

2. Geoffrey Blodgett, "The Political Leadership of Grover Cleveland," *South Atlantic Quarterly* 82 (Summer 1983): 292.

3. Ibid., pp. 293, 298.

4. Rexford G. Tugwell, *Grover Cleveland* (New York: Macmillan, 1968), p. 139.

5. See scrapbook of "Cleveland Obituaries," Special Collections, Firestone Library, Princeton University, Princeton, N.J.

6. See, e.g., *New York World*, 25 June 1908; *New York Evening Post*, 24 June 1908; *Philadelphia Public Ledger*, 25 June 1908; *London Daily Telegraph*, 25 June 1908.

7. Robert H. Wiebe, *The Search for Order, 1877–1920* (New York: Hill & Wang, 1967), p. 93.

BIBLIOGRAPHICAL ESSAY

PRIMARY SOURCES

The major manuscript collection for any study of the Cleveland presidency is obviously the Papers of Grover Cleveland in the Library of Congress (Manuscript Division, James Madison Building). They comprise over 87,000 items. The use of these papers is greatly facilitated by the published *Index to the Papers of Grover Cleveland* (Washington, D.C.: U.S. Government Printing Office, 1965), which includes a lengthy Introduction, explaining the manner in which the collection was assembled and the division of the collection into various categories and series. The Cleveland Papers have been microfilmed, and the *Index* indicates the general content of each of the 164 reels. In addition to the Cleveland Papers at the Library of Congress, there are a few letters to and from Grover Cleveland in the Andre De Coppet Collection at the Firestone Library, Princeton University, Princeton, New Jersey.

Several other collections at the Library of Congress contain important material for a study of the Cleveland presidency, especially the papers of Daniel S. Lamont, Richard Olney, and William C. Whitney. Also useful was the diary of Charles S. Hamlin, in the Charles S. Hamlin Papers, for the years when Hamlin was assistant to Secretary of the Treasury John G. Carlisle.

There are a number of published collections of Cleveland's letters and speeches. Far and away the most valuable is *Letters of Grover Cleveland, 1850–1908*, edited by Allan Nevins (Boston, Mass.: Houghton Mifflin, 1933), which includes all of Cleveland's more important and revealing letters, except for a handful to be found in the Olney and Whitney Papers, and is edited with meticulous care. The present author found no errors of transcription nor any important elisions when comparing Nevins's *Letters* with the original manuscripts. In preparation for Cleveland's campaign for the Democratic nomination in 1892, his self-appointed aide, George F. Parker, edited *The Writings and Speeches of Grover Cleveland* (New York: Cassell, 1892). This volume covers Cleveland's major public addresses from 1882 through 1891. It is without scholarly annotation, as is true of a later collection, *Letters and Addresses of Grover Cleveland*, edited by Albert Ellery Bergh (New York: Unit Publishing Co., 1909). Bergh's collection suffers from erratic deletions but is wider in coverage than Parker's.

Cleveland's more important state papers will be found in *Public Papers of Grover Cleveland, Twenty–second President of the United States, 1885–1889* (Washington, D.C.: U.S. Government Printing Office, 1889), and *Public Papers of Grover Cleveland, Twenty-fourth President of the United States, 1893–1897* (Washington, D.C.: U.S. Government Printing Office, 1897), and in Volumes 8 and 9 of James D. Richardson, compiler, *A Compilation of the Messages and Papers of the Presidents, 1789–1897*, 10 volumes (Washington, D.C.: U.S. Government Printing Office, 1897–1907). Important diplomatic papers of the Cleveland administrations will be found in the series *Papers Relating to the Foreign Relations of the United States* for 1885–88 and 1893–96 (Washington, D.C.: Government Printing Office, 1886–89, 1894–97).

Apart from letters, speeches, and public papers, Cleveland's writings include a number of essays published in such journals as the *Century* during the years of his retirement. Four of his public lectures at Princeton University were subsequently published under the title *Presidential Problems* (New York: Century Co., 1904). Interesting for its insight into Cleveland's effort to reconcile republican equality and economic progress is Cleveland's essay *The Self-made Man in American Life* (New York: T. Y. Crowell, 1897).

One may also classify among primary sources the giant scrapbook of "Obituaries of Grover Cleveland," to be found in Special Collections, Firestone Library, Princeton University. In the same provenance are scrapbooks of newspaper clippings concerning Cleveland's public career and his retirement years in Princeton, New Jersey.

SECONDARY SOURCES

There have been a number of biographies of Grover Cleveland, good, bad, and indifferent. The best written is Allan Nevins's magisterial effort *Grover Cleveland: A Study in Courage* (New York: Dodd, Mead, 1933). Nevins can be criticized for exaggerating Cleveland's virtues and minimizing his limitations, but all students of the Cleveland presidency must acknowledge a large debt to Nevins. There are two other scholarly biographies of divergent value: Robert McElroy, *Grover Cleveland: The Man and the Statesman*, 2 vols. (New York: Harper & Bros., 1923), and Horace Samuel Merrill, *Bourbon Leader: Grover Cleveland and the Democratic Party* (Boston, Mass.: Little, Brown, 1957). McElroy's is an authorized biography, dutifully admiring of Cleveland's strength and policies and useful for its many quotations and chronological detail. Merrill's is a much shorter and more opinionated work. It is Merrill who succeeded in fastening the label "Bourbon" on Cleveland and the Cleveland Democrats. The present author finds the label erroneous and unhelpful, but Merrill's is a challenging interpretation that demands respect.

Three other biographical efforts are of little or no value: Ronald Hugins, *Grover Cleveland: A Study in Courage* (Washington, D.C.: Anchor-Lee Publishing Co., 1922); Dennis T. Lynch, *Grover Cleveland: A Man Four Square* (New York: H. Liveright, 1932); and Rexford G. Tugwell, *Grover Cleveland* (New York: Macmillan, 1968). Hugins's effort was apparently designed for the grammar-school library, and Lynch's book suffers from an excessive reliance on undocumented anecdotes and a determination to stress the beer-swilling Grover of the Buffalo years. In some ways the most disappointing effort is that of Tugwell, a man with wide political experience and the author of several excellent volumes on Franklin D. Roosevelt and the New Deal. Tugwell presumably hoped to find in Cleveland a forerunner of Roosevelt and, failing to do so, offers an appraisal that reflects a large element of personal irritation.

A few memoirs are useful for anecdotal materials. Four of these are by Cleveland's contemporaries: E. Jay Edwards, "The Personal Force of Cleveland," *McClure's Magazine*, Nov. 1893, pp. 493–500; Richard Watson Gilder, *Grover Cleveland: A Record of Friendship* (New York: Century, 1910); Hilary A. Herbert, "Grover Cleveland and His Cabinet at Work," *Century Magazine*, Mar. 1913, pp. 740–44; George F. Parker, *Recollections of Grover Cleveland* (New York: Century Co., 1909). The sketch of Cleveland in De Alva S. Alexander's *Four Famous New Yorkers: The Political Careers of Cleveland, Platt, Hill and Roosevelt* (New York: H. Holt, 1923) is pedestrian and disappointing, as is the capsule biography in Robert I. Vexler, editor, *Grover Cleveland, 1837–1908: Chronology, Documents, Bibliographical Aids* (Dobbs Ferry, N.Y.: Oceana Publications, 1968).

Three interesting doctoral dissertations treat various aspects of Cleveland's presidential career: George Roscoe Dulebohn, *Principles of Foreign Policy under the Cleveland Administrations* (Philadelphia: University of Pennsylvania Press, 1941); Orville T. Payne, "The Administrative Theory and Practice of Grover Cleveland" (Ph.D. dissertation in Political Science, University of Chicago, 1951); Pearl L. Robertson, "Grover Cleveland as a Political Leader" (Ph.D. dissertation in Political Science, University of Chicago, 1937). A portion of Robertson's dissertation was published by the University of Chicago Press in 1938 under the same title. Dulebohn's admiration for Cleveland's diplomatic policies is somewhat exaggerated, as is Payne's emphasis on Cleveland's contribution to civil-service reform and Robertson's application of Freudian psychology to explain Cleveland's personality and policies. Nevertheless, all three of these dissertations have provided appreciated assistance in the preparation of this study.

Of the scores of articles and books that deal in whole or part with Cleveland's presidency, I am most indebted to the works of Geoffrey Blodgett and Robert Kelley. Blodgett's *Gentle Reformers: Massachusetts Democrats in the Cleveland Era* (Cambridge: Harvard University Press, 1966) is an insightful study of the party supporters and Mugwump allies of Cleveland in the Bay State; and Blodgett's article "The Political Leadership of Grover Cleveland," *South Atlantic Quarterly* 82 (Summer 1983): 288–99, is a brilliant example of the interweaving of political and intellectual history. Blodgett perhaps exaggerates the influence of Cleveland's anxiety to "sanitize" his Buffalo reputation, but the present study is much indebted to Blodgett's thought-provoking analysis of the sources of Cleveland's weaknesses and strengths as a political leader. It is equally indebted to Robert Kelley's essay "Presbyterianism, Jacksonianism and Grover Cleveland," *American Quarterly* 18 (1966): 615–36. The present study rejects Kelley's emphasis on the impact that Cleveland's Calvinist background had on his political opinions, but it borrows, with grateful acknowledgment, Kelley's interpretation respecting the Jacksonian strain in Cleveland's political ideas and objectives. Kelley offers a more extended treatment of the Cleveland years in his book-length study *The Transatlantic Persuasion: The Liberal-Democratic Mind in the Age of Gladstone* (New York: Knopf, 1969). This is an ambitious attempt at comparative intellectual history which seeks to demonstrate the correspondence between British, Canadian, and American political thought during the last quarter of the nineteenth century.

Another author who has made important contributions to the literature on Grover Cleveland is Vincent P. De Santis, who wrote the essay on Cleveland in *America's Ten Greatest Presidents*, edited by Morton Borden (Chicago: Rand McNally, 1961) and a subsequent evaluation, "Grover Cleveland: Another Look," for the *Hayes Historical Journal* 3 (Winter 1983): 41–50. Although his strictures on Cleveland's "conservatism" have become increasingly severe, DeSantis is one of the scholars who has promoted a healthy revision of the political history of the decades following Reconstruction. There are interesting observations on Cleveland's policies and historical contribution in the following works: Thomas A. Bailey, *Presidential Greatness: The Image and the Man from George Washington to the Present* (New York: Appleton-Century, 1966); Marcus Cunliffe, *American Presidents and the Presidency* (New York: American Heritage Press, 1968); Matthew T. Downey, "Grover Cleveland and Abram S. Hewitt: The Limits of Factional Consensus," *New-York Historical Society Quarterly* 54 (Summer 1970): 222–40; Robert F. Durden, "Grover Cleveland and the Bourbon Democracy," *South Atlantic Quarterly* 57 (Summer 1958): 333–38; Gerald G. Eggert, "I Have Tried So Hard To Do Right," *American History Illustrated* 12 (Jan. 1978): 10–23; Richard Hofstadter, *The American Political Tradition and the Men Who Made It* (New York: Knopf, 1948). Older assessments that continue to be of value are Gamaliel Bradford, "Grover Cleveland," *Atlantic Monthly*, Nov. 1920, pp. 654–65; William Allen White, "Cleveland," *McClure's Magazine*, Feb. 1902, pp. 322–30; Woodrow Wilson, "Mr. Cleveland's Cabinet," *The Review of Reviews*, Apr. 1893, pp. 286–97; Woodrow Wilson, "Mr. Cleveland as President," *Atlantic Monthly*, Mar. 1897, pp. 289–300.

Among biographies of Cleveland's political allies and enemies, the following give varying degrees of attention to Cleveland's presidential role and policies: Harry Barnard, *"Eagle Forgotten": The Life of John Peter Altgeld* (Indianapolis, Ind.: Bobbs–Merrill, 1938); James A. Barnes, *John G. Carlisle: Financial Statesman* (New York: Dodd, Mead, 1931); Herbert J. Bass, *"I Am A Democrat": The Political Career of David Bennett Hill* (Syracuse, N.Y.: Syracuse University Press, 1961); Gerald G. Eggert, *Richard Olney: Evolution of a Statesman* (University Park: Pennsylvania State University Press, 1974); Ray Ginger, *The Bending Cross: A Biography of Eugene Victor Debs* (New Brunswick, N.J.: Rutgers University Press, 1949); Dewey W. Grantham, Jr., *Hoke Smith and the Politics of the New South* (Baton Rouge: Louisiana State University Press, 1958); Matilda Gresham, *Life of Walter Quintin Gresham, 1832–1895* (Chicago: Rand, McNally, 1919); Mark D. Hirsch, *William C. Whitney, Modern Warwick* (New York: Dodd, Mead, 1948); John R. Lambert, *Arthur Pue Gorman* (Baton Rouge: Louisiana State University Press, 1953); Edward Mayes, *Lucius Q. C. Lamar . . .* (Nashville, Tenn.: Methodist Episcopal Church South, 1896); Horace Samuel Merrill, *William Freeman Vilas: Doctrinaire Democrat* (Madison: State Historical Society of Wisconsin, 1954); Harry J. Sievers, S.J., *Benjamin Harrison*, 3 vols. (Indianapolis, Ind.: Bobbs-Merrill, 1961); Homer E. Socolofsky and Allen B. Spetter, *The Presidency of Benjamin Harrison* (Lawrence, Kans.: University Press of Kansas, 1987); Joseph Frazier Wall, *Henry Watterson: Reconstructed Rebel* (New York: Oxford University Press, 1956). Interesting sketches of two Cleveland aides will be found in Michael Medved, *The Shadow Presidents* (New York: Times Books, 1979), in a chapter on the career of Daniel S. Lamont; and in Gordon A. Moon II, "George F. Parker: A 'Near Miss' as First White House Press Chief," *Journalism Quarterly* 41 (Spring 1964): 183–90.

Over the last quarter-century, the political and social history of the Gilded Age has experienced an important reassessment. No longer are historians content to accept the scornful evaluation offered by Matthew Josephson in his study *The Politicos, 1865–1896* (New York: Harcourt,

Brace, 1938). Many historians have contributed to this reassessment. Worthy of special notice are Vincent P. De Santis, H. Wayne Morgan, Lewis L. Gould, R. Hal Williams, and Morton Keller. De Santis's publications include the best bibliography of the Gilded Age years, *The Gilded Age, 1877–1896* (Northbrook, Ill.: AHM Publishers, 1973), and an excellent review essay, "American Politics in the Gilded Age," *Review of Politics* 25 (1963): 551–61. Among Morgan's many important contributions is a skillfully organized general survey, *From Hayes to McKinley: National Party Politics, 1877–1896* (Syracuse: Syracuse University Press, 1969), and an original synthesis of cultural and political history, *Unity and Culture: The United States, 1877–1900* (London: Penguin, 1971). Morgan has edited a valuable collection of essays entitled *The Gilded Age: A Reappraisal*, rev. ed. (Syracuse: Syracuse University Press, 1970). Among the best of those essays are Lewis L. Gould's "The Republican Search for a National Majority" (pp. 171–87) and R. Hal Williams's " 'Dry Bones and Dead Language': The Democratic Party" (pp. 129–48). Neither writer has many kind words for Grover Cleveland, but both have made a significant contribution to a better understanding of national politics in the Gilded Age. Also useful is Williams's summary analysis of the political upheaval of the 1890s: *Years of Decision: American Politics in the 1890s* (New York: John Wiley, 1978). Morton Keller's most important contribution to the reassessment of Gilded Age politics will be found in *Affairs of State: Public Life in Late Nineteenth Century America* (Cambridge, Mass.: Harvard University Press, 1977); but of continued interest is his earlier essay "The Politicos Reconsidered," *Perspectives in American History* 1 (1967): 401–8.

Students of the political and social history of the Gilded Age should also consult Geoffrey Blodgett, "A New Look at the Gilded Age: Politics in a Cultural Context," in *Victorian America*, edited by Daniel Walker Howe (Philadelphia: University of Pennsylvania Press, 1976), pp. 95–108, and "Reform Thought and the Genteel Tradition," in *The Gilded Age: A Reappraisal*, pp. 55–76; John M. Dobson, *Politics in the Gilded Age: A New Perspective on Reform* (New York: Praeger, 1972); John A. Garraty, *The New Commonwealth, 1877–1900* (New York: Harper & Row, 1968); Ray Ginger, *Age of Excess* (New York: Macmillan, 1965); Robert D. Marcus, *Grand Old Party: Political Structure in the Gilded Age, 1880–1896* (New York: Oxford University Press, 1971); Walter T. K. Nugent, *From Centennial to World War: American Society, 1876–1917* (Indianapolis, Ind.: Bobbs-Merrill, 1977), and "Politics from Reconstruction to 1900," in *The Reinterpretation of American History and Culture*, edited by William H. Cartwright and Richard L. Watson, Jr. (Washington, D.C.: National Council for the Social Studies, 1973), pp. 377–99; John G. Sproat, *"The Best Men": Liberal Reformers in the Gilded Age* (New York: Oxford University Press, 1968). Robert H. Wiebe's *The Search for Order, 1877–1920* (New York: Hill & Wang, 1967) is an influential synthesis of American political history from the Gilded Age through the Progressive Era.

In addition to general accounts of the Gilded Age, the last three decades have seen the publication of a large number of books and articles analyzing special features of its political history and offering new insights respecting the relationship between politics and social-cultural developments. Lee Benson, Walter Dean Burnham, and Samuel P. Hays have made important contributions with respect to research methodology in such articles as Benson, "Research Problems in American Political Historiography," in *Common Frontiers of the Social Sciences*, edited by Mirra Komarovsky (Glencoe, Ill.: Free Press, 1957), pp. 113–83; Burnham, "Party Systems and the Political Process," in *The American Party Systems: Stages of Political Development*, edited by William N. Chambers and Walter Dean Burnham (New York: Oxford University Press, 1967), pp. 277–307; Hays, "Political Parties and the Community Society Continuum," in *The American Party Systems*, pp. 152–81, and "The Social Analysis of American Political History, 1880–1920," *Political Science Quarterly* 80 (Summer 1965): 373–94. Leonard D. White explores the administrative history of the national government during the post–Civil War generation in *The Republican Era, 1869–1901: A Study in Administrative History* (New York: Macmillan, 1958); and David J. Rothman has corrected various misconceptions respecting the strength of national party organizations in *Politics and Power: The United States Senate, 1869–1901* (Cambridge, Mass.: Harvard University Press, 1966). Three scholars have contributed to our understanding of the influence of ethnic-cultural issues on political allegiance in the Middle West and the Northeast: Richard Jensen, *The Winning of the Midwest: Social and Political Conflict, 1888–1896* (Chicago: University of Chicago Press, 1971); Paul Kleppner, *The Cross of Culture: A Social Analysis of Midwestern Politics, 1850–1900* (New York: Free Press, 1970); Samuel McSeveney, *The Politics of Depression: Political Behavior in the Northeast, 1893–1896* (New York: Oxford University Press, 1972). Gerald W. McFarland offers an interesting footnote on the rise and fall of Cleveland Democrats in a New England state in "The Breakdown of Deadlock: The Cleveland Democracy in Connecticut," *Historian* 31 (Summer 1969): 381–97. Other important regional studies are Horace Samuel Merrill, *Bourbon Democracy of the Middle West, 1865–1896* (Baton Rouge: Louisiana State University Press, 1953); R. Hal Williams, *The Democratic Party and California Politics, 1880–1896* (Stanford, Calif.: Stanford University Press, 1973); C. Vann Woodward, *Origins of the New South, 1877–1913* (Baton Rouge: Louisiana State University Press, 1951). The last cited is deservedly one of the most highly praised works in American historical literature during the twentieth century.

George Sinkler's study *The Racial Attitudes of American Presidents: From Abraham Lincoln to Theodore Roosevelt* (Garden City, N.Y.: Doubleday, 1971) offers some interesting observations about Cleveland's attitude toward blacks, immigrants, and Jews; and Joseph P. O'Grady assesses "The Roman Question in American Politics, 1885" in *Journal of Church and State* 10 (Summer 1968): 365–77.

The presidential campaigns of the years 1884 through 1896 have elicited the attention of many scholars. Statistical data for the first three of those elections will be found in Walter Dean Burnham, *Presidential Ballots, 1836–1892* (Baltimore, Md.: Johns Hopkins University Press, 1955). For the campaign of 1884 the best summary is Mark D. Hirsch, "Election of 1884," in *History of American Presidential Elections, 1789–1968*, edited by Arthur M. Schlesinger, Jr., and Fred L. Israel, 4 vols. (New York: Chelsea House/McGraw-Hill, 1971), 2:1561–81. Additional material will be found in John M. Dobson, "George William Curtis and the Election of 1884," *New-York Historical Society Quarterly* 52 (Summer 1968): 214–34; Thomas J. Osborne, "What Was the Main Reason for Cleveland's Election Victory in 1884?" *Northwest Ohio Quarterly* 45 (Spring 1973): 67–71; Marvin Rosenberg and Dorothy Rosenberg, "The Dirtiest Election," *American Heritage*, Aug. 1962, pp. 4–9, 97–100. For the campaign of 1888 see Robert Wesser, "Election of 1888," in *History of American Presidential Elections, 1789–1968*, 2:1615–52; James L. Baumgardner, "The 1888 Presidential Election: How Corrupt?" *Presidential Studies Quarterly* 14 (Summer 1984): 416–27; T. C. Hinckley, "George Osgoodby and the Murchison Letter," *Pacific Historical Review* 27 (Nov. 1958): 359–70. The standard account of the campaign of 1892 is George Harmon Knoles, *The Presidential Campaign and Election of 1892* (Stanford, Calif.: Stanford University Press, 1942). It can be supplemented by H. Wayne Morgan, "Election of 1892," in *History of American Presidential Elections, 1789–1968*, 2:1703–32; and Robert Bolt, "Donald M. Dickinson and the Second Election of Grover Cleveland, 1892," *Michigan History* 49 (Winter 1965): 28–39. Many books previously cited analyze the division of the Democratic party and the election of 1896. In addition see Stanley L. Jones, *The Presidential Election of 1896* (Madison: University of Wisconsin Press, 1964); Paolo E. Coletta, "Bryan, Cleveland and the Disrupted Democracy, 1890–1896," *Nebraska History* 41 (Mar. 1960): 1–29; J. Rogers Hollingsworth, *The Whirligig of Politics: The Democracy of Cleveland and Bryan* (Chicago: University of Chicago Press, 1963).

A number of important books and articles examine specific features and problems of the Cleveland presidency. For Cleveland and civil-service reform see Ari Hoogenboom, *Outlawing the Spoils: A History of the Civil Service Reform Movement* (Urbana: University of Illinois Press, 1961), and "The Pendleton Act and the Civil Service," *American Historical Review* 44 (Jan. 1959): 301–18; Justus D. Doenecke, "Grover Cleveland and the Enforcement of the Civil Service Act," *Hayes Historical Journal* 4 (Spring 1984): 45–58; Leonard S. Schulp, "Vilas, Stevenson and Democratic Politics, 1884–1892," *North Dakota Quarterly* 44 (Winter 1976): 44–52. For Cleveland's fight with the Senate over the revised Tenure of Office Act see Louis Fisher, "Grover Cleveland against the Senate," *Congressional Studies* 7 (Winter 1979): 11–25; and John F. Marszalek, Jr., "Grover Cleveland and the Tenure of Office Act," *Duquesne Review* 15 (Winter 1970): 206–19. For Cleveland's effort to reform veterans' pension policy and his stormy relations with the Grand Army of the Republic see Mary R. Dearing, *Veterans in Politics: The Story of the G.A.R.* (Baton Rouge: Louisiana State University Press, 1952); C. Joseph Pusateri, "Public Quarrels and Private Plans: The President, the Veterans, and the Mayor of St. Louis," *Missouri Historical Review* 62 (Winter 1967): 1–13; P. L. Robertson, "Cleveland's Constructive Use of the Pension Vetoes," *Mid-America* 44 (Jan. 1962): 33–45. For Cleveland's cancer operation the basic source is William W. Keen, *The Surgical Operations on President Cleveland in 1893* (Philadelphia: G. W. Jacobs, 1917); but see also Wilbur Cross and John Moses, "My God, Sir, I Think the President Is Doomed!" *American History Illustrated* 17 (Nov. 1982): 40–45, and John Stuart Martin, "When the President Disappeared," *American Heritage*, Dec. 1957, pp. 10–13, 102–3.

Milton Friedman and Anna Jacobson Schwartz, in *A Monetary History of the United States, 1867–1960* (Princeton, N.J.: Princeton University Press, 1963), provide the necessary background for Cleveland's long struggle against unlimited silver coinage. There is important material on Cleveland's monetary policy in Barnes's *Carlisle*, as well as in the biographies by Nevins, McElroy, and Merrill, cited earlier. An old but still useful article is Jeanette P. Nichols, "The Politics and Personalities of Silver Repeal in the United States Senate," *American Historical Review* 41 (Oct. 1935): 26–53. For background on Cleveland's faltering crusade for tariff reform see Robert Higgs, *The Transformation of the American Economy, 1865–1914: An Essay in Interpretation* (New York: John Wiley, 1971), and the classic surveys, Edward Stanwood, *American Tariff Controversies in the Nineteenth Century* (Boston, Mass.: Houghton Mifflin, 1903), and Frank W. Taussig, *The Tariff History of the United States*, 5th ed. (New York: G. P. Putnam, 1910). An important and original contribution to the subject has been made by Tom E. Terrill in his book *The Tariff, Politics, and American Foreign Policy, 1874–1901* (Westport, Conn.: Greenwood Press, 1973) and in his earlier article "David A. Wells, the Democracy, and Tariff Reduction, 1877–1894," *Journal of American History* 56 (Dec. 1969): 540–55. Terrill relates Cleveland's interest in tariff reduction to his anxieties respecting the expansion of foreign markets. A contrasting interpretation will be found in Festus P. Summers, *William L. Wilson and Tariff Reform* (New Brunswick, N.J.: Rutgers University Press, 1953), and in A. T. Volwiler, "Tariff Strategy and Propaganda in the United States, 1887–1888," *American Historical Review* 36 (Oct. 1930): 76–96. An excellent and well-written account of the unhappy fate of the Wilson tariff bill of 1894 will be found in Warren Hamill Wilson, "Grover Cleveland and the Wilson-Gorman Tariff" (Master's thesis, University of Texas, Austin, 1977). Wilson's carefully researched essay was made available to the author through the kindness of Professor Lewis L. Gould.

The most detailed account of the Pullman strike and the response that it inspired from the second Cleveland administration is Almont Lindsey's *The Pullman Strike* (Chicago: University of Chicago Press, 1942); but additional material will be found in Arnold M. Paul, *Conservative Crisis and the Rule of Law: Attitudes of Bar and Bench, 1887–1895* (Ithaca, N.Y.: Cornell University Press, 1960), and in Bennett M. Rich, *The Presidents and Civil Disorder* (Washington, D.C.: Brookings Institution, 1941). Paul also offers an excellent analysis of the controversy over the income-tax case.

Since 1960 there has been a perceptible increase of interest among American diplomatic historians in the foreign policy of the Cleveland years; this has been due in large part to the studies of Walter LaFeber, which emphasize the economic motivation of Cleveland's diplomacy.

Students of Cleveland's diplomacy can best approach the subject by means of two excellent general accounts of American foreign policy in the post–Civil War generation: Robert L. Beisner, *From the Old Diplomacy to the New, 1865–1900*, rev. ed. (Arlington Heights, Ill.: Harlan Davidson, 1986); and Charles S. Campbell, Jr., *The Transformation of American Foreign Relations, 1865–1900* (New York: Harper & Row, 1976). Beisner's insightful analysis has proved especially useful. The doctoral dissertation of George Roscoe Dulebohn, previously cited, was of assistance; but the essays by Montgomery Schuyler on Walter Quintin Gresham and Richard Olney in *American Secretaries of State*, vol. 8 (New York: Knopf, 1928), are outdated and of little value. This cannot be said of Charles C. Tansill's *The Foreign Policy of Thomas F. Bayard, 1885–1897* (New York: Fordham University Press, 1940), a study of continuing merit. Brief but perceptive comments on Bayard, Gresham, and Olney will be found in Alexander DeConde, *The American Secretary of State: An Interpretation* (New York: Frederick A. Praeger, 1962).

Since 1963, however, the book that all students of Cleveland Diplomacy must confront is Walter LaFeber's *The New Empire: An Interpretation of American Expansion, 1860–1898* (Ithaca, N.Y.: Cornell University Press, 1963). The present author believes that LaFeber seriously exaggerates the influence of domestic overproduction and the economic surplus on Cleveland's foreign policy, but there can be no doubt that LaFeber's revisionist analysis is brilliantly written and skillfully argued. Two of the more successful efforts to rebut his interpretation are William H. Becker, "American Manufacturers and Foreign Markets, 1870–1900: Business Historians and the 'New Economic Determinists,' " *Business Historical Review* 47 (Winter 1973): 466–81; and Paul S. Holbo, "Economics, Emotion, and Expansion: An Emerging Foreign Policy," in *The Gilded Age: A Reappraisal*, pp. 199–221.

Cleveland's long and unsuccessful effort to solve the North Atlantic fisheries dispute is best followed in Charles C. Tansill's *Canadian-American Relations, 1875–1911* (New Haven, Conn.: Yale University Press, 1943) and his *The Foreign Policy of Thomas F. Bayard, 1885–1897*, previously cited. Additional material will be found in Charles S. Campbell, Jr., "American Tariff Interests and the Northeastern Fisheries, 1883–1888," *Canadian Historical Review* 45 (Sept. 1964): 212–28. The standard account of the Samoan problem is Paul M. Kennedy's *The Samoan Tangle: A Study in Anglo-German-American Relations, 1878–1900* (New York: Barnes & Noble, 1974). All of the many accounts of Hawaiian-American relations give attention to Cleveland's Hawaiian diplomacy. Most useful for this study were Thomas J. Osborne, *"Empire Can Wait": American Opposition to Hawaiian Annexation, 1893–1898* (Kent, Ohio: Kent State University Press, 1981), and the chapter on Hawaii in John A. S. Greenville and George Berkeley Young, *Politics, Strategy and American Diplomacy: Studies in Foreign Policy, 1873–1917* (New Haven, Conn.: Yale University Press, 1966). See also William A. Russ, Jr., *The Hawaiian Revolution, 1893–94* (Selinsgrove, Pa.: Susquehanna University Press, 1959), and "The Role of Sugar in Hawaiian Annexation," *Pacific Historical Review* 12 (1943): 339–50; Sylvester K. Stevens, *American Expansion in Hawaii, 1842–1898* (New York: Russell, 1968); Charles C. Tansill, *Diplomatic Relations between the United States and Hawaii, 1885–1889* (New York: Fordham University Press, 1940).

The most controversial feature of Cleveland's foreign policy—his intervention in the British-Venezuelan boundary dispute—has understandably elicited the greatest scholarly attention. In addition to a summary discussion in *The New Empire*, Walter LaFeber has written two interesting essays on Cleveland's Venezuelan policy: "The American Business Community and Cleveland's Venezuelan Message," *Business History Review* 34 (Winter 1960): 393–402, and "The Background of Cleveland's Venezuelan Policy: A Reinterpretation," *American Historical Review* 66 (July 1961): 947–67. Most useful for the present author were the interpretations by Gerald Eggert, Dexter Perkins, and George Berkeley Young. Eggert's analysis will be found in his biography of Richard Olney, previously cited; Perkins's most detailed analysis is *The Monroe Doctrine, 1867–1907* (Baltimore, Md.: Johns Hopkins University Press, 1937); Young's evaluation of the strategic motivation of Cleveland's policy was first offered in his essay, "Intervention under the Monroe Doctrine: The Olney Corollary," *Political Science Quarterly* 57 (1942): 247–80, and then in the Venezuelan chapters of *Politics, Strategy and American Diplomacy*, previously cited. Of less persuasiveness are Nelson M. Blake, "Background of Cleveland's Venezuelan Policy," *American Historical Review* 47 (Jan. 1942): 259–77; and Joseph J. Mathews, "Informal Diplomacy in the Venezuelan Crisis of 1896," *Mississippi Valley Historical Review* 50 (Sept. 1963): 195–212. Important studies that seek to place Cleveland's Venezuelan diplomacy in the broader context of Anglo-American relations are Alexander E. Campbell, *Great Britain and the United States, 1895–1903* (London: Longmans, 1960), and Bradford Perkins, *The Great Rapprochement: England and the United States, 1895–1914* (New York: Atheneum, 1968).

Two excellent articles that deal with other features of Cleveland's diplomacy are Nelson M. Blake, "The Olney-Pauncefote Treaty of 1897," *American Historical Review* 50 (Jan. 1945): 228–43; and Charles S. Campbell, Jr., "The Dismissal of Lord Sackville," *Mississippi Valley Historical Review* 44 (Mar. 1958): 635–48.

Those who enjoy playing the game of ranking presidents and assaying "greatness" will wish to consult Arthur M. Schlesinger, "Our Presidents: A Rating," *Life*, 1 Nov. 1948, pp. 65–66, 68, 73–74; and Robert K. Murray and Tim H. Blessing, "The Presidential Performance Study: A Progress Report," *Journal of American History* 70 (Dec. 1983): 535–55.

INDEX

257

Raw materials, duty-free, 130, 131, 132, 133, 134, 135, 138
Recessions, 45
Reconcentrado policy (Cuba), 194
Reconstruction, 2, 7, 65
"Redeemers," 7, 66
Reed Rules, 101
Reform Darwinism, 113
"Relief, Recovery and Reform," 128
Religion, 10, 16
Republican Independents, 26, 29
Republican party, 1, 2, 4, 7, 20, 38, 41, 45, 46, 94, 95, 97, 201; dissidents in, *see* Mugwumps; of 1890s, 102; and federal aid, 95; National Committee of, 39; nominees of, *see* Blaine, James G.; Harrison, Benjamin; McKinley, William; platform of, in 1884, 32, in 1888, 93, 95; and protective tariffs, 83–84, 88, 93, 95, 107–8, 132, 137; and veterans, 64
Republicans, 67, 90, 115, 122, 125, 133, 164, 185, 189, 194, 202, 218
Retaliation Act (1887), 162, 163
Rio de Janeiro (Brazil), 179
Robber barons, 2
Robbins, Henry S., 203
Rogers, Bowen, and Rogers (law firm), 22
Roosevelt, Franklin D., 77, 111, 221
Roosevelt, Theodore, 5, 61, 76, 164, 192, 224
"Rum, Romanism, and Rebellion," 40
Russell, William E., 210
Russia, 164, 165, 166

Sabbatarian laws, 95, 102
Sackville-West, Lionel, 96, 214
St. John, John P., 40
Salisbury, Lord, 184, 186, 189, 193
Samoa, 166–69, 189
Sanborn letter, 34
San Joaquin Forest (Calif.), 76
Santos (Brazil), 67
Saturday Evening Post, 121
Scalawags, 66
Schlesinger, Arthur M., 5
Schlesinger, Arthur M., Jr., 6
"Schlesinger poll," 5
Schomburgk, Robert, 180, 187
Schurz, Carl, 30, 56, 57, 71, 170
Scott, William L., 73
Scruggs, William L., 181
Seals, 161, 164–65, 166, 169
Second Bank of the United States, 16

Second Industrial Revolution, 224
Secret Service, 150
Secular schools, 95
Segregated public education, 68, 151
Seigniorage bill, 124, 125, 127, 204
Self-help, 13
"Self-Made Man in American Life, The" (Cleveland), 153–54
Sellers, Beriah, 2
Senate, 53, 54, 56, 57, 89, 123, 133, 134, 136, 163, 196, 206–7, 217; Finance Committee of, 133, 134, 138; Foreign Relations Committee of, 159, 171, 174; Judiciary Committee of, 54, 55
Separation of powers, 11, 20, 53
Sheehan, William, 110
Sheridan, Fort, 145
Sherman Anti-Trust Act (1890), 151
Sherman Silver Purchase Act (1890), 101, 108, 116, 117, 118, 119; repealed (1893), 11, 122, 123, 124, 127, 134, 137, 208, 218
Silver, 11, 32, 48, 77, 81–82, 85, 88, 101, 103, 108, 116, 117–18, 119, 122, 123, 125, 202, 203, 204, 208, 209, 210, 211; Acts (1878, 1890), 124; certificates, 116
"Silver Letter" (1891), 103
Simpson, Jerry, 132
Sinclair, William, 65
Sino-Japanese War (1894/95), 166
Slocum, Henry W., 25
Smith, Hoke, 71, 115, 153, 203, 212
Social division, 2, 3, 47
Social equality, 14
Socialism, 14
Socialist party, 146
Social sciences, 113
Sound money. *See* Cleveland, Grover, and currency
Southern Education Society, 68
Southern Farmers' Alliance, 103, 110
Southwest, 74, 75
Spain, 192, 194, 195, 196, 197, 198
Spanish-American War (1898), 198
Spanish Antilles, 179
Sparks, W. A. J., 74, 75
Specie certificates, 82
Spencer, Herbert, 113
Spoils system. *See* Political spoils
Springfield (Mass.) *Republican*, 185
Sproat, John G., 6
Stalwart Republicans, 50
Standard of living, 47
Standard Oil Trust, 45
State bank notes, 108